H. G. Wells and Rebecca West

By the same author:

An H. G. Wells Companion
An Edgar Allan Poe Companion
A George Orwell Companion
A Robert Louis Stevenson Companion
H. G. Wells: Interviews and recollections (editor)
The Man With a Nose And Other Uncollected Short Stories of H. G. Wells (editor)
H. G. Wells: An annotated bibliography of his works
H. G. Wells and the Modern Novel

H. G. Wells and Rebecca West

J. R. Hammond

ST MARTIN'S PRESS
New York

Printed in Great Britain

Library of Congress Cataloging-in-Publication Data
Hammond, J. R. (John R.), 1933-
    H. G. Wells and Rebecca West/J. R. Hammond.
        p.   cm.
    Includes bibliographical references and index.
    ISBN 0-312-07163-9
    1. Wells, H. G. (Herbert George), 1866-1946—Relations with women.
2. West, Rebecca, Dame. 1892-   —Relations with men.   3. Novelists,
English—20th century—Biography.   4. Journalists—Great Britain-
-Biography.   5. Authorship—Collaboration.   I. Title.
PR5776.H36   1991
823'.91209—dc20   91-27232
[B]   CIP

Historians publicly pretend that they can give an exact account of events in the past, though they privately know that all the past will let us know about events above a certain degree of importance is a bunch of alternative hypotheses.

Rebecca West, A Train of Powder

What personalities you will encounter in life, and have for a chief interest in life, is nearly as much a matter of chance as the drift of a grain of pollen in the pine forest . . . These unknowns are the substance of your fate. You will in extreme intimacy love them, hate them, serve them, struggle with them, and in that interaction the vital force in you and the substance of your days will be spent.

H. G. Wells, The Passionate Friends

Contents

Illustrations

Preface

The literary partnership between H. G. Wells and Rebecca West was a passionate friendship between two unusually gifted and imaginative writers. Their partnership lasted almost exactly ten years, from the autumn of 1913 to the autumn of 1923, but its repercussions extended far beyond this period. From the time of their first meeting they were drawn together by bonds of affection and attraction that remained with them for the rest of their lives.

I would like to make it clear at the outset that the present study is primarily a *literary* biography. I regard Wells and West essentially as *writers* who profoundly influenced each other's creative lives, rather than as two individuals who were caught up in an unhappy affair. This book is the story of a partnership between two of the most significant literary figures of the twentieth century and how their fiction, their attitudes and their lives were affected by each other. The book frequently draws on their fiction to account for, explain and illustrate aspects of their lives, since I take the view that a biographer can gain useful insights about a writer's life from his or her writings, though clearly we must regard the episodes and characters which might reasonably be said to be based on fact as *fictionalised* accounts which are not unproblematic.

Many individuals and institutions have contributed to the making of this volume. My principal debt is to Jackie Jones, Senior Acquisitions Editor at Harvester Wheatsheaf, who invited me to undertake it in the first place and has proved a constant source of advice, assistance and encouragement. Rebecca West's biographer Victoria Glendinning and the late Anthony West have both been unfailingly kind and helpful.

I must also thank the members and officers of the H. G. Wells Society for allowing me to share with them my discoveries about Wells and for the stimulus of many helpful conversations. I am particularly indebted to Dr Patrick Parrinder, former Chairman of the Wells Society and Head of the English Department at the University of Reading, and the late A. H. Watkins, former librarian of the London Borough of Bromley, both of whom have contributed advice of material assistance to this project.

I would like to thank the staff of the following libraries for their assistance: Beinecke Rare Book and Manuscript Library, Yale University; McFarlin Library, University of Tulsa, Oklahoma; University of Illinois Library; Bromley Central Library; and the National Newspaper Library, Colindale. I am particularly indebted to Gene Rinkel, Curator of Special Collections at Illinois, for his courteous co-operation over a long period and especially for making available a microfilm of Sarah Wells's diaries; and to Alex Freeman, Local Studies Librarian at Bromley, for responding to many tedious requests with promptness and efficiency. Lori N. Curtis, Assistant Curator of Special Collections at the University of Tulsa, has been a tower of strength in providing xerox copies of fugitive material and general advice and help. All the librarians I have encountered have been helpful and forthcoming beyond the call of duty.

I have also to thank the West Sussex Record Office and the Registrar of Norfolk County Council for their helpfulness in tracing elusive birth and marriage certificates.

Finally I would like to thank my wife for her patience during the many silent hours I spent writing and for her assistance in reading through and commenting on the various drafts. The book has benefited greatly from her judicious scrutiny.

J. R. Hammond

Acknowledgements

The extracts from the works of H. G. Wells are reproduced by permission of the Literary Executors of the Estate of H. G. Wells and the following copyright holders: Chatto and Windus and the Hogarth Press for the extracts from *Apropos of Dolores, The Bulpington of Blup, The Dream, Marriage, Mr Blettsworthy on Rampole Island, Mr Britling Sees It Through, The Passionate Friends;* Faber and Faber Ltd and Little, Brown and Co. for the extracts from *Experiment in Autobiography* and *H. G. Wells in Love.* A. P. Watt Ltd for all other works by H. G. Wells.

The extracts from the works of Rebecca West are reproduced by permission of A. D. Peters & Co. Ltd on behalf of the Rebecca West Estate. The author and publishers wish to thank the following who have kindly given permission for the use of other copyright material: Eyre and Spottiswoode (Publishers) Ltd for the extracts from *Principles and Persuasions* by Anthony West; Martin Secker & Warburg Ltd for the extracts from *Heritage* by Anthony West; Hutchinson & Co. (Publishers) Ltd for the extract from *H. G. Wells: Aspects of a life* by Anthony West; William Heinemann Ltd for the extracts from *An Estonian Childhood* by Tania Alexander; Routledge & Kegan Paul Ltd for the extract from *The Novelist at the Crossroads* by David Lodge.

Part I:
Beginnings

Chapter 1

A Man of His Time

To understand my father and his personal history one must look back beyond his origins to those of his parents. Things that had happened to them before he was born had made them the people he knew, and what he saw them do and heard them say to each other left him marked for life.

Anthony West, *H. G. Wells: Aspects of a life*

In that English countryside of my boyhood every human being had a 'place'. It belonged to you from your birth like the colour of your eyes, it was inextricably your destiny.

H. G. Wells, *Tono-Bungay*

I

Bromley in the mid-nineteenth century was a town in transition. For centuries its High Street had been 'a narrow irregular little street of thatched houses strung out on the London and Dover Road, a little mellow sample unit of a social order that had a kind of completeness, at its level, of its own'.[1] It was typical of English market towns of its period in that its population was engaged almost entirely in agriculture and ancillary trades. Situated twelve miles from London – three or four hours' walking before the advent of the railway – Bromley was a rural community, pleasantly situated above the valley of the River Ravensbourne. The name 'Bromley' literally means 'the heath where broom grows', and many of H. G. Wells's early memories were of the despoliation of a countryside he had come to know and love. The coming of the railway in 1858 meant the beginning of the end of the town's existence as a separate, identifiable community, for it was now possible for people living there to travel daily to London to earn their living. The population of 5,505 in 1861 had doubled by 1871 and increased to 15,000 by 1881. The Ravensbourne, which Wells remembered in his boyhood as 'a beautiful stream' leading to 'pampas grass, yellow and crimson spikes of hollyhock, and blue suggestions of wonderland'[2] was diverted and became at least a mere trickle. The open fields which had surrounded Bromley became increasingly submerged under housing to meet the needs of its rapidly expanding population. From the 1850s onwards it was a community in a state of flux, a microcosm of a society caught up in the metamorphosis from rural to urban. To this town in 1855, while it was poised on the brink of irrevocable change, came Joseph and Sarah Wells, two innocents in search of a livelihood.

Joseph Wells was born at Penshurst, Kent, on 14 July, 1828, the son of the head gardener to Lord de Lisle at Penshurst Place. He was trained to his father's profession and held a number of transitory appointments as a gardener between 1847 and 1851. The fact that he moved in and out of several different posts in rapid succession suggests the restlessness of youth but also hints at a mercurial temperament. All his life Joseph Wells was remembered as a man who did not like to be given orders, who wished to be his own master and, his son records, 'combined practical incompetence, practical enterprise and a thoroughly sanguine temperament, in a manner that I have never seen paralleled in any human being'.[3] Contemporary photographs show him to have been a jovial-looking man with a short crisp beard, an upright bearing and penetrating eyes. He held decided opinions and was not afraid to voice them; it is this characteristic, one suspects, which did not endear him to his employers. He was enthusiastic, intelligent and eager to learn, but subservience did not come easily to him. In June 1851 he was engaged as gardener by Miss Featherstonhaugh of Uppark, Sussex, and there he remained for two years. It was at Uppark that he met Sarah Neal, a quiet, gentle woman, five years older than himself, who was employed at the great house as a lady's maid.

Uppark was by no means typical of country houses of that era. It was a microcosm of an earlier age, frozen in a time warp. The house, which was built *circa* 1690, stands in a commanding position overlooking the village of South Harting and the great ridge of the South Downs. Surrounded by walled gardens, a deer park and undulating countryside it was remote from urbanity or any intrusive influence. The widowed Lady Featherstonhaugh, who lived there with her sister, Frances Bullock, had been working at the house as a dairymaid when Sir Harry Featherstonhaugh met her and proposed marriage. She was then aged 20 and he was 72. They remained happily married for twenty years until his death in 1846, after which she and her sister 'lived like dried-up kernels in the great shell'[4] of the house, and continued to do so until the end of the century. It was a world of attenuated ritual, a world in which nothing changed from decade to decade and where the prevailing tone was that of Dickens's *Bleak House*. House parties, shooting, hunting, balls and dinners formed the substance of its life.

Sarah Neal was born in 1822, the daughter of George Neal, an innkeeper first at Chichester and then at Midhurst, Sussex. She attended a finishing school for young ladies at Chichester where she learned to write in copperplate handwriting, to read, to do arithmetic and elementary geography. After leaving school she had four years' apprenticeship as a dressmaker (1836–40) and went into service as a lady's maid in various parts of England and Ireland before being appointed personal maid to Frances Bullock at Uppark in September 1850. Here she was happy, developing a warm affection for Miss Bullock and delighting in the house. 'The place is pretty and the house large', she wrote in her diary, 'and a beautiful park with deer.'[5] From Uppark she could visit her parents regularly and was unfailing in her attendance each Sunday at Harting parish church, a fine cruciform building dating from the fourteenth century.

A contemporary of Joseph and Sarah who knew them both records that Joseph was 'a dictatorial, overbearing man, quite overawing his delicately made and lady-like wife'.[6] On the face of it, the engagement between this oddly matched couple does seem unusual. Joseph was an out-of-doors man, vigorous, sceptical and unconventional. Sarah was small, quietly spoken and self-effacing, determined to do her duty and to know her place in a rigidly hierarchical world. 'Her mind was fixed and definite', Wells recorded, 'she embodied all that confidence in church and decorum and the assurances of the pulpit which was characteristic of the large mass of the English people . . . in early Victorian times.'[7] The gardener and the lady's maid struck up a friendship in which she was presently calling him 'Joe' and he was calling her 'Saddie'. He was a good looking young man, not unattractive to women and more articulate than many in his station in life. The two exchanged serious letters in which they discussed not only their courtship but such weighty topics as the Sacrament or the text of last Sunday's sermon. 'He seems *peculiar*', she confided in her diary, but despite the contrast between their temperaments and attitudes to life there seems little doubt that he was pressing her to become engaged.

In 1853 Sarah's world collapsed about her. She left her situation at Uppark to look after her invalid mother; her parents died within a few weeks of each other and she discovered to her horror that her father had been heavily in debt. The inn and all her parents' possessions had to be sold in order to meet the creditors' demands. With no home and no situation Sarah evidently felt she had little alternative but to accept Joe's offer of marriage. They were married at St Stephen's Church, London, on 22 November 1853, seventeen days after her mother's death. The marriage certificate records Joseph's occupation simply as 'gardener'. Why the wedding took place in London is not clear; evidently they both took lodgings nearby for the purpose. For a time they were unable to live together – Joseph had obtained a post at Trentham in Staffordshire but it had no married quarters with it – until, in April 1854, he was appointed to a post at Shuckburgh Park in Warwickshire. Here they were very happy in their little cottage on the Park estate, and a daughter, Fanny, was born in 1855. The dream could not last, however, for in August 1855 Joseph lost his situation again and the couple were homeless once more. At this point George Wells (a cousin of Joseph's father) offered what seemed to be a solution to their crisis. He owned a china and glassware shop at 47 High Street, Bromley (pretentiously named Atlas House) which they could purchase, if they wished, on attractively easy terms. Joseph took little time to consider. He spent all his savings and reserves on acquiring the business and, together with his wife and infant daughter, moved into the shop. For the first time in his life he was master of his destiny. 'Dined at Mr G. Wells', Sarah wrote on 9 October, 'after which we came to Bromley. May it prove with God's blessing a happy home for us.' Alas, it proved to be nothing of the kind.

Sarah sensed from the outset that they had made a mistake. 'I fear we have done wrong', she wrote. 'How sad to be deceived by one's relations. They have got their money and we their old stock.'[8] In addition to glassware, china, crockery and paraffin the shop soon began selling cricket bats and balls, for Joseph was a keen cricketer and was a member of the Kent team in 1862 and 1863. He supplemented the shop's income by earning money as a cricket coach and bowler, and for some years went each summer to Norwich Grammar School as a professional cricketer. It seems clear that the shop survived only in the most precarious way despite this additional income, for Joseph was no businessman. Had he had more business acumen and drive the venture would probably have succeeded. As it was, the shop simply ticked over, drifting on from year to year until Joseph was finally sold up (May 1887) for failing to pay his quarterly rent. Wells recorded of his father: 'he had a light and cheerful disposition, and a large part of his waking energy was spent in evading disagreeable realisations.'[9] Much of the work of running the shop and managing the home fell to Sarah, for Joseph was frequently absent. 47 High Street was an awkward building for a household with no servant – it was 'a big clumsy residence in the earliest Victorian style, interminably high and with deep damp basements and downstairs coal-cellars and kitchens that suggested an architect vindictively devoted to the discomfort of the servant class'[10] – but Sarah was a woman of some determination and did her utmost to keep up appearances. It was into this home that Frank (1857) and Fred (1862) were born, and finally Herbert George on 21 September 1866.

H. G. (or Bert as he was usually called) was thus the youngest of four children. Sarah's beloved daughter Fanny died suddenly and tragically of appendicitis in 1864, whereupon she heaped all her devotion on her youngest son in the hope that he would grow up, like Fanny, a model of infant piety. In this she was to be cruelly disappointed. Bert inherited much of his father's scepticism and wilfulness, and displayed little interest in the religious beliefs which were so important to her. At the same time he inevitably spent much time in her company and his early vision of the world derived largely from her teachings. He wrote in his autobiography: 'My own beginnings were shaped so much as a system of reactions to my mother's ideas and suggestions and feelings that . . . I arose mentally, quite as much as physically, out of her.'[11] Throughout her life the relationship between mother and son was a complex mixture of exasperation and love.

Young Bert was sent to a dame school at 8 South Street, Bromley (1871–2) where he learned to read and do simple arithmetic, and then became a pupil at Mr Thomas Morley's Academy situated further up the High Street. Here he remained for six years (1874–80). Between leaving the dame school and becoming a day boy at Morley's Academy there occurred an interregnum of crucial importance to his life. In 1874, when he was aged 7, he sustained a fractured leg which necessitated a lengthy convalescence and his absence from all active games (the bone was badly set by the local doctor and had to be rebroken and set again). During these months of enforced idleness he discovered the pleasures of reading and would let his imagination soar over Wood's *Natural History*, the works of Washington Irving, and bound volumes of *Punch* and *Fun*. Joseph Wells had a taste for reading and would bring books home from sales or from the Bromley Literary Institute. 'The home was poverty-struck and shabby but not unhappy', Wells recorded later, 'if food was sometimes rather short there was plenty to read.'[12] Morley's school, though grandly termed an Academy, seems to have been no better and no worse than many private schools of its time. Its prospectus boasted 'Writing in both plain and ornamental style, Arithmetic logically, and History with special reference to ancient Egypt'. Thomas Morley, an irascible Scot, was a strict disciplinarian with little patience with dullards. With pupils who showed promise he was however prepared to make an effort and he soon singled out Wells as a boy of exceptional gifts, encouraging him in the solution of mathematical and grammatical problems. By the time he left the school at the age of 13 Wells had acquired the basis of an education but was still intensely curious about the world of science and discovery unfolding all about him. Throughout his school years he supplemented his daytime learning with perfervid reading at home. Among the books he recalled particularly was the poetry of Sir Walter Scott, Chaucer, Humboldt's *Cosmos*, George Eliot's *Middlemarch*, Captain Cook's *Travels* and Grote's *History of Greece*. He was also dipping eagerly into Dickens's novels and imbiding a fascination with literature which remained with him throughout his life. A humorous story of some 100 pages, *The Desert Daisy*, written and illustrated by Wells at the age of 12 or 13, survived among his papers and was published in facsimile in 1957.

In 1877 disaster came to the Wells family and necessitated the breakup of the household. Joseph fell one Sunday morning and broke his leg while attempting to prune a grapevine which grew against the back of the house. It soon became clear that from now on, though he could walk, he would be permanently and heavily lame. His lameness meant that his days as a cricketer and coach were over and thus the shop's income, at best a meagre one, was severely reduced. Frank and Fred were by this time apprenticed to the drapery trade, for Sarah's overriding ambition for her sons was that they should be drapers – this she considered to be a gentlemanly and respectable occupation. It was decided that Bert must follow in his brothers' footsteps as soon as his schooling could be terminated. At this point, Wells recalled later, 'the heavens opened and a great light shone on Mrs Sarah Wells'.[13] Sarah's former employer, Frances Bullock, had inherited Uppark on the death of Lady Feathers-tonhaugh. She was in need of a housekeeper and wrote to her former maid offering her the post. This seemed to be the solution to all Sarah's worries. She had always hated Bromley and her life of drudgery in the shop, and the chance of leaving all this behind her and returning to Uppark where she had been so happy must have come to her like the answer to her dreams. She decided to accept the offer, having little compunction in leaving Joe behind to run the shop on his own and thrusting Bert out into the world (June 1880) to become a draper's apprentice at Windsor. Sarah became housekeeper at Uppark in the summer of 1880 and continued in that capacity until February 1893.

Young Wells's arrival at Windsor as a shop assistant 'on trial' was the first of a series of false starts in life. Shop assistants at that time had to work a thirteen-hour day, from 7.30 a.m. to 8.30 p.m. (the Shop Hours Act limiting the working week to seventy-four hours was not introduced until 1892, and weekly half-day holidays for employees did not become compulsory until 1911). To the 13-year-old Wells, cut off from his schooling just when his curiosity and imagination had been most aroused, the days must have seemed endless. On his own admission however he was clearly a misfit as a draper, displaying little or no aptitude for the work and making it all too clear that his interests lay elsewhere. At every opportunity he slipped away from the shop to visit his uncle who kept a riverside inn, Surly Hall, on the Thames near Eton. *Dickens's Dictionary of the Thames* (1880) describes Surly Hall as 'A tavern well-known to all oarsmen, and especially dear to every Etonian'. At Surly were books and music and the stimulating company of his cousins. He wrote pathetically to his mother that he found the inn 'much better than I used to think it, in fact a perfect heaven [compared] to Rodgers & Denyers'. The letter is signed formally 'H. G. Wells' followed by a terse postscript: 'N.B. My washing will be twelve shillings a quarter.'[14] He proved so unsuitable as a draper that at the end of the trial month his employers rejected him, finding him 'untidy and troublesome'.

His next false start was to be sent to Wookey in Somerset, where a distant relative of his mother's, Alfred Williams, was the only school-master at the National School. The plan was that Wells would live at the school house while his 'Uncle' Williams coached him to be an usher (or pupil-teacher as they were then termed). This plan also came to grief after only three months. An inspector discovered that Williams's certificates were suspect. The schoolmaster was dismissed and Bert had to pack his bags once more.

For a while his mother was at a loss what to do with him and he spent some weeks at Uppark, reading voraciously, going for long walks, exploring the house and building a miniature theatre to entertain the maids with a shadow play in the housekeeper's room. A snowstorm kept him housebound for a fortnight and he produced a facetious newspaper, *The Uppark Alarmist*, to keep the servants entertained. Uppark possessed a fine eclectic library, once the property of Sir Harry Featherstonhaugh who had been a freethinker. Many of his books had been relegated to an attic and Wells was allowed to rout among these abandoned volumes. Here he discovered Paine's *Rights of Man*, an unexpurgated edition of *Gulliver's Travels*, Johnson's *Rasselas* and William Beckford's *Vathek*. He dipped into Gibbon and Plutarch's *Lives*, and improved his French by reading Voltaire's *Candide* in the original. Here also he discovered a forgotten Gregorian telescope, pieced it together through a process of trial and error, and was found by his mother in the small hours studying the craters of the moon. It would be difficult to exaggerate the impact of Uppark on Wells's imagination; indeed it would not be too much to say that it was the greatest single influence on his early life. The great house with its deer park and woodlands, its library and paintings, its air of leisured civilisation, affected him enormously and played a considerable part in stimulating his imagina-tion. 'For me at any rate', he wrote, 'the house at Uppark was alive and potent. The place had a great effect upon me; it retained a vitality that altogether overshadowed the insignificant ebbing trickle of upstairs life . . . .'[15] The house also made a deep impression on him because of its rigid hierarchical structure of staff and servants, and the sharp contrast between life above and below stairs. In the basement are a series of underground passages constructed in 1810 to link the kitchen with the service stairs. These tunnels are ventilated by deep shafts letting in light from the surface. As a boy he would have been very familiar with this system of tunnels and may well have derived the idea of the

Morlocks with their underground passages from this eerie below-stairs world. Anthony West wrote many years later that *The Time Machine* could be regarded as 'a violent gut reaction'[16] to the world of Uppark.

Later he was to portray Uppark as Bladesover House in *Tono-Bungay*, Burnmore Park in *The Passionate Friends* and Mowbray in *The World of William Clissold*. Its effect on a 14-year-old boy who had spent all his life in Bromley had the force of a revelation. It awakened him to the importance of social relationships and led him to speculate about the country house and its role in English history. Throughout his mother's tenure as housekeeper he spent many of his holidays at the house, familiarising himself more and more with its library and slowly modifying his first uncritical impressions. He wrote in *Tono-Bungay* that he was glad he had seen so much of Uppark because

> seeing it when I did, quite naively, believing in it thoroughly, and then coming to analyse it, has enabled me to understand much that would be absolutely incomprehensible in the structure of English society . . . it is one of those dominant explanatory impressions that make the framework of my mind.[17]

The interlude at Uppark – the first of many over the next thirteen years – came to an end in January 1881 when he was sent on trial to a chemist's shop belonging to Samuel Evan Cowap at Church Street, Midhurst. Wells took a liking to Midhurst, then a peaceful, mellow town untouched by industrialisation: the fact that it had been the home of his grandparents gave him a sense of belonging there. He was happy in the shop and the little house – lovingly described in the 'Wimblehurst' chapters in *Tono-Bungay* – but soon came to the conclusion that the fees required in order for him to qualify as a chemist would be beyond his mother's means. The experiment came to an end on Wells's own initiative after only one month, although it did have significant consequences for English literature. Writing to Cowap's son many years later he confided: 'Your mother was a delightful person. One never puts real people into novels but I got the idea of my Aunt Ponderevo (in *Tono-Bungay*) from a nonsensical way she had of talking.'[18] He remained in Midhurst for a further seven weeks, studying at the Grammar School under the guidance of the headmaster, Horace Byatt. (By an odd coincidence Byatt had been a headmaster in Burslem and had numbered among his pupils a young man named Arnold Bennett. Later Wells and Bennett were to have a long and cordial friendship.) Wells was one of only ten pupils and made the most of his brief respite there, studying Latin, physiology and physiography and astonishing Byatt by his facility in absorbing textbooks and mastering abstract ideas. He would have liked his stay at the Grammar School to continue indefinitely for his eagerness for knowledge and sense of wonder had been keenly aroused by this experience, his 'first systematic acquaintance with modern science',[19] but his mother was still determined that he should become a draper. Unknown to him she had been busy making enquiries to this end and had consulted Sir William King, agent to the Uppark estate and an important man in local affairs. King in turn recommended her to Edwin Hyde, proprietor of a drapery emporium in King's Road, Southsea. Wells left the school in April and travelled to Southsea with his portmanteau, bound as an apprentice to a draper for four years.

His dismay can be imagined. He felt he had been swallowed up by the retail trade and that the path of educational advancement was closed to him for ever. He had promised his mother that this time he would make a real effort, and he held to his promise for two long years. Something of the atmosphere of his life as a draper's apprentice can be derived from the opening chapters of *Kipps* and *The History of Mr Polly*, though Wells is careful to point out in his autobiography that Hyde was an enlightened employer for his time and that working conditions were greatly superior to those he had known at Windsor. It was a life made up of stock keeping, window dressing, tidying up, fetching and carrying, making up parcels, running errands and endless small fussy chores. 'It was not excessively laborious', he wrote, 'but it was indescribably tedious . . . I recall those two years of incarceration as the most unhappy hopeless period of my life.'[20] A thirteen-hour working day left little time or energy for reading, but he pored over his Latin grammar whenever he could and struggled with Spencer's *First Principles*. The emporium possessed a library for use by the assistants consisting mainly of popular novels. He left the novels severely alone, feeling that his time was so precious he could not afford to be seduced by a good story, and concentrated instead on an encyclopaedia which contained long summaries of philosophy and science. At last he wrote to Byatt at Midhurst enquiring whether a post might be found for him as a school usher. Byatt replied that he could come to the Grammar School as a student assistant without pay. Wells went over to Midhurst to see him, and the two continued to correspond. Wells also wrote to his mother and father begging them to cancel his indentures and allow him to accept Byatt's offer. After some reflection the schoolmaster improved his original offer by suggesting a commencing salary of £20 a year rising to £40 after twelve months: clearly he had considerable faith in Wells's ability and promise. Still Sarah Wells prevaricated. She had, after all, undertaken to pay Hyde a premium of £50, of which £40 had already been paid. She resisted her son's entreaties, begging him to be patient and try again. His letters to her became increasingly agitated. At last, one Sunday morning in July or August 1883, he decided he could endure the situation no longer, slipped away from the emporium before breakfast and walked the seventeen miles to Uppark to present her with an ultimatum. Either she must consent to the termination of his apprenticeship, he declared, or he would end his life. During his two years at Southsea he had had abundant opportunity to think over his life and to weigh the possibilities before him and when he used suicide as a threat it was only after much earnest meditation. His tramp to Uppark and his thoughts on that memorable journey are described in some detail in *Tono-Bungay*. He waylaid his mother and the servants as they straggled up the hill from Harting church:

> Standing up to waylay in this fashion, I had a queer feeling of brigandage, as though I was some intrusive sort of bandit among these orderly things. It is the first time I remember having that outlaw feeling distinctly, a feeling that has played a large part in my subsequent life. I felt there existed no place for me – that I had to drive myself in.[21]

Clearly he felt he had reached a turning point in his life and that his letters to his mother had failed to convince her of his grim determination to improve his lot. Perplexed by him as always, at last and with great reluctance she consented to his demands, though inwardly she must have felt that her youngest son was making a grave mistake. In her eyes he was abandoning a secure, respectable occupation in favour of an uncertain future as a teacher. Frank and Fred were trying hard to make a success of the drapery trade – why could not Bert do the same? The crisis between Wells and his mother ended as so often in her grudging acquiescence. It was not until years later when he had become a successful novelist and a world figure that, looking back on this episode, he was able to place it in perspective and try to understand his mother's feelings. However misguided he felt her behaviour and attitudes to have been, he had to concede that throughout his life she had been motivated by her deep love for him and her concern for his happiness.

One further hurdle lay ahead of him. Byatt advised Wells that the statutes of the Grammar School required that all members of the teaching staff must be communicants of the Church of England. His young pupil balked at this: all his reading and thinking led him more and more to a profound disbelief in the scheme of redemption taught by orthodox Christianity; his mother's fanatical devotion to the Church had merely strengthened his own scepticism. He realised, however, that he had no alternative but to acquiesce. To have refused to comply would have meant the abandonment of all his hopes of escape. It was a reluctant and secretly very embittered young man who was confirmed as a member of the Church of England at the age of 17. The wound to his honour rankled in his mind for many years and aggravated his hostility to organised religion.

He remained at Midhurst for a year, lodging in a room over a sweet shop adjoining the Angel Hotel – the same room which is described with such affection in *The Wheels of Chance* and *Love and Mr Lewisham*. On the wall of his room he pinned, as Lewisham did, a 'Schema' allocating his hours of study. The 'Schema' specified the year in which he proposed to take his BA degree at London University with 'hons. in all subjects', followed by 'pamphlets in the Liberal interest'. A text on the wall above the wash-hand stand proclaimed 'Who would control others must first control himself.'[22] Throughout his time there he worked extremely hard – teaching, studying, reading, thinking and going for headlong walks, timed to last one hour at a pace of four miles an hour. In addition to teaching a class of junior boys he attended evening classes under Byatt's nominal tuitition, classes in which for the most part he was the solitary student. He studied physiography, physiology, geology, chemistry and mathematics among other subjects, working his way through textbooks and checking his progress by submitting to the discipline of written examinations. He was aware that this fanatical dedication to study and the pursuit of knowledge was in large measure a response to his obsessive quest to escape from drapery. At the age of 14, he wrote,

> when so many boys are at a public school, I was precipitated by my father's financial troubles into a driving, systematic, incessant draper's shop, and given so bad a time as to stiffen my naturally indolent, rather slovenly, and far too genial nature into a grim rebellion against the world – a spurt of revolt that enabled me to do wonders of self-education before its force was exhausted.[23]

Nor was science his only preoccupation at Midhurst. It was at about this time, when he was aged 17, that he encountered Plato's *Republic* and Henry George's *Progress and Poverty* – books of a very different complexion which awakened him to ideas of social reform and reconstruction. With all the idealism and earnestness of youth he had a blinding vision of an Age of Reason: he became a socialist. It was an essentially crude, naïve vision – as yet he saw life 'with a divine simplicity'.[24] His conception of the world at this time must have resembled that of Willie Leadford in his novel *In the Days of the Comet*; he was filled with a dream of the world remade – a dream fed on socialist pamphlets and desultory reading of Shelley and Carlyle.

Presently his life at Midhurst was transformed by

> a marvellous blue document from the Education Department promising inconceivable things. He was to go to London and be paid a guinea a week

for listening to lectures – lectures beyond his most ambitious dreams! Among the names that swam before his eyes was Huxley – Huxley and then Lockyer! What a chance to get![25]

He had been awarded a scholarship to the Normal School of Science at South Kensington (now the Imperial College of Science and Technology) as a teacher in training. This meant that he had to uproot himself from Midhurst, say farewell to Byatt, and become a full-time student in London. After a summer vacation spent partly at Uppark with his mother and partly at Bromley with his father (where the shop 'was in a sort of coma')[26] he arrived in London in September 1884, a pale, earnest young man consumed with unrealised dreams and a burning desire to learn.

II

The three years he spent as a science student under Huxley, Lockyer and others exercised a profound influence upon Wells and shaped his outlook and attitudes for the remainder of his life. Fifty years later, in *The Fate of Homo Sapiens*, he recalled that 'by 1887 the world as I saw it had become something altogether greater, deeper and finer than the confused picture I had of it in 1880 . . . There has been a lot of expansion and supplementing since, but nothing like a fundamental reconstruction.'[27] His first year under Huxley in particular gave him a vision of the universe as a single biological process and an evolutionary approach to life and history which affected all his writings. Huxley was a brilliant and inspiring teacher who imparted to his students a vision of the world as an unfolding panorama which 'is not made and dead like a cardboard model or a child's toy, but a living equilibrium; and every day and every hour, every living thing is being weighed in the balance and found sufficient or wanting'.[28] It is this austere vision of life which permeates such works as *The Time Machine, The Island of Doctor Moreau* and *The War of the Worlds* and shaped him indelibly as man and writer. His formative years were lived against a background of social and intellectual ferment. John Stuart Mill's *The Subjection of Women* was published in 1869, Darwin's *The Descent of Man* in 1871, and Henry George's *Progress and Poverty* in 1879. The Fabian Society was founded in the same year in which Wells commenced his studies at South Kensington, a year which also saw the publication of Herbert Spencer's *Man Versus the State* and the anarchist writings of Kropotkin. The debate on evolution generated by the teachings of Darwin and Huxley was raging all through Wells's boyhood and adolescence. This ferment of ideas all around him convinced him that he was living in an epoch of change and that the rigid, pre-ordained world of his mother's generation was visibly passing away.

His second and third years under Professors Guthrie (physics) and Judd (geology) failed to capture his imagination as Huxley had done and he found an outlet for his energies in a complex of emotional and intellectual distractions. Throughout most of his time as a student Wells lodged with an uncle and aunt at 181 Euston Road, a menage he was later to describe with fascinating particularity in his account of the lodging house kept by Matilda Good in *The Dream*. Here he met his cousin Isabel Mary Wells, a shy and beautiful girl of his own age, and with her he fell deeply in love. From 1884 until their marriage in October 1891 he 'tethered [his] sexual and romantic imagination to her'.[29] Mentally and temperamentally profound incompatibilities lay between them yet they were deeply attracted to one another; their kinship and daily physical proximity gave them a sense of belonging. Facets of Isabel's character are drawn in the portraits of 'Ethel' in *Love and Mr Lewisham* and 'Marion' in *Tono-Bungay*, and the former novel conveys much of the atmosphere of Wells's life during his student years. Continually he must have felt torn between the disinterested quest for scientific truth: the dazzling vision which had beckoned him onwards since his arrival at Midhurst, and his deep and irrational fixation for his cousin. As Lewisham expresses it: 'On the one hand that shining staircase to fame and power, that had been his dream from the very dawn of his adolescence, and on the other hand – Ethel.'[30] This choice between duty and romance was one which exercised him at intervals throughout his life.

He was, moreover, being distracted from his studies in other directions. He became an active member of the Debating Society and took a leading part in discussions on a wide range of social and political questions (it was in the Debating Society that he first encountered the notion of a four-dimensional universe which became the germ of the idea for *The Time Machine*). He made a number of lasting friendships including Arthur Morley Davies, William Burton, Elizabeth Healey, Richard Gregory and others, who joined him in lengthy discussions about socialism, religion, evolution, Ruskin, William Morris and a host of other topics. He was reading widely among authors and subjects utterly remote from his ostensible studies – Goethe, Shelley, Blake, Carlyle and Milton. He was also the founder and first editor of the college magazine, the *Science Schools Journal*, to which he contributed both under his own name and a variety of pseudonyms. A cartoon of himself drawn at this time shows him sitting in a field deep in thought surrounded by copies of his works: 'How I could save the nation', 'All about God', 'Wells's design for a new framework for society', 'Whole duty of man', 'Key to politics' and 'Secret of the cosmos'. The cartoon is headed 'Incidents in the lives of great men: H. G. Wells FOM [Friend of Mankind?] meditating on his future'.[31] Through all his student years his health was deteriorating. He took little exercise, ate scamped meals and worked irregular hours in rooms which were frequently cold, draughty and ill-lit. It is hardly surprising that after three winters spent in this fashion the combination of poor health, mental and emotional turmoil, inability to concentrate on his studies and a nagging awareness that he was losing his direction in life culminated in setback. In the June 1887 finals he only succeeded in obtaining a second class in astronomical physics and failed altogether in advanced geology.

His disappointment at this turn of events can be imagined. How could he possibly break the news to his parents after their bitter resistance to his pursuit of an educational career? Yet despite his failure to obtain a degree he was still determined to become a teacher and after some searching secured a post at a small private school near Wrexham, the Holt Academy. The school proved to be a bitter disappointment and was apparently little improvement on Dotheboys Hall in Dickens's *Nicholas Nickleby*. He spent his twenty-first birthday ill in bed, having been badly fouled while playing football and sustained a crushed kidney, from the effects of which he suffered for many years.

Despite poor health he remained at Holt from July to November 1887, than travelled to Uppark for a long convalescence. He was by this time suffering from haemorrhages and for some months lived the life of a semi-invalid. From April to July 1888 he stayed with his friend William Burton at Etruria in the Staffordshire Potteries. All these experiences – his sojourn in North Wales, his convalescence at Uppark and his stay in the Potteries – had an enormous impact on him, for throughout this time he was reading and writing voraciously, and gaining valuable experience in expressing his thoughts and ideas in essays, verse and short stories.

His reading at this time included Keats, Spenser, Heine, Emerson, Rousseau, Stevenson, Carlyle and Hawthorne. As George says of himself in *Tono-Bungay*: 'My ideas were made partly of instinct, partly of a romantic imagination, partly woven out of a medley of scraps of suggestion that came to me haphazard. I had read widely and confusedly.'[32]

Perhaps the strongest literary influences on him during these months were Stevenson and Hawthorne. Throughout his student years – and the years immediately following – he had contributed facetious articles, verse and stories to the *Science Schools Journal* under a variety of pseudonyms: Walker Glockenhammer, Septimus Browne, Sosthenes Smith, Tyro and H. G. Wheels, as well as contributions published under his own name.

These pieces include two short stories, 'The devotee of art' and 'Walcote, A tale of the twentieth century', which is a farcical account of the application of a perpetual motion machine to the London Underground, and 'A vision of the past', a remarkable piece of writing in which the narrator dreams he is in an age of reptilian monsters who are convinced that *they* are the lords of creation and that the world was made for *them*. In later years Wells was inclined to be very disparaging about these early writings. They were, he said, 'imitative puerile stuff'.[33] Despite his reservations there is much of considerable interest in these early essays and stories. In such pieces as 'A talk with Gryllotalpa' and 'A vision of the past' there is abundant evidence of the narrative skill and facility with words which was later to stand him in such good stead, and in a story such as 'Walcote' – over elaborate in style though it may be – there is ample promise of greater things to come. During the year he spent at Holt, Uppark and Stoke-on-Trent his literary efforts continued and a number of short stories were written at this time. None of these has seen the light of day and we know that some of them were burnt by Wells himself. A number of novels were also commenced at this time. One of them, *Lady Frankland's Companion*, ran to 35,000 words. Another, which he described as 'a vast melodrama in the setting of the Five Towns, a sort of Staffordshire *Mysteries of Paris* conceived partly in burlesque, with lovely and terrible passages'[34] ran to 25,000 words and was also subsequently destroyed. Yet another was the story known as 'The chronic argonauts', which appeared as a serial in *The Science Schools Journal* in April, May and June 1888 but was left unfinished. The significance of these early literary efforts is that throughout this time Wells was gaining increasing self-confidence in self-expression and, secondly, that he did not give up, however discouraging his continual rejections must have been. He says in his autobiography:

> With every desire to be indulgent to myself I am bound to say that every scrap of writing surviving from that period witnesses that the output was copious rubbish, imitative of the worst stuff in the contemporary cheap magazine. There was not a spark of imagination or original observation about it.[35]

In saying this he was doing less than justice to himself. Immature 'The chronic argonauts' certainly is; but it could hardly be described as 'copious rubbish'. It contains evidence of considerable descriptive and narrative power – and it contains the germ of the idea which was to become *The Time Machine*, Wells's first novel, and the work which first earned him a reputation as an imaginative writer.

III

For five years Wells held to his career as a teacher. From the beginning of 1889 to the summer of 1890 he was an assistant master at the Henley House School, Mortimer Road, Kilburn, where he taught science and resumed his studies for a London University degree. Throughout his time at Henley House he lived in lodgings with his aunt and uncle at Fitzroy Road, Primrose Hill, and here again was in daily contact with his cousin Isabel. From 1890 until May 1893 he taught biology for the University Correspondence College (a precursor of the National Extension College), conducting cramming classes at Red Lion Square and marking correspondence-course papers. There is no doubt that these years, from the age of 23 to 27, were years of active mental growth in which he was working extremely hard and coming to an increasing awareness of his ambitions and desires.

Academically they were years of growth and promise. As a teacher he worked diligently, helping students with their difficulties and showing a genuine understanding of their problems. In his first published book, *Textbook of Biology* (1893), he wrote:

> No method of studying – more especially when the objects of study are tangible things – can rival that prosecuted under the direction and in the constant presence of a *teacher* who has also a living and vivid knowledge of the matter which he handles with the student.[36]

He took a keen interest in educational theory and practice, contributing essays on pedagogic and scientific topics to such journals as the *University Correspondent*, the *Educational Times* and *Chambers's Journal*. Meanwhile his own studies continued apace. He gained his BSc. degree in October 1890 with first-class honours in zoology and second-class honours in geology. For a time he seemed reconciled to a career as a teacher and writer on educational topics.

But simultaneously with his academic career he continued to worry away at his literary ambitions. In July 1891 came his first real breakthrough with the publication of 'The rediscovery of the unique' in Frank Harris's influential journal the *Fortnightly Review*. This essay, which Wells described as his 'first quarrel with the accepted logic',[37] postulated the uniqueness of all living things and the error inherent in rigid classifications. Since all individuals are unique, he argued, it follows that there can be no such thing as universally applicable moral laws: 'we cannot think of regulating our conduct by wholesale dicta'. In its insistence on the provisionality of man and of logical processes and language 'The rediscovery of the unique' is characteristic of attitudes he was to hold throughout his life. In place of a confident faith in social advance the essay reveals a profound sense of doubt, a troubled awareness of a universe in which there can be no certainties:

> The neat little picture of a universe of souls made up of passions and principles in bodies made of atoms, all put together so neatly and wound up at the creation, fades in the series of dissolving views that we call the march of human thought.

This sense of a society in process of fragmentation is a frequently recurring theme in his early writings and one to which he returned many times as a mature writer. Though he was greatly elated by Frank Harris's acceptance of the essay, his attempt to follow it up with 'The universe rigid' – an account of a four-dimensional time–space system – came to nothing, for this was rejected by Harris as unreadable.

Between 1889 and 1892 Wells rewrote 'The chronic argonauts' twice under the same title (unfortunately these versions do not survive) and then between 1893 and 1894 rewrote it again four times before he was satisfied. Geoffrey West wrote: 'This struggle to embody satisfactorily the brilliantly original idea of time travelling might in itself be said almost to constitute his literary apprenticeship.'[38] It says much for Wells that he continued working on this story – revising, reshaping and polishing – often in the most lonely and dispiriting circumstances: at Holt, at Uppark, while he was a full-time schoolteacher at Henley House School in Kilburn, and during his unhappy first marriage. Clearly he was reluctant to abandon the idea, and sensed that in the concept of time travelling he had hit upon something original and important. With hindsight we can only be thankful for his patience and determination. Many aspiring writers would have given up after an apprenticeship lasting eight years.

Writing in her diary at the beginning of 1892 and looking back on the past year Sarah wrote: 'My loved ones have had numerous blessings. My dear Bertie's illness caused us alarm but it has pleased God to spare him and to become the husband of our dear Isabel. May it please God to give them a happy life.' Through these years in which he pursued his educational and literary ambitions Isabel was never far from the surface of his mind. 'There was', he wrote, 'a deep-seated fixation of my mind upon her.'[39] He was quite simply *obsessed* with her, as his autobiography and the 'Marion' chapter of *Tono-Bungay* make clear. For him she was the embodiment of all his sexual and emotional dreams; his ambition to marry and possess her became his consuming object in life. After their marriage in 1891 came swift disillusionment. Wells must have quickly realised that in his determination to make Isabel his wife he had made a grave mistake and was repeating the same error his father had made forty years earlier. Indeed the more one reflects on Wells and his cousin the more one is struck by the parallels between Joseph and Sarah. Wells, like his father, was sceptical, impatient, wayward and untidy; Isabel, like his mother, was conventional, meek, submissive and dutiful. There was a deeply passionate strand in Wells's make-up which found its expression in romantic daydreams of Isabel released from her earthly self and transformed into the woman of his desires. 'I had let myself come to want her, my imagination endowed her with infinite possibilities', writes the narrator in *Tono-Bungay*, 'I wanted her and wanted her, stupidly and instinctively.'[40] To him the physical and emotional expression of his love was of consuming importance; to Isabel it was a distasteful intrusion. For his part he was frustrated and disappointed by her apparent frigidity and her indifference to his ideas. For her part she was perplexed and hurt by his untidiness, his bouts of ill temper, his gnawing dissatisfaction with life. Above all she could not come to terms with his driving impatience and his increasing tendency to mock at conventional institutions. The marriage struggled on for two years but both husband and wife must have been increasingly exasperated by the latent and surface tensions. Sooner or later the marriage would have come to an end, but matters were precipitated by the entry into Wells's life of Amy Catherine Robbins.

She came to his tutorial class as a student in the autumn of 1892, intending to study for a degree and earn her living as a teacher. This grave little figure, dressed in mourning (her father had been recently killed in a railway accident) soon came to fascinate him for she seemed to embody all that intellectual curiosity and unconventionality which Isabel lacked. She had read widely and seemed keenly interested in topics which were anathema to his wife: evolution, theology, and social and political issues. After their initial meetings he sought more and more opportunities for conversation with her. They lent each other books and exchanged notes; they went for walks together; he confided to her his dissatisfaction with his life and his literary hopes and dreams. 'It was a friendship,' he wrote, 'that assured itself with the most perfect insincerity that it meant to go no further, and it kept on going further.'[41] His situation had reached this point when his health suddenly deteriorated. Late one evening in May 1893 he was hurrying down the slope of Villiers Street on his way to Charing Cross Underground Station carrying a heavy bag of geological specimens (he had been coaching a pupil) when he was siezed by a violent bout of coughing. The coughing fit ended in a haemorrhage and, though he succeeded in reaching home, the haemorrhage became steadily worse. That night he realised he was extremely near to death. Eventually the bleeding was arrested by the application of ice bags to his chest. Slowly and precariously he recovered but had to face the fact that his teaching career was over. From now onwards he would have to find some other way of earning a living.

As soon as he had recovered sufficiently to make travel feasible, he and his wife and aunt set off to Eastbourne for a fortnight's holiday to enable him to convalesce. Here he lay on the beach each day reading and thinking and – quite by chance – encountered a book which transformed his life. This was J. M. Barrie's *When a Man's Single*, an account of Barrie's early days as a journalist, which contained the valuable hint that material for articles and stories could be found in the everyday things of life rather than in abstract topics. Wells took the hint, realising that his own mistake had lain in composing arcane scientific essays instead of articles based on more humdrum themes. He wrote a humorous essay 'On the art of staying at the seaside: a meditation at Eastbourne' and submitted it to the *Pall Mall Gazette*, one of the popular London dailies of the time. This was accepted and the Editor asked for more. Newspapers and journals were then on the look out for new writers who could produce bright, entertaining stories and sketches – at last he had discovered the desired formula. This first success was quickly followed by others. Within a matter of months he was earning far more than he had done as a teacher, writing in rapid succession articles, sketches and short stories with an amazing fertility of invention. Much of this material – but by no means all – was subsequently reprinted in three collections: *Select Conversations with an Uncle* (1895), *The Stolen Bacillus and Other Incidents* (1895), and *Certain Personal Matters* (1897). For Wells the years 1893 and 1894 were notable for their prolific journalism. He quickly followed up his success with the *Pall Mall Gazette* by producing a series of facetious essays and sketches on topics ranging from house-hunting to cricket and from coal scuttles to modelling in clay. Interspersed with these he wrote vivid prophetic articles on such themes as 'The man of the year million', 'The advent of the flying man' and 'The extinction of man'. Since the comic stories written in his boyhood he had possessed the ability to laugh at himself, and in such essays as 'The education of novelists', 'On the writing of essays' and 'The pose novel' he gently deflated the pretensions of the literary aesthete. In such tales as 'A family elopement' he was also producing engaging short stories which contain abundant evidence of his understanding of human foibles.

Matters had reached this point when his marriage collapsed. He wrote in his autobiography: 'It came to me quite suddenly one night that I wanted the sort of life Amy Catherine Robbins symbolised for me and that my present life was unendurable. That was the realisation of a state of affairs that had been accumulating below the level of consciousness for some time.'[42] In January 1894 he left Isabel – the termination is described with complete honesty in George Ponderevo's account of his leaving Marion in *Tono-Bungay* – and went to live in lodgings with Amy, first at 7 Mornington Place and later at 12 Mornington Road (now Terrace), Camden Town. Their decision to elope and live together without being married was a bold one by the standards of the time and was strongly resisted by Amy's mother. Mrs Robbins and various members of the Robbins family remonstrated with Wells and pleaded with Amy to return to the family fold – all in vain. Amy was strongly attracted to this unusual man and was firmly resolved to throw in her lot with his in the full knowledge that he was married and that his health was precarious. Photographs of him taken at this time show that he was not unhandsome, with a thin, eager face, a sensitive mouth and a penetrating gaze. Contemporary accounts agree that he was a gifted talker and that, in congenial company, he could be a man of great charm. The attraction was reciprocal. To him she held a promise of companionship and partnership he had never attained in his marriage. She encouraged him in his literary ambitions, understood his moods and sympathised with his unconventional outlook on life. She shared Isabel's qualities of gentleness and quietness but possessed, in addition to these, a gift for organisation and real strength of mind.

However painful his parting from Isabel must have been he realised that the marriage could not possibly have lasted. He acknowledged that one of the fundamental defects in his own personality was 'a superficial volatility and a profound impatience in my make-up that would have taxed her ultimately beyond the limit of her adaptability'.[43] For both Wells and Isabel the separation was a traumatic emotional upheaval for, despite their differences of opinion, they were deeply attached to one another. But he was determined on the course he had chosen.

Together he and Amy embarked on their new life, he writing articles, stories and book reviews and she working for her degree and assisting him in every way she could. To this period, at the outset of his literary career, belong such tales as 'A slip under the microscope', 'The flowering of the strange orchid', 'The diamond maker', and 'Aepyornis island' – stories which are known wherever the English language is read. In the summer of that year came his lucky break.

W. E. Henley, who was then one of the leading figures in London journalism, invited him to write a serial for his new monthly *The New Review*. Wells accepted at once, rewriting his time-travelling articles which had been published in the *National Observer* under the title 'The time traveller's story' and reshaping them as a gripping narrative. The *National Observer* pieces were a recasting of the 'Chronic argonauts' material, containing a series of prophetic visions of the future but not linked together into a coherent story. Henley grasped that the articles could be immeasurably improved by retaining the central concept of travelling through time but recasting the individual chapters as a continuous story narrated by the inventor. Greatly encouraged by Henley's enthusiasm Wells set to work on a thorough revision. After several weeks of hectic writing, while staying in lodgings with Amy and her mother at Tusculum Villa, Eardsley Road, Sevenoaks, he succeeded in recasting the story into the form known today throughout the world as *The Time Machine*. Not only was this accepted for serial publication but Heinemann agreed to bring it out as a book in July 1895. With the publication of this, his first novel, at the age of 28, he was firmly launched on a literary career.

Chapter 2

The Divided Self

Uncle Wells arrived always a little out of breath, with his arms full of parcels, sometimes rather carelessly tied, but always bursting with all manner of attractive gifts that range from the little pot of sweet jelly that is *Mr Polly*, to the complete meccano set for the mind that is in *The First Men in the Moon*.

Rebecca West, 'Uncle Bennett'

Then very haltingly at first, but afterwards more easily, he began to tell of the thing that was hidden in his life, the haunting memory of a beauty and a happiness that filled his heart with insatiable longings, that made all the interests and spectacle of worldly life seem dull and tedious and vain to him.

H. G. Wells, 'The door in the wall'

I

There can be no doubt that for Wells what he termed the 'fugitive impulse' was a powerful element in his make-up. Thinking aloud in his autobiography he posed the questions: 'Is there a strain of evasion in my composition? Does the thought of being bound and settling down, in itself, so soon as it is definitely presented, arouse a recalcitrant stress in me?'[1] His life thus far had been a series of escapes – from Bromley, from Midhurst, from South Kensington, from Holt, from teaching, from marriage. Although he had left Isabel in favour of Amy there was still a marked reluctance on his part to settling down. He and Amy commenced their life together in January 1894 but it was not until the autumn of 1895 that they ceased to live in lodgings and acquired a home of their own, a semi-detached villa on Maybury Road, Woking (they married as soon as he was free to do so in October 1895). For the next five years the story of his life is one not only of rapidly growing literary success but of a continuing attempt to reconcile the contradictions within his personality and to arrive at a *modus vivendi* with his second wife.

He was tied to her with bonds of deep affection and respect but not with the overwhelming passion he had felt for Isabel. He and Amy 'worked in close association and sympathy', he wrote, 'but there arose no such sexual fixation between us as still lingered in my mind towards my cousin.'[2] He disliked both her first names, Amy and Catherine, and after some experimenting with alternative names (one of which was Euphemia) he presently hit on Jane as her epithet. She was known as Jane from then until her death in 1927. Jane Wells was small, fragile and gentle but had a mind of her own and was a capable organiser and manager. She became a real helpmate, typing his manuscripts, checking his proofs and coping with a multitude of secretarial tasks. Where he was untidy, headstrong and temperamental she was tidy, calm and even-tempered. Where he was impatient, mercurial and prone to moods of self-doubt she was placid, tolerant and constant in her devotion to him. She exerted a steadying influence upon him, surrounding him with order and peace in which he could write. He was under no illusions of what he owed to her. 'To her sympathy, loyalty, co-operation, and capable management of my affairs', he wrote many years later, 'my success in the world is very largely due.'[3] The first few years of adjustment to one another cannot have been easy, for beneath an outwardly cheerful persona he was a man of many contradictions. On the one hand he possessed a genuine literary talent, formidable energy, and a sense of wonder which led him to produce a series of brilliant mythopoeic visions. He was capable of exploiting the teeming possibilities of science and invention in a rich vein of novels, fantasias, speculations and short stories. On the other hand he was deeply divided within himself and not at all certain of the direction he wished to follow. As a writer he was still feeling his way, consciously experimenting with a range of styles and genres. Emotionally he still yearned for what he termed 'the deep desired embraces of Venus Urania', a passionate reciprocity based on mutually desirable minds and bodies.[4] Psychologically he was increasingly aware of an ambivalence in his character between romantic and classical drives: between the world of the imagination as exemplified by Shelley and Blake, and the world of science as exemplified by Huxley and Darwin. And behind these emotional and artistic dichotomies lay a profound, unspoken claustrophobia and a manifest dislike of domesticity.

Meanwhile he was working extremely hard and establishing a name for himself on the London literary scene. The publication of *The Time Machine* was followed in swift succession by another novel, *The Wonderful Visit*, and a collection of short stories, *The Stolen Bacillus*. Soon he was at work on a satirical fable in the vein of Swift, *The Island of Doctor Moreau*, and a bicycling romance, *The Wheels of Chance*. The 1890s saw the increasing popularity of cycling and he and Jane took up the hobby with enthusiasm, exploring the lanes of Surrey and Sussex together on a tandem. Looking back with hindsight on his astonishing literary performance it is tempting for a biographer to see *The Time Machine* as the first of a series of novels in which Wells, with increasing ease and confidence, dazzled the world and won for himself a pre-eminent place among writers. To Wells himself, 'writing away for dear life', the situation at the time must have seemed far less certain. There was, after all, no guarantee that he would succeed; the literary life was notoriously unpredictable. To abandon a secure income as a teacher in favour of a fluctuating income as a writer was an enormous gamble. He was moreover a man with increasing responsibilities. He was now a married man with a household; he was paying alimony to his first wife; and he was maintaining his mother and father in a cottage at Liss, Hampshire, which he first rented and later bought for them. In addition to writing novels, fantasias and short stories he was contributing regular book reviews to Frank Harris's *Saturday Review* and a considerable amount of miscellaneous journalism to the leading London weeklies. The book reviewing was extremely important to him – during his two-year tenure as fiction critic for the *Saturday Review* he contributed some ninety-two essays containing 285 reviews – coinciding with a period of seminal importance in his own literary development.

During these years he was shaping and refining his critical approach to the art of fiction, continually testing his own work against that of established novelists such as Hardy, James, Stevenson and Meredith. As his income and reputation steadily increased he was able gradually to shed the journalism and concentrate his energies on the writing of full-length works. However, he continued to write short stories for many years and between 1895 and 1911 published five collected editions: *The Stolen Bacillus and Other Incidents, The Plattner Story and Others, Tales of Space and Time, Twelve Stories and a Dream* and *The Country of the Blind and Other Stories*, containing between them fifty-five stories. For a time, he wrote, he found the writing of short stories 'a very entertaining pursuit indeed . . . I would discover I was peering into remote and mysterious worlds ruled by an order logical indeed but other than our common sanity'.[5] Ideas for short stories continually bubbled to the surface of his mind, ranging from the horror of 'Pollock and the Porrah man' and 'The red room' to the disquieting vision of such tales as 'Under the knife', 'The crystal egg' and 'The story of the late Mr Elvesham'. The common element in these tales is their ability to *disturb*: to unsettle the reader by displaying life from an unusual perspective or introducing hitherto unexplored facets of behaviour. Behind the short stories and the science fiction – or, as he preferred to term them, 'fantasias of possibility' – lay a mind increasingly curious about human potentialities and eager to engage in speculations concerning life and society. It is a mind which sees life with pitiless clarity and is deeply aware of the irrational drives underlying the veneer of civilisation: the drives towards cruelty, violence and pain. His early novels – *The Island of Doctor Moreau, The Invisible Man, The War of the Worlds* and *When the Sleeper Wakes* – are notable for their austere scientific vision, their insight into the human predicament. They are imbued both with a sombre pessimism and a stoical detachment. 'At times I suffer from the strangest sense of detachment from myself and the world about me', writes the narrator of *The War of the Worlds*, 'I seem to watch it all from the outside, from somewhere inconceivably remote, out of time, out of space, out of the stress and tragedy of it all.'[6]

But simultaneously with this sombre mood a very different Wells is discernible, a Wells who is fascinated with quirks of behaviour and wellsprings of emotion, a man filled with a deep affection for rural England. Consider the descriptions of the Sussex countryside in *The Wheels of Chance*, the description of Whit Monday and the village of Iping in *The Invisible Man*, the portrayal of Lady Hammergallow in *The Wonderful Visit* or the opening chapters of *The War of the Worlds* depicting the impact of the coming of the Martians on a cross-section of ordinary people. These reveal a novelist's eye for detail and a shrewd understanding of human nature. It is this fusion of the stoical detachment of Huxley with the warm humanitarian vision of Dickens which makes Wells such a fascinating writer and a significant transitional figure between the Victorian and the modern novel.

Despite his material success his health remained indifferent – a particularly serious bout of illness occurred in 1898, culminating in two months' convalescence – and domestic claustrophobia underlay much of his restlessness. Between 1894 and 1900 he changed his address no fewer than eight times, either because of the urge to move to larger premises or for the sake of his health. From Woking he moved to Worcester Park, Surrey, but finding this unsuitable for his catarrh he moved to Sandgate, near Folkestone (September 1898) having been advised by his doctor that he must live in a dry climate, on sand or gravel, and in a high, sheltered position. A letter to George Gissing written at this time wistfully conveys his longing for sunnier climates:

> I mean to lead a great multitude of selected people out of this reek, sooner or later, artists and writers and decent souls and we will all settle in little houses along and up a slope of sunlight all set with olives and vines and honey mellowed marble ruins between the mountains and the sea.[7]

Love and Mr Lewisham, published in 1900, is a carefully written account of a youthful love affair modelled on his own student years in London. It was meticulously planned and wrought over a period of four years and remains one of the most consciously 'written' of all his works. In a letter to Elizabeth Healey while it was in process of composition he confided: 'Heaven knows when it will get done, for writing fantastic romance is one thing, and writing a novel is quite another.' In a real sense *Love and Mr Lewisham* can be seen as the workshop in which a tyro taught himself the art of the realist novel. As he worked on draft after draft, revising and reshaping, he found himself becoming increasingly fascinated by the characters he had created and the ability of the novel to depict problems of human behaviour. When it was published he sent a copy to Henry James, who praised it fulsomely. 'I have found in it great charm and a great deal of the real thing', wrote James, 'the thing is a bloody little chunk of life, of no small substance, and I wish it a great and continuous fortune.'[8] Though he and James remained on terms of friendship for some years, corresponding regularly and visiting each other, there were profound temperamental differences between them and a fundamental divergence in their attitudes to the novel. To James the novel was an art form, the highest of all art forms, and the only kind of novel worthy of the name was the wholly symmetrical, beautifully constructed edifice as exemplified by the works of Jane Austen. All other types of fiction – the romances of Defoe and Stevenson, for example – were inferior imitations and could not properly be regarded as novels. To Wells on the other hand, the novel was a medium of expression. His background and reading led him more and more to the recognition that his mentors were Dickens, Fielding and Sterne; to this discursive tradition of the English novel he felt he belonged. This irreconcilable divergence of view continued to exercise the two writers until James's death in 1916.

The Wellses lived in rented houses in Sandgate until December 1900, when they moved into Spade House, Radnor Cliff Crescent, a substantial stone-built house designed for them by the architect Charles Voysey. Situated in a commanding position overlooking the English Channel, Spade House was built on a split level to utilise the slope of the ground and to take advantage of the splendid views. With rising fame and success he felt, as he put it, that he was 'fairly launched at last'. He decided to settle. Spade House remained his home for almost ten years: a decade of crucial importance to his development as an imaginative writer and a public figure. Two sons were born at Spade House: George Philip in 1901 and Frank Richard in 1903.

The move to Sandgate not only brought about a marked improvement in his health but, equally important, brought him within the ambit of Joseph Conrad, Henry James and Ford Madox Ford, each of whom lived within cycling distance of his home. The friendships with them, which developed in the ensuing years, together with his friendships with Arnold Bennett, George Gissing and Dorothy Richardson, sustained him during one of the most creative periods of his life. Early in the new century he embarked on a series of sociological essays, published in book form in 1901 under the title *Anticipations*. These remarkable forecasts covering such topics as the rise of suburbia, warfare in the twentieth century, changes in methods of transport and the growth of technocracy, brought him to the attention of a wide audience and revealed his growing interest in social and political matters. The birth and upbringing of his sons revived his interest in education, and in *Mankind in the Making* (1903) he set forth his ideas on the teaching of the young. This was followed two years later by *A Modern Utopia*, a persuasively written description of an ideal world ruled by a dedicated elite, the Order of the Samurai, a twentieth-century rendering of the Guardians in Plato's *Republic*. In these writings he insisted again that every individual was unique and reiterated the implications of this idea upon personal morality:

> The last temporary raft of a logical moral code goes to pieces at this, and its separated spars float here and there . . . Each life, it seems to me, in that intelligent, conscious, social state to which the world is coming, must square itself to these things in its own way, and fill in the details of its individual moral code according to its needs.[9]

This insistence that there could be no universally applicable moral laws was one of his most fundamental convictions. It was a conviction which, together with his rejection of orthodox religious belief and his growing interest in socialist ideas, earned him the respect and support of many among the young but the hostility of many among the establishment.

II

With all his ambience of comfort and success Wells should have been a deeply happy man. He had a wife who cared for him intensely, a family, a beautiful home and material prosperity. He was writing well and producing some of his finest work. To the Spade House years belong such works as *The First Men in the Moon*, *The Food of the Gods*, *Kipps*, *In the Days of the Comet* and *The War in the Air*. He was also turning his attention to social, philosophical and political issues in *A Modern Utopia*, *New Worlds for Old* and *First and Last Things*. Yet deep inside his make-up he was troubled with profound discontents; he was aware of a very real but unspoken sense that something was missing from his life. In a short story written at Sandgate but not published until many years later, 'The wild asses of the devil', he describes an author 'who pursued fame and prosperity in a pleasant villa on the south coast of England':

Sometimes – in the morning sometimes – he would be irritable and have quarrels with his shaving things, and there were extraordinary moods when it would seem to him that living quite beautifully in a pleasant villa and being well-off and famous, and writing books . . . was about as boring and intolerable a life as any creature with a soul to be damned could possibly pursue.[10]

This gnawing discontent with life comes to the surface in a number of the novels and stories written at this time. *Love and Mr Lewisham* tells the story of a conflict between the pursuit of a career and the quest for romance – a conflict which he described in his autobiography as his 'Compound Fugue' – which ends in an uneasy victory for domesticity. The short story 'The door in the wall' (1906) describes a successful politician, Lionel Wallace, who is haunted by an intolerable longing for an enchanted garden he had glimpsed as a child. One of his most revealing novels in this connection is *The Sea Lady*, published in 1902 but planned two years earlier, in which a rising politician, Chatteris, abandons his career in pursuit of a mermaid. Chatteris is described as a man 'divided against himself' who is continually seeking an elusive vision of lost happiness; he is troubled by a longing 'that tears at the very fabric of this daily life'. For him the mermaid is the embodiment of the beauty and mystery lacking in his world. Beckoned by her into the sea on a warm summer's night, he follows her and is drowned. The Sandgate setting of the story and the close similarities between Chatteris's personality and Wells's leave little doubt that, consciously or unconsciously, he was sublimating his own desires in the form of an allegory. *The Sea Lady*, he acknowledged later, revealed 'a craving for some lovelier experience than life had yet given me'. He added significantly: 'Not only Catherine Wells but I too could long at times for impossible magic islands.'[11] This yearning for 'magic islands', for beauty and romance, was to haunt him throughout his life. It found its expression in *Tono-Bungay* and *The History of Mr Polly*, in 'Mr Skelmersdale in fairyland' and 'The door in the wall', and in his continual quest for emotional completion. This quest, which he described as 'the mixture of sexual need and the hunger for a dear companion that has so disturbed me',[12] came to obsess him increasingly during these years.

After the birth of their first child he and Jane arrived at a compromise which would enable him to remain married to her and at the same time be free to find an outlet for his emotional restlessness. He was to be free to have *passades*, to indulge in affairs with other women, so long as Jane continued to be Mrs H. G. Wells and their home remained the centre of his life. In the chapter of his autobiography describing this compromise, '*Modus vivendi*', he mentions apparently casually 'I have published only four lines of verse in my life' but does not go on to say what the lines of verse are. In fact they appeared in the *Pall Mall Gazette* on 13 March, 1894, and – since they seem to me to be extremely significant in the light of his subsequent emotional history – they are worth quoting in full:

Episode
A meeting under the greenwood tree
In a soft, leaf-filtered light;
A meeting or so, and a passion to know
If I read your eyes aright.

A parting under the greenwood tree
A delicate passion of pain
And soberly I return to my
Mature and elegant Jane.

Here surely is a prefigurement in unmistakable terms of the tensions latent in his marriage. The romantic encounter in 'a soft, leaf-filtered light'; the parting in 'a delicate passion of pain'; and the return to his 'mature and elegant' wife – this pattern is repeated again and again in the story of Wells's relationships with women from 1900 onwards. Jane remained the anchor, the unfailing companion who stabilised his life. Together, he wrote, they contrived 'in the absence of a real passionate sexual fixation, a binding net of fantasy and affection that proved in the end as effective as the very closest sexual sympathy could have been in keeping us together'.[13] She and the home she created for him at Spade House remained the centre of his world. But outside this he was free to have affairs – that the verses are entitled 'Episode' suggests an assumption, which Jane seems to have shared, that the affairs would be transitory. This was indeed the pattern of his life for some years, and with Violet Hunt, Dorothy Richardson and others he indulged in passing affairs. But though episodic in nature it would be misleading to see them as merely a symptom of a man who was continually seeking sexual gratification. For Wells each of these affairs was a search for fulfilment, for intellectual and emotional completion. All his life was a search for what he termed 'the Lover-Shadow', the embodiment of the romantic longings which had disturbed him since adolescence. The quest was never wholly realised. 'The fundamental love of my life is the Lover-Shadow', he wrote towards the end of his life, 'and always I have been catching a glimpse of her and losing her in these adventures.'[14]

It may be questioned why his marriage held together for so long when Jane had every provocation to bring it to an end. Clearly there was a deep emotional bond between them, a bond so strong that it endured through all the strains Wells placed upon it. Despite his numerous infidelities their partnership continued unimpaired. That it did so is evidence not only of the fact that Jane was a very remarkable person but that she and Wells were both deeply complex individuals. Behind the public mask which each presented to the world was a private self – one that provided a reserve of reassurance and solace in times of difficulty.

Jane Wells had two selves – the public self, Jane, and the private one, Catherine. Jane was the efficient organiser and secretary, the helpmate who coped with all his administrative and business affairs, tackled his voluminous correspondence, was a capable hostess at house parties and shielded him from the petty irritations which afflict a famous writer. This was the Jane the world saw – practical, wise and unflappable. Behind this self lay a much more private person, the Catherine whom Wells rarely glimpsed. Catherine was prone to reverie, to dreams of romantic encounters and elusive happinesses. She expressed this hidden side of her nature in writing short stories, poetry and fantasies, many of which he collected together after her death and published under the title *The Book of Catherine Wells*. The stories possess a haunting quality, a striving for lost contentment and completion. Though her marriage brought her much material happiness – a fine house, costly clothes, foreign travel and a wide and growing circle of friends – clearly there were aspects of her personality that remained unfulfilled. As the years went on she found she could only express these secret longings through her writing.

Just as there were two sides to Jane's personality so there were two Wellses – a truth which Kingsley Martin grasped when he wrote: 'I once told H. G. Wells and, after reflection, he agreed with my analysis, that at least two people struggled inside him, Herbert and George. Bert reacted; George dreamed.'[15] The public Wells was the successful writer, the sage who commanded a world audience for his novels and journalism, who hobnobbed with the leading politicians and writers of the day and whose name was known throughout the English-speaking world. The private Wells was a very different figure, a man who loved rural scenery and English villages, who delighted in simple pleasures – walking, cycling, reading and listening to classical music – and who was at his best when conversing with a small circle of intimate friends. The private Wells yearned for 'impossible magic islands', indulged in romantic fantasies about elusive goddesses and was haunted by tantalising visions of lost beauty. It is partly because Jane understood and sympathised with this side of his nature, that she tolerated the claustrophobia which at times overwhelmed him, that their partnership continued harmoniously for so many years. 'But if she did not understand my ideas', he wrote,

she came to understand many things in my character that are still hidden from me. She controlled me for my own happiness, invisibly, imperceptibly. She gave me a disinterested friendship, which is so much greater a thing to give than sexual love. While she lived my discontent with life was greatly allayed. I never worked so well as I did during those years.[16]

Gordon Ray, in the introduction to his study of Wells and Rebecca West, remarks that after the birth of their two sons Wells and Jane 'ceased to be lovers'. In the physical sense this is probably true but it is a mistake to infer from this that they no longer loved one another. It is impossible to understand the marriage between Wells and Jane without grasping that there was between them a very powerful bond of love, affection and respect. There is abundant testimony to the web of emotion and understanding that held them together, to the fact that he depended on her more and more for companionship and intellectual affinity, and to his realisation that she was 'the strongest secondary system of reference I ever developed . . . the moral background of half my life'.[17] A letter she wrote to him in April 1906 during one of his absences abroad is typical of many: 'I feel tonight *so* tired of playing wiv making the home comfy & as if there was only one dear rest place in the world, & that were in the arms & heart of you.' After asking him why he puts up with such an unsatisfactory wife she signed the letter 'Your very loving Bits'. Bits was his private nickname for her; her name for him was Bins. This extraordinary marriage survived the vicissitudes and tensions of more than thirty years and was only severed by her death.

The death of his mother Sarah Wells in June 1905 and the consequent cessation of the web of affection that had held mother and son together exercised a releasing influence upon him and for the first time in his life he felt able to place his feelings towards her in perspective. In the figures of Willie Leadford's mother in *In the Days of the Comet*, Mrs Ponderevo in *Tono-Bungay* and Remington's mother in *The New Machiavelli* he presented aspects of her character with a verisimilitude he had never previously attained. In these portraits he tried to make amends for his wilfulness in the past and to convey the love for her he had rarely expressed in her lifetime. It is clear from these portrayals and the account of her in his autobiography that while she lived he had been unable to acknowledge the deep bonds of attachment which bound him to her. George Ponderevo in *Tono-Bungay* writes of his mother after her death:

Suddenly I saw her tenderly; remembered not so much tender or kindly things of her as her crossed wishes and the ways in which I had thwarted her. Surprisingly I realised that behind all her hardness and severity she had loved me, that I was the only thing she had ever loved, and that until this moment I had never loved her.[18]

1. Joseph Wells (H. G. Wells's
father).

2. Sarah Wells (H. G. Wells's
mother).

3. Isabella Campbell Mackenzie (Rebecca West's mother).

4. Charles Fairfield (Rebecca West's father).

5. Uppark, Sussex. The house was partially destroyed by fire in August 1989 but is to be rebuilt by the National Trust.

6. H. G. Wells, *circa* 1896. He was then aged 30 and at the beginning of his extraordinary literary career.

7.   H. G. Wells and Sarah Wells. The photograph was taken at Spade House, Wells's home from 1900–9.

8.   Easton Glebe, Dunmow, Wells's home from 1912–27. Here Wells and Rebecca first met on 27 September 1912, following her review of his novel, *Marriage*.

Throughout Sarah's life her references to Wells in her diaries are invariably in affectionate terms. As a boy he is 'my dearest child' and as an adult he is 'dear Bertie'. Though she had longed for another daughter after Fanny's death and Wells's scepticism on religious matters must have deeply disappointed her it seems fair to conclude that of all her offspring she was closest to her youngest son. Emotionally and psychologically the bonds between them were deep and enduring. Sarah Wells's passing removed one of the emotional cornerstones of his life. From henceforward, probably quite unconsciously, he transferred the dependence and affection he had felt towards her increasingly upon his wife. Jane became a mother-figure, a steadfast source of companionship, counsel and reassurance.

III

His years at Spade House were torn by two events which dominated his life and exercised a lasting influence upon him as both man and writer. These were, first, his unsuccessful attempt to transform the Fabian Society from a drawing-room debating society to a crusading political force; and, second, his friendship and love affair with Amber Reeves. Interwoven with these events was his continuing struggle to find himself as a creative artist, culminating in the writing of his masterpiece, *Tono-Bungay*.

For in spite of these and other distractions he was working steadily at Sandgate on the writing of fiction. As early as 1900 in a letter to his friend Arnold Bennett he declared: 'I want to write novels and before God I *will* write novels. They are the proper stuff for my everyday work, a methodical careful distillation of one's thoughts and sentiments and experiences and impressions.'[19] It is clear that the creation of scientific romances and fantasias – with which his career had begun so amazingly – failed to satisfy some deep inner need, and throughout the first decade of the new century he increasingly turned his energies and imagination to the writing of novels in the realist tradition. The first of these, *Kipps*, published in 1905, had an even longer gestation than *Lewisham*. Originally conceived in 1898 under the title *The Wealth of Mr Waddy*, it passed through a series of metamorphoses before it appeared under the title *Kipps: The story of a simple soul* seven years later. Planned on a much broader canvas than *Lewisham* it is far more evidently a novel in the vein of Dickens. The opening chapter, 'The little shop at New Romney', is a touching evocation of innocence, describing the childhood love between Arthur Kipps and Ann Pornick with a fidelity he rarely surpassed. The chapters depicting Kipps's adolescence and early

manhood draw freely on his own experiences as a drapery assistant at
Southsea but it is rather more than an autobiographical novel. In its
portrayal of the playwright Chitterlow, Chester Coote, Helen Walsing-
ham and her circle, and Kipps's slow realisation that he does not belong
in the world of polite society, Wells is exploring ground he had not
entered before and displaying a growing preoccupation with questions
of conduct and motivation.

In the Days of the Comet, written in 1905, is a curious hybrid possessing
the characteristics of a realist novel and a scientific romance. The first
two-thirds of the book describing a tale of love and intrigue set against
the background of the Staffordshire Potteries is a fine piece of
storytelling, conveying in unforgettably vivid terms the life and times
of an idealistic but poor young man in the opening years of the century.
The final chapters depicting an England miraculously transformed as a
result of a beneficient gas emanating from a comet are much less
convincing. By common consent these chapters mar an otherwise
memorable novel, notable for its gripping account of industrial strife
seen from the vantage point of an underdog and its sensitive evocation
of the youthful love affair between Willie Leadford and Nettie Stuart.
Nettie, with her indefinable beauty and simple charm, is another sketch
of Wells's first wife Isabel – a sketch he was to elaborate in much
greater depth in *Tono-Bungay* – and in the account of the narrator's
fascination with her there are unmistakable echoes of Wells's obsession
with his cousin. But already in this novel there are hints of the
disingenousness which was to land Wells in so much hot water with the
publication of *Ann Veronica* and *The New Machiavelli*. The narrator falls in
love with a girl called 'Anna Reeves' who bears a close resemblance to
the young bluestocking Amber Reeves whom Wells was seeing at this
time. Nor is this all. At the conclusion of the book Leadford, Anna,
Nettie and her lover Verrall live together in a *ménage à quatre*. The
narrator makes the point explicit when he comments in the Epilogue:
'But we four from that time were very close, you understand, we were
friends, helpers, personal lovers in a world of lovers.' This was siezed
on by a number of reviewers hostile to Wells who accused him of
advocating promiscuity. *The Times Literary Supplement*, for example, on 14
September 1906 proclaimed: 'Socialistic men's wives, we gather are, no
less than their goods, to be held in common. Free love, according to Mr
Wells, is to be of the essence of the new social contract.'

Angry at this charge he hastened to defend himself and in a paper
delivered to the Fabian Society – subsequently published as a booklet
under the title *Socialism and the Family* – he spelt out his conviction that in
a socialist society the role of women would be radically different:

My concern now is to point out that socialism repudiates the private ownership of the head of the family as completely as it repudiates any other sort of private ownership. Socialism involves the responsible citizenship of women, their economic independence of men, and all the personal freedom that follows that . . . Socialism indeed proposes to abolish altogether the patriarchal family amidst whose disintegrating ruins we live, and to raise women to an equal citizenship with men. It proposes to give a man no more property in a woman than a woman has in a man.

This was the germ of the idea he was later to elaborate as the Endowment of Motherhood – the proposal that married women bearing children should be paid a wage by the state to be financed by a special income tax. Increasingly in his novels he came to be preoccupied with the relationships between men and women, with the nature of marriage in the twentieth century and the labyrinth of problems connected with sexual morality.

Tono-Bungay, completed in the spring of 1908 and published early in the following year, is widely regarded as the high water mark of his achievement as a novelist. In its pages all the different Wellses – the humorist, the sociologist, the scientific romancer, the prophet, the novelist – fuse together in a narrative of compelling richness and power. A. C. Ward described it as 'the central point at which all Wells's competing interests met and united'.[20] The planning and writing of it occupied a total of four years, for again and again he was interrupted by diversions: the writing of *In the Days of the Comet* and *New Worlds for Old*, a visit to the United States in 1906, the Fabian episode and a considerable amount of journalism. Despite these interruptions it remains one of the most carefully planned and executed of all his books, and there can be no doubt that he held for it very high ambitions. 'Presently I was finishing *Kipps*', he wrote in his autobiography, 'and making notes for what I meant to be a real full-length novel at last, *Tono-Bungay*, a novel, as I imagined it, on Dickens-Thackeray lines . . .'[21] What is so remarkable about the novel is not only its *David Copperfield*-like evocation of the adult world seen through the eyes of a child but the austere scientific detachment with which the narrator contemplates the decline and breakup of Victorian England. In its extraordinarily ambivalent portrayal of Bladesover House (Uppark), its account of the rise and fall of the Tono-Bungay empire, its perceptive account of the narrator's loveless marriage and, above all, its eloquent coda 'Night and the open sea' it is one of the most far-seeing of twentieth-century novels.

The narrator, in common with Wells himself, is a deeply divided personality, for there is evident in *Tono-Bungay* a continuing (and unresolved) attempt to reconcile the sceptical and romantic elements in his make-up. George Ponderevo describes himself as 'a spiritual gutter-snipe in love with unimaginable goddesses'. As a student, an aeronaut and an engineer he is consumed by the idea of scientific research, the disinterested quest for reality. He does his utmost to maintain a pose as a man of science: sceptical, detached, critical, rational. Yet he is continually distracted by a yearning for beauty which, though he cannot define it, is always present. When he falls in love with Marion he sees her in his dreams as a romantic vision, 'beautiful, worshipful, glowing'. He is distracted from his marriage by a promise of sensuous attraction, and from his scientific research by the enigmatic Beatrice Normandy. But it is the great house and its surrounding parkland which become a fitting symbol for his ambivalence:

> About that park there were some elements of a liberal education; there
> was a great space of greensward not given over to manure and food
> grubbing; there was mystery, there was matter for the imagination . . .
> There were corners that gave a gleam of meaning to the word forest,
> glimpses of unstudied natural splendour. There was a slope of bluebells in
> the broken sunlight under the newly green beeches in the West Wood
> that is now precious sapphire in my memory; it was the first time that I
> knowingly met Beauty.[22]

In this one short passage occur a cluster of key romantic concepts: mystery, imagination, nature, splendour, beauty. In the image of the house and the park can be seen a summation of the contradictions which divide the narrator (and, by implication, his creator). The mansion with its classical architecture, its scholarly library, its order and symmetry, represents all that is rational and disciplined in man: a perfect symbol of the Age of Reason. The park encapsulates the opposite values – wildness, loveliness, romance, uncertainty. All his life Wells was haunted by the enchanted garden as a literary and imaginative motif, and the idea recurs again and again in his work: in *The Time Machine*, 'The door in the wall', *The Passionate Friends*, *Men Like Gods*, *The Happy Turning*. This dichotomy between the scientist and the artist, between reason and imagination, fractured his work and thought to the end of his life.

But now his writings were bringing him to the attention of the Fabians. The Fabian Society was founded in January 1884 and remained for many years a small, exclusive society of intellectual socialists pledged to work for empirical reforms through a policy of permeation. Its membership has never risen higher than four thousand, yet it has exercised an influence out of all proportion to its size, partly owing to brilliant leadership and partly because it has concentrated on building up a body of doctrine based upon meticulous study and thought. In the late nineteenth and early twentieth centuries it included in its leading elite some of the shining intellectual lights of the age: Bernard Shaw, Sidney and Beatrice Webb, Graham Wallas, Annie Besant and many others. They were the spearhead of the intelligentsia, seeking to transform Britain into a socialist polity through writing, speaking, preaching, pamphleteering and the dissemination of their ideas. Wells became a member in February 1903, having been jointly sponsored by Shaw and Graham Wallas. He had been introduced to the Society by the Webbs, who had been greatly interested by his *Anticipations* and its sequel *Mankind in the Making*. It was the serialisation of the former in the *Fortnightly Review* which first brought Sidney and Beatrice Webb into his world. He recorded later that 'they appeared riding very rapidly upon bicycles, from the direction of London, offering certain criticisms of my general forecast and urging me to join and stimulate the Fabians'.[23] Their criticisms are recalled with some rancour in *The New Machiavelli*.

Wells played little part in the Society until February 1906 when he read a critical paper to members, 'Faults of the Fabian'. In his address he urged the Society to conduct 'a vigorous socialistic propaganda among all the more educated and intelligent sections of our population' and outlined a series of proposals designed to enthuse new life and purpose into the organisation. 'Faults of the Fabian' was written with all his persuasiveness and eloquence, and when one adds to this his attractive personality and the fact that the younger Fabians, at least, regarded him as their hero in their struggle against tradition, it is not difficult to understand the furore his paper aroused. There was nothing inherently unsound in any of his proposals for reform. But he was an unconvincing public speaker and organiser and it was this factor, plus a natural incapacity for leadership, which proved to be his undoing.

The Executive – the 'Old Guard' as Wells dubbed them – agreed to set up a special committee 'to consider what measures should be taken to increase the scope, influence, income and activity of the Society'. This consisted of three members of the Executive plus seven others including Wells and Jane. The committee, when it reported in October, endorsed his detailed proposals but the Executive published a reply amounting to a complete rejection of all the committee's recommendations. Wells and his supporters had advocated the formation of local groups, a vigorous propaganda campaign, more frequent publications, an increased subscription and a simpler membership procedure: all proposals designed to transform the Society into an aggressive propagandist organisation with a wide membership. The Executive in its reply – clearly drafted by Shaw – would have none of this, dismissing the committee's recommendations as impracticable. The debate within the Society raged for some months but Wells was no match for Shaw's oratory and in the end had to concede defeat. His resignation came in a letter to 'Fabian News' in September 1908, when he announced that 'I want very much to concentrate myself now upon the writing of novels for some years.'

Wells himself had gone but his ideas remained, a source of ferment and inspiration for many years to come. The wound rankled deeply in his mind (and still rankled when he came to write his autobiography more than twenty years later). He had wanted to revolutionise the Fabian Society – no less. And revolution was the last thing its leaders wanted. He was seeking to transform it into a dedicated, militant, crusading Order akin to the Samurai of *A Modern Utopia* – an Order which would be the spearhead of a socialist revival. With the wisdom of hindsight it is easy to say that the Society was no place for Wells. It was far too respectable and cautious a body for one so capricious and impatient of gradual change. The truth is that he was constitutionally incapable of working with societies, organisations and committees. His distinctive role was to stimulate thought, to provide ideas and inspiration, to portray the vision and the ideal. During his years of activity membership increased substantially, and there can be no question that many younger members were attracted to the Society through his fame and influence, two of whom – Amber Reeves and Rebecca West – were destined to play decisive roles in his life.

Amber Reeves, whom he first met in 1904, was the daughter of the prominent Fabians Maud and Pember Reeves. Maud had been an ally of Wells's in his attempts to rejuvenate the Society and her daughter inherited much of her idealism and unconventionality. Amber, a student at Newnham College, Cambridge, became an active member of the Fabian Nursery and a staunch advocate of Wells's ideas. For some years she remained on the fringe of his world, one of a group of young people who had been inspired by such works as *A Modern Utopia, In the Days of the Comet* and *This Misery of Boots*. Gradually their friendship became more and more intimate until in 1907 they became lovers in the fullest sense. Amber was then 20, an intensely idealistic and single-minded young woman filled with intellectual curiosity and passionate feminist convictions. She told Wells she was in love with him and he was deeply flattered, feeling towards her a strong physical and mental attraction. For some time they contrived to keep the affair secret, but after some months Amber unwisely began to talk; a whispering campaign began to develop around him. Wells describes the affair and its consequences with some frankness in *Ann Veronica*, where he appears in the guise of Capes and Amber as the spirited heroine. The story is then retold with even more candour in *The New Machiavelli*, where he is cast as Richard Remington and Amber as Isabel Rivers. His inability to keep his private life out of his novels makes the fiction of the Edwardian years an extremely interesting guide to his state of mind at this time. The narrator of *The New Machiavelli* comments ruefully:

And then we found, as all those scores of thousands of people scattered about us have found, that we could not keep it to ourselves. Love will out. All the rest of this story is the chronicle of that. Love with sustained secrecy cannot be love. It is just exactly the point people do not understand.[24]

The scandal of his affair with Amber began to be whispered not only among the Fabians but beyond, greatly fuelled by the publication of *Ann Veronica* in October 1909. What so many readers found distasteful about the novel was that the heroine practically throws herself at a married man and lives with him in open defiance of convention. Capes, the biology tutor with whom Ann Veronica falls in love, begs her to discuss their situation calmly and not to rush into precipitate action. Ann Veronica will have none of it: ' "I want you. I want you to be my lover. I want to give myself to you. I want to be whatever I can to you." She paused for a moment. "Is that plain?" she asked.'[25]

It was this frankness which caused such a furore. In a society which preached that a wife was a man's property, that to live together outside wedlock was to 'live in sin', that an unmarried mother was 'a fallen woman', Ann Veronica's behaviour was scandalous and outrageous. The novel was denounced from pulpits and many libraries refused to stock copies. *The Spectator* denounced it as 'a poisonous book', claiming that 'His is a community of scuffling stoats and ferrets, unenlightened by a ray of duty or abnegation'. Wells was deeply torn. On the one hand he passionately desired and needed Amber, who in his eyes was the Venus Urania of his adolescent dreams. On the other hand he dearly loved his wife and sons and refused to leave them. For a time he sought to have the best of both worlds but when Amber gave birth to a baby daughter in December 1909 matters became impossibly complicated. Pulled asunder by incompatible emotional needs he was unable to settle on a clear course of action; in the end it was Amber who arrived at a solution to their dilemma. A friend and admirer of long standing, Rivers Blanco White (Arnold Shoesmith in *The New Machiavelli*) offered to marry her, in full knowledge of the circumstances. She decided to accept him. On the face of it this seemed a tidy way of resolving the problem but in real life, as no one knew better than Wells, solutions to emotional problems are rarely tidy and are not achieved without pain. He was still riven by competing desires and for long afterwards was tormented by intolerable longings. 'I've had rather a bad time', he wrote to Mrs J. M. Barrie, 'Amber and I are being forced never to see or write to each other. I suppose it's the same thing in the long run – except that I rather hanker after bolting – but it hurts horribly and leaves one the prey to all sorts of moods.'[26]

The affair left him in a phase of restlessness during which he sold Spade House – 'because I felt that otherwise it would become the final setting of my life'[27] and moved to London, to 17, Church Row, Hampstead. But at the same time it stimulated him to write some of his finest work. *The History of Mr Polly*, by common consent one of his most enduring achievements, was written during the affair's immediate aftermath (he recalled later that the description of Mr Polly's wedding, one of the most memorable episodes of the novel, was written while he was 'weeping bitterly like a frustrated child'.)[28] The novel, published in 1910, is in part an affectionate tribute to the memory of Joseph Wells. In the story of a failed shopkeeper who escapes from a humdrum marriage to find happiness as a handyman at a country inn Wells incorporated memories of his father and also embodied many of his own childhood fantasies. Alfred Polly, a bookish dreamer who never loses sight of the idea that 'somewhere – magically inaccessible perhaps, but still somewhere – were pure and easy and joyous states of body and mind' is a quintessentially Wellsian hero. In its description of his romantic daydreams, its loving evocation of the English countryside, its deep insight into Mr Polly's mind and its idyllic picture of the ultimate haven of the Potwell Inn it is one of the most intimate of his works. The novel has been seen by some critics as an escape from reality, a deliberate rejection of duty and responsibility. But it is in another sense a wish fulfilment, for there can be no doubt that in writing the novel Wells gave expression to some of his deepest unspoken desires. His biographer Geoffrey West recorded that '*Mr Polly* is what it is because it is neither what Wells thought nor what he believed, but what he knew.'[29]

The New Machiavelli, written in 1908–9, though flawed by an excessive amount of homily contains some very fine descriptive passages, especially in the chapters portraying the narrator's childhood in Bromstead (Bromley). In its moving account of his mother and father, his boyhood home and his adolescent dreams *The New Machiavelli* is an intensely personal document. Here Wells is looking back with mingled affection and disenchantment on the world of his childhood and attempting to place it in perspective. At last he felt able to write about his parents with complete openness, and in the picture of Remington's parents we have what is surely an authentic portrait drawn from life. His mother's attitude to his father, he wrote in the novel, 'seems to me one of the essentially tragic things that have come to me personally, one of those things that nothing can transfigure, that *remain* sorrowful, that I cannot soothe with any explanation, for as I remember him he was indeed the most lovable of weak spasmodic men'.[30] In the novel he is clearly trying to reach inside his parents' minds, to understand their motivations and dreams. It is as if he is consciously seeking to place them in perspective and to define his feelings towards them. *The New Machiavelli* is one of the most personal and revealing of his novels not only in the sense that the story is partly autobiographical but also because its central character, Richard Remington, embodies many of Wells's contradictions. Idealistic, sceptical, imaginative, he is torn by the conflict between duty and passion until in the end his career is wrecked. In the portrait of a statesman who abandons his career in pursuit of love Wells is rendering in fictional form some of his deepest unformulated dreams and repeating on an ampler scale the fantasy of *The Sea Lady*.

After his affair with Amber – an affair which brought him both great happiness and great sorrow – he embarked on a much more lighthearted liaison with Elizabeth von Arnim, the authoress of *Elizabeth and her German Garden* and its sequels. Her real name was Elizabeth Mary Beauchamp; she was Irish and the same age as Wells. Wise, witty, vivacious and small in stature she proved to be a cheerful companion who distracted his mind from the immense upheaval of his entanglement with Amber Reeves and left his mind free to concentrate on his novels. He nicknamed her 'Little e'. She was estranged from her marriage to the German Count von Arnim and had settled in England where she continued to write fiction and engaging sketches of domestic life. Later Wells was to satirise her as Mrs Harrowdean in *Mr Britling Sees It Through*. Elizabeth was no intellectual, in the sharpest contrast to Amber. She had an easy-going attitude to life which at first he found appealing but soon tired of. The affair continued through 1911 and 1912 but by the autumn of the latter year was beginning to deteriorate. She began to be jealous of Jane and to make hurtful comments about her. When they were abroad together she resented the daily letters he wrote to his wife. She developed a habit of making sudden unaccountable changes to their arrangements – deliberately, it seemed, to annoy him. His growing disenchantment with Little e became one more symptom of his developing restlessness – a phase of discontent in which he felt at odds with the world. He began to chafe at his Church Row house, to draw up plans for a world tour (plans which never materialised), to embark on hectic rounds of country house weekends and to set off on flights by aeroplane – then a relatively new form of transport. He was clearly dissatisfied with his world but unable to define in his own mind what was wrong. Though he did not rationalise his situation in these terms he had reached a watershed in his life.

The Fabian imbroglio had left him with a profound animus towards organisations and the administrative habit of mind – an animus he was able to exorcise to some extent in caricaturing Sidney and Beatrice Webb as Oscar and Altiora Bailey in *The New Machiavelli*. His disillusionment with the socialist movement had left him with a vague sense of discontent in which he cast about for other progressive causes. To him socialism was a project for the reconstruction of human society – in

This Misery of Boots he had denounced those 'who will assure you that some odd little jobbing about municipal gas and water is socialism' – and he had no patience with those who argued for a gradual process of permeation. In his literary work also he was dissatisfied with his own efforts and uncertain that he was applying his energies in the right direction. The writing of *Tono-Bungay* had cost him an immense effort but its sales had been disappointing. Its successor, *The New Machiavelli*, had been accompanied with equally high ambitions but had been rejected by several publishers before its final acceptance by John Lane. *Ann Veronica* had sold well but had earned him vilification in many influential quarters. With the dust from the latter controversy gradually dying down he seems to have felt the need for a period of consolidation both in his private and public life and to turn over a new chapter in his career.

In March 1912 he was invited to become a member of the Academic Committee of the Royal Society of Literature. At that time the Committee included among its members Henry James, J. M. Barrie, John Galsworthy, Thomas Hardy and Bernard Shaw. Wells politely declined, whereupon James wrote him an impassioned letter begging him to change his mind. Wells still declined, saying

> I have an insurmountable objection to Literary or Artistic Academies as such, to any hierarchies, any suggestion of controls or fixed standards in these things . . . This world of ours, I mean the world of creative and representative work we do, is I am convinced best anarchic.

James still persisted, pleading with him to reconsider his attitude 'for the general amenity and civility and unimportance of the thing, giving it the benefit of the doubt – for the sake of the good-nature'.[31] But Wells was not to be moved. The following day he buttonholed James at the Reform Club and made it clear that all entreaties would be in vain. James wrote resignedly to Edmund Goose: 'He has cut loose from literature clearly – practically altogether; he will still do a lot of writing probably – but it won't be *that*.' James's impression that Wells was distancing himself from the world of literature was both right and wrong. He was certainly distancing himself from the intensely art-conscious conception of the novel as exemplified by James in such works as *The Ambassadors* and *The Golden Bowl*. But his work continued to be shaped by artistic concerns. In 1912 he was feeling his way towards a new type of novel, the 'discussion novel', through which it would be possible to examine the problems of human relationships by presenting varieties of behaviour and looking at them from different angles. In groping towards this concept he was harking back, consciously or unconsciously, to the conversational novels of W. H. Mallock and

Thomas Love Peacock and to the discursive fiction of Laurence Sterne, the man he described as 'the subtlest and greatest *artist* that Great Britain has ever produced in all that is essentially the novel'.[32]

IV

It was not until the autumn of 1912 that the restless phase showed signs of coming to an end with the decision to leave Church Row and move into Little Easton Rectory near Dunmow, Essex. The Rectory, soon renamed Easton Glebe, was a pleasant Georgian house overlooking a deer park belonging to the Countess of Warwick, an eccentric aristocrat who espoused socialism and philanthropy. Here he was free to write in beautiful surroundings, to widen his circle of friends and to entertain on a large scale. Originally taken as a weekend retreat, he and Jane found they both liked the house and the Essex countryside so much that they decided to settle. Easton Glebe remained his family home until Jane's death fifteen years later. He retained a flat at St James's Court as his London base.

In September of that year his novel *Marriage* was published. This was a carefully written study of middle-class marriage problems and contained none of the controversial matter which had made *Ann Veronica* such a *cause célèbre*. It tells the story of Trafford, a young professor engaged in scientific research who meets and falls in love with Marjorie Pope, one of Wells's most engaging and convincingly drawn heroines. Their marriage begins harmoniously but disillusionment sets in when Trafford has to curtail and eventually abandon his disinterested pursuit of knowledge in order to take up lecturing work to supplement his income. While he becomes more and more overworked his wife is bored by too much leisure. Trafford becomes wealthy and influential but his marriage to Marjorie is increasingly empty. At last he and his wife journey to the solitudes of Labrador to think out their problems. They talk through their difficulties and decide that henceforward their marriage will be a real partnership, Trafford turning his energies to the study of contemporary thought and Marjorie assisting by writing and research. The novel is solidly written on a spacious canvas and is dedicated to Arnold Bennett, as if as an indication that a new leaf has been turned over and the indiscretions of *Ann Veronica* are a thing of the past. The *Spectator* in its review praised the book, adding pointedly: 'Mr Wells has put all his cleverness into this long story of an engagement and marriage between two attractive and, we may add, perfectly moral young people.' *T. P.'s Weekly* said it was a book 'that can be placed on a puritan's family bookshelf'. One assessment which was not so enthusiastic was by a young writer named Rebecca West who reviewed the novel in *The Freewoman* on 19 September 1912. The review began in characteristic forthright style:

> Mr Wells's mannerisms are more infuriating than ever in *Marriage* . . . Of course, he is the old maid among novelists; even the sex obsession that lay clotted on *Ann Veronica* and *The New Machiavelli* like cold white sauce was merely old maid's mania, the reaction towards the flesh of a mind too long absorbed in airships and colloids . . . And then there is Mr Wells's habit of spluttering at his enemies.

The review went on to castigate the central character, Marjorie, as mean and parasitic, and to comment on her unreality as a woman and as a lover. Wells's worst sin, in her eyes, was to pretend that Marjorie was normal or typical in accepting an inferior role: 'That is the terrible thing, for there is no author who has a more religious faith; nor one who speaks his gospel with such a tongue of flame.' Wells was intrigued by this review and promptly invited Rebecca West to Easton Glebe. The name cannot have been unknown to him for he had been a regular reader of *The Freewoman* since its inception and must have been familiar with her astringent criticism. He had been an occasional contributor to the paper himself and had aired his views on 'the Endowment of Motherhood' and on the suffragette question in its pages. In his article 'Mr Asquith will die' (*The Freewoman*, 7 December 1911) he had criticised the violent behaviour of the militant suffragettes and added: 'Humanity is obsessed by sex. I have always been disposed to take sex rather lightly, and to think we make a quite unnecessary amount of fuss about it.' When he invited Rebecca to his home he must have been intensely curious about her. He had probably imagined a waspish spinster hiding behind a pen-name. Instead he found a determined young woman who was both physically attractive and surprisingly mature for her age. Mathilde Meyer, the governess to his sons, noted in her diary for September 27th: 'Miss Rebecca West arrived today. She looks about twenty two years of age, and is very vivacious.' In fact she was 19 – passionate, intelligent, eager, and already making a name for herself as a writer on political and feminist issues. Wells recalled later:

> She talked well and she had evidently read voraciously – with an excellent memory. We argued and she stood up to my opinions very stoutly but very reasonably. I had never met anything quite like her before, and I doubt if there ever was anything like her before.[33]

He did not realise it at the time, but he had made one of the crucial encounters of his life.

Chapter 3

A Free Woman

There was something about her, too, which he could not identify, which made him feel the sharp yet almost anguished delight that is caused by the spectacle of a sunset or a foam-patterned breaking wave, or any other beauty that is intense but on the point of dissolution.

Rebecca West, The Judge

Always through my fuller years there was a feeling, a confidence I never had the power or will to analyse, that somewhere among womankind there was help and completion for me. How shall I express it? The other half of my androgynous self I had lost and had to find again.

H. G. Wells, The World of William Clissold

I

In order to understand Cicely Isabel Fairfield – for that was her real name – one needs to take a closer look at her ancestry. As with Wells, the forces that had shaped her parents and grandparents marked her indelibly and contributed in a significant way to the fashioning of her personality and attitudes.

Her mother, Isabella Campbell Mackenzie, was one of six children, the daughter of Alexander and Janet Mackenzie of Edinburgh. Isabella's father was a violinist, song-writer and editor of *The National Dance Music of Scotland*. His death in 1857 at the early age of 37 left his wife Janet with a large family to raise. Isabella was then aged 3. Janet's father was a wealthy lace merchant and, though he had disapproved of her marriage to an impecunious musician, he offered her the post of manageress of one of his retail shops on George Street. She accepted the challenge with enthusiasm and made a success of it. She had been left a widow with a family of six all under the age of 10 but seems to have been a woman of iron determination, making the best of the situation and bringing up her children in a harmonious environment. It was the income from the lace shop which helped them to survive.

The Mackenzies settled at 41 Heriot Row, Edinburgh (Robert Louis

Stevenson and his parents were also living on the same road) and remained there for thirty years. It was a happy, musical household; Isabella inherited from her parents their keen interest in music and became an accomplished pianist and linguist. Before her marriage she taught music to the daughters of a wealthy Jewish family in London, Emily and Clara Heinemann. The Heinemann family were cultured and urbane; all her life Isabella was happiest in an atmosphere of books and music and intelligent conversation. In later years she became something of a connoisseur of art and architecture, an interest she may well have imbibed from the years she spent with the Heinemanns in their comfortable menage. She enjoyed her time in London but when she was in her late twenties ill health compelled her to resign her post and return to Edinburgh. She stayed at Heriot Row for a short time, undecided about her future, then resolved to travel to Australia. This decision was taken partly on health grounds and partly to enable her to visit her unmarried brother, John, who had gone to Australia some years earlier in the hope that the climate would alleviate his tuberculosis. It was at Melbourne that she met Charles Fairfield, a tall, romantic Irishman who was working there as an artist and journalist. After a swift courtship she accepted his proposal of marriage. The wedding took place at Melbourne on 17 December 1883; Charles was 42 and Isabella 29.

Charles Fairfield was born in Tralee in 1841, the son of a professional soldier. He had been brought up in Kerry and Dublin – he recalled it later as a happy childhood spent in an idyllic countryside – but his father died when he was 12, leaving his mother and her four sons homeless. His mother, Arabella Rowan Fairfield, was a devout woman of grim determination. She became a member of the Plymouth Brethren, an intensely puritanical sect vividly described by Edmund Gosse in his memoir *Father and Son*. It is a sect characterised by fervent prayer, abstinence from worldly pleasures and belief in the devil. She derived a small income from the rents of various tumbledown properties in Dublin inherited from earlier Fairfields but this income was unreliable and insufficient to sustain the family. Arabella decided to uproot the household and start a new life in London. Charles, like his father, joined the army. He enlisted in the Prince Consort's Own Rifle Brigade in 1863 and served as a rifle instructor in Canada and Europe before resigning his commission four years later. For some years he lived a nomadic existence, travelling in the United States and Mexico and earning a living as an itinerant man of all work. He finally sailed for Australia and settled in Melbourne as an artist and reporter on the staff of the influential *Melbourne Argus*.

Many years later Rebecca described the union between Isabella and Charles Fairfield as 'the marriage of loneliness to loneliness'.[1] In fact it was a fusion of emotions and attitudes – hereditary, temperamental and psychological – which marked her indelibly as a woman and as a writer, and whose combination helped to mould one of the most remarkable figures of the twentieth century. From her mother's side, the Mackenzies and the Campbells, she derived her love of music and the fine arts, her capacity for pleasure and her intense vitality. She also imbibed qualities of resilience and independence which served her well during a long and active life. There was within her make-up a strong element of self-reliance derived from her Scottish ancestry; a resource that proved indispensable to her during her ten-year partnership with H. G. Wells and the difficult years of unmarried motherhood. From her father's side, the Fairfields and the Rowans, she derived a love of ideas, a decided unconventionality of mind, and a fearlessness in criticising respected institutions. A tendency to question received wisdom, to strike at the root of ideas and forces underlying current affairs, became one of her most characteristic traits. She also imbibed a lifelong preoccupation with good and evil, light and darkness. This Manichean view of the world, a belief that mankind is governed by opposing forces of life and death, was one of her most unshakeable convictions and coloured all her work. From both her parents she inherited a love of rural scenery, a delight in the countryside which deepened with the passing of the years. It is this combination of elements, part Scottish and part Irish, part dour and part romantic, which made Rebecca West what she was.

II

For a few years after his marriage Charles continued as a journalist for the *Argus*, writing (under the pseudonym 'Ivan') articles on economics, art and topical questions of the day. The Fairfields lived at St Kilda near Melbourne, a sparsely populated settlement on a flat coastline. In her last work, *Family Memories*, Rebecca gives a heavily romanticised description of St Kilda based on a watercolour she believed to be of the town. It seems that the watercolour is in fact a painting of an English coastal scene, and that in reality St Kilda has a featureless sandy shoreline utterly different from the hilly, wooded landscape of her imagination. The newly married couple settled in a small wooden house with a diminutive garden and here two daughters were born to them, Letitia (Lettie) in 1885 and Winifred (Winnie) in 1887. Shortly after Winnie's birth Charles was dismissed from his post with the *Argus*. Apparently his outspoken views on religion and politics did not find favour with the newspaper's owners; he was also accused of leaking confidential information about alleged bank irregularities. They returned to Britain with no money and no prospects, living for a time in Glasgow where Charles found work on the *Glasgow Herald*. Isabella's health was still precarious and when she found she was pregnant again the Fairfields decided to move to London. Here, they felt, they could make a fresh start far away from the cold climate of Scotland and with a better chance of finding work. It was at 28 Burlington Road, Westbourne Park, a furnished house paid for by the Heinemann's, that their third daughter, Cicely Isabel Fairfield, was born on 21 December 1892. She was known as Cissie.

Cissie loved her mother with an intensity which never left her. Through all the tribulations of her later life – her own illnesses, her mother's illness, her love affair with Wells, her public controversies and her efforts to come to terms with the contradictions within her personality – the emotional bond between them was profound and unshakeable. Something of Cissie's love for her mother is expressed in the description of Ellen Melville's mother in *The Judge*:

> And she was so good, so good – even divinely good. Life had given her so little beyond her meagre flesh and breakable bones that it might have seemed impossible that she should satisfy the exorbitant demands of her existence. But she had done that; she had reared a child, and of the wet wood of poverty she had made a bright fire on her hearthstone. She had done more than that: she had given her child a love that was unstinted good living for the soul. And she had done more than that: to every human being with whom she came in contact she had made a little present of something over and above the ordinary decent feelings arising from the situation, something which was too sensible and often too roguish to be called tenderness, which was rather the handsomest possible agreement with the other person's idea of himself, and a taking of his side in his struggle with fate.[2]

It was this gut feeling – a complex mixture of love, tenderness, gratitude and admiration – which held her to her mother through thick and thin. She never lost her respect for Isabella for having given her 'a love that was unstinted good living for the soul' and for creating a bright fire from 'the wet wood of poverty'. As Cissie grew into adulthood she came to be increasingly conscious of the debt she owed to her mother; a sense of gratitude that was tinged with guilt as they grew mentally more and more apart. However much they diverged in their attitudes to life and morality nothing could change the fundamental love between them. The bond between mother and daughter continued until Isabella's death in 1921.

Charles's political views were fiercely individualist and conservative. Had he lived in the eighteenth century he would have been called a Whig for his great hero was Edmund Burke. He was a member of the

Liberty and Property Defence League (a society fanatically opposed to socialist ideas) and strongly disapproved of women's suffrage. The outward respectability of his political beliefs contrasts oddly with his Bohemian private life, for outside the home he was a compulsive gambler and womaniser. Cissie did not become aware of this until years later when she must have been struck by the contrast between outward probity and inward laxity: a dichotomy which had fascinated Robert Louis Stevenson and formed the substance of one of his most powerful tales, *Dr Jekyll and Mr Hyde*.

Looking back on her father many years later she wrote of him: 'The detachment of my father from the consequences of his actions was almost a cause, like his anti-socialism. The whole strength of his being was turned in a direction which led him away from his wife and children.'[3] In his refusal to face up to the consequences of his behaviour, his lack of concern for his wife and his reluctance to grapple with disagreeable realities one is reminded irresistibly of Joseph Wells. Yet there is no doubt that Cissie loved him deeply. She was powerfully attracted by his manliness, his romantic charm, his gifts as a raconteur and his stories of childhood life in Ireland. Photographs of him taken in the 1890s show an upright, handsome figure with a military bearing and penetrating eyes. One senses a definite *presence*: a man who possessed charisma and was aware of it. Women found him extremely attractive; Cissie wrote with some bitterness 'he was continually and frenetically unfaithful to my mother, who was in love with him'.[4]

Cissie owed him much, not least her interest in ideas and her questioning attitude to life. Her father was a born storyteller and was passionately interested in life and society. He talked to his children as equals and encouraged them to be curious about the world around them. It was a home filled with books and talk and ideas. 'I cannot remember a time', she wrote, 'when I had not a rough idea of what was meant by capitalism, socialism, individualism, anarchism, liberalism and conservatism . . . I grew up with a knowledge of politics and economics comparable to the knowledge of religion automatically acquired by children in a churchgoing and Bible-reading household.'[5] The continual talk of newspapers and current affairs inevitably coloured her view of life. Her father encouraged her to ask questions about ideas and movements, to think for herself and to justify her own opinions. 'He was interested in nothing about us except our looks and our capacity to absorb ideas', she wrote in *The Fountain Overflows*. 'If . . . our comments were intelligent, then he burned with love for us, and if they were stupid, he shook his head like a horse rebelling against the bit and went away to be alone.'[6] When one recalls that she saw him for the last time in 1901, when she was 8, it is clear that these conversations with him made a deep and lasting impression. Throughout her life she never lost her enthusiasm for abstract ideas, her propensity to question the assumptions underlying movements and forces and the ability to grasp the essentials of an argument.

Cissie had no memories of the Westbourne Park house for the family moved before she was 2 and settled at 21 Streatham Place, near Brixton Hill, where they remained until 1898. Her father had resumed his employment with the *Melbourne Argus*, contributing articles on social and political subjects, and also edited an anti-socialist newspaper. He began a habit of speculating with what little money he had in stocks and shares: a habit he concealed from his wife. Cissie looked back on the Streatham Place house with affection and nostalgia. This is the home of the Aubrey family in *The Fountain Overflows*, a home described with all the roseate tints of a lovingly recalled childhood:

> I remember those wild tints, for like my sisters I was looking at the scene with an exalted vision. We were experts in disillusion, we had learned to be cynical about fresh starts even before we had ourselves made our first start, but this house gave us hope. Indeed, it gave us back our childhood. Papa swung me up on his shoulder as he stood behind us, and I was proud, I was wrapped in delight, as if I knew no ill of him.[7]

21 Streatham Place was a tall semi-detached villa with a veranda screening its lower floor and handsome pediments above the bedroom windows. Cissie loved the garden with its roses and chestnut trees, the neat terraces of Georgian houses, the rural nature of the surrounding landscape, the atmosphere of order and symmetry. The ornamental urns adorning the roof balustrade and the elaborately decorated ironwork surrounding the front door gave an air of classical elegance to the building which pleased her greatly. A photograph of her parents taken outside the house shows them standing at the front gate: Charles upright and aloof, Isabella smiling and relaxed. For them the house represented a new beginning, a chance to bring up their daughters in a healthy environment within walking distance of open meadowland. The six years they spent at Streatham Place were years of happiness and growth for all of them: a memory that remained even more poignantly in her mind by the fact that the house was destroyed during the Second World War. For her it was a memory to be treasured into old age, a recollection of a time when she still had her father, when she was surrounded with affection, when all seemed for the best in the best of all possible worlds. 'Mamma watched us in ecstasy', she wrote in *The Fountain Overflows*, 'when our family life was as it is supposed to be on earth she was as if lifted to heaven.'[8]

But the idyll could not last. In 1897 Cissie's two elder sisters were seriously ill with meningitis. At the same time the family income was considerably reduced by the termination of Charles's contract with the *Argus*. He was still an occasional contributor to the *Glasgow Herald* and the London *St James's Gazette* but his earnings from these sources were hardly sufficient to keep the wolf from the door. Early in the following year, when Cissie was 5, the family uprooted themselves once again and moved to a smaller and less desirable house in Richmond-on-Thames (9 Hermitage Road). Here the three girls attended the Church of England High School and, with their father's encouragement, continued their voracious reading. History and literature were their staple diet; Cissie recalled later that the novels of Dumas 'taught one in the nursery what romance was'.[9] Other enthusiasms included the works of Robert Louis Stevenson and George Borrow. Despite their comparative poverty it seems odd by twentieth-century standards that even during the years when they were most penurious they employed a nurse and a maid-of-all-work. Recording this fact in *Family Memories* Rebecca admits that it seems extraordinary but adds laconically: 'Girls were so eager to get into domestic service that they worked for pitiful wages.'[10] For her, Richmond was not a place of happy memories: she disliked the school, finding it strict and starchy, and was already aware that all was not well with her father. At Richmond his income declined even further and the family had to penny-pinch in a host of irritating minor ways.

The menage which Cissie loved and remembered as a child was decidedly odd by the standards of late Victorian England. Her father did not go out to work: he worked from home. Their home was full of books and conversation about books and art, yet they never seemed to have any money. Their parents were intelligent and well read yet poor; conversely, households as cultured as theirs were usually better off and lived in a visibly grander style. It was a home that was neither working class nor middle class but in a kind of limbo. They were short of money but surrounded by the trappings of learning; urbane and respectable yet living on the brink of penury.

One morning in 1901, apparently without telling his wife and daughters in advance, Charles Fairfield left his home and set sail for Sierra Leone in search of a new life. This traumatic event is vividly recalled in *The Fountain Overflows*:

> This was something new and worse than anything which had happened to us before. We could not advance in intelligence and worldly knowledge without becoming daily more conscious of how much less he was doing for us than other fathers did for their children. But to have lost him was terrible. He had apparently given us more than we knew, for now we felt bitterly cold.[11]

He left a letter telling his wife that he had gone to Africa to take up a temporary post at a pharmaceuticals factory, but in fact the family never saw him alive again. He returned to England after only four months and settled in Liverpool, living in cheap lodgings and eking out a precarious existence as a solicitor's clerk. He remained in Liverpool for the next five years in declining health, writing home occasionally but giving little concrete information as to his work or future plans. At last, in October 1906, came a pencilled note: 'Goodbye Lettie, Winnie, Cissie. I am dying. I loved you. Papa.' He died shortly afterwards, apparently of heart disease, at the age of 63. Isabella travelled alone to Liverpool to arrange the funeral and collect his few pathetic possessions. It was clear that he had died in poverty.

This event and its consequences had a profound effect on the family and particularly upon Cissie, the youngest and most sensitive of the daughters and the one who had perhaps been closest to her father. When Charles walked out, abandoning his wife and family, Mrs Fairfield decided to uproot herself and the girls and move to Edinburgh, where it was possible to live much more cheaply than in London. Inwardly she must have felt very bitter indeed at her husband. From her point of view his abandonment of his family must have seemed an act of treachery. To leave her and the girls without resources was an abdication of his responsibilities: an unforgiveable act which she deeply resented. To make matters worse his rare letters had been addressed to his eldest daughter rather than herself: Lettie had had to play the unenviable role of mediator between husband and wife. But the wound of his departure and death was for Cissie a lifelong trauma. For a long time she was unable to come to terms with his apparent rejection of his family, presenting it in her recollections and correspondence as merely a mutually agreed separation. The fact that her autobiographical work *Family Memories* was left unfinished at her death and she is known to have toiled away at the various drafts over a period of many years, revising and polishing, reveals a profound uncertainty, an evident reluctance to express her feelings about her father in a definitive form. As it is, the chapters about him in *Family Memories* are deeply ambivalent, a strange mixture of affection and repugnance. She adored him for his manly qualities, his warmth, his willingness to discuss every subject under the sun, his aura of bookish wisdom. But she despised him for his sexual infidelity and the flaws in his make-up that led to his failure as a husband. That her own father could have abandoned them all with such apparent lack of compunction left her with an ambivalence towards the male sex which nothing could eradicate. Men, she felt, should be strong and dependable; deep inside herself she sensed that they were not to be trusted. Moreover, the comparative poverty of the Fairfield household had the effect of strengthening her reliance on material possessions. She was determined that, whatever the future held for her and whatever her relationships with men, never again would she be left penniless. What mattered was *security*.

Edinburgh was the Fairfields' home from 1901 to 1910: the most formative years of Cissie's life. These years from 8 to 18 were years of intellectual and emotional growth in which she developed from a gawky schoolgirl to a young woman with a mind of her own and passionate political convictions.

The family must have become quickly aware that the town is not a single entity but a duality, and that the contrast between the two Edinburghs encapsulates a divergence of attitudes to life and behaviour. On the one hand was the New Town, a cluster of gracious eighteenth-century squares and terraces occupied exclusively by comfortably off professional people living respectable lives: the New Town stood for all that was formal, orderly and correct. The Old Town, in complete contrast, was louche and disreputable, an area of insanitary tenements in which drunkenness and prostitution were rife. As she grew into adolescence Cissie must have been increasingly conscious of this sharp contradiction between decorum and disreputability. All her life she was exercised by the duality between good and evil, between light and darkness, truth and falsehood. In Edinburgh the duality was visible in all its simplified rawness; a cleavage between wealth and poverty, respectability and licence, which left her irrevocably marked.

Buccleuth Place, where the Fairfields made their home, was neither in the Old Town nor the New but in an area of elegant Georgian terraces to the South of the Old Town. Here, at number 24, the family occupied a flat in a menage which Cissie described later as a 'mean life of hopeless thrift'.[12] It was from Buccleuth Place that she took the short daily walk to George Watson's Ladies' College (in George Square) where she became a pupil in 1903 at the age of 11. She remained a pupil at the College for five years.

Edinburgh left an indelible impression upon her, colouring her attitudes in ways which did not become apparent until many years later when she felt able to distil her memories in the novel *The Judge*, published in 1922. The opening chapters with their vivid evocation of the city, part affectionate and part withdrawn, are written with a detachment unusual in her writing, as if the narrator is uncertain what to make of this most intriguing of cities. This ambivalence was characteristic of her feelings towards Scotland, an amalgam of pride and distaste; a deep affection for Scottish scenery coupled with a profound antipathy towards the superficial conventionality of Edinburgh society. Some of her most treasured memories were of walks and cycle rides to the countryside loved by Stevenson: to the Pentland Hills, to Colinton, to Prestonpans. Ellen Melville in *The Judge* recalled the happiness of these explorations, remembering a day when she 'had just walked between the snow that lay white on the hills and the snow that hung black in the clouds, and had seen no living creature save the stray albatross that winged from peak to peak'.[13]

All three sisters were prone to tuberculosis and Cissie wrote later that 'we thought we were going to pass out like *La Bohème*'.[14] Though they all lived to an advanced age their health remained delicate for some years and Cissie in particular suffered from recurrent haemorrhages from the mouth until well into adult life. These attacks came without warning and were a source of distress and inconvenience.

At the College Cissie received a sound education by the standards of the time, taking lessons in English, mathematics, science, art, Latin and music. She particularly enjoyed poetry, learning by heart long passages from Tennyson, Whitman, Browning and Shakespeare. Music was another enthusiasm. She took piano lessons at school and loved hearing her mother play the piano at home: Mendelssohn's *Songs Without Words* was a special delight. 'Music', she wrote later, 'is part of human life and partakes of the human tragedy . . . Music partakes also of the human mystery.'[15] Playing the piano gave her mother so much pleasure that Cissie never forgot the sense of elation; the giving and receiving of pleasure she held to be one of life's greatest gifts.

The death of her father occurred when she was 14, mid-way through her school career. The releasing effect on her emotions took the form of a surge of interest in radical politics: she and her sisters became ardent socialists and advocates of women's suffrage. In 1907 she became a member of the Votes for Women Club – a militant suffragette society – and joined the National Women's Social and Political Union (NWSPU), the leading organisation campaigning for the franchise, which had been founded by Emmeline and Christabel Pankhurst in 1903. She wore a NWSPU badge at school – a courageous thing to do at the time, for she risked the opprobrium of her teachers and the ridicule of her schoolmates – and sold their journal *Votes for Women* on the streets of Edinburgh. She attended suffragette meetings in Yorkshire and Scotland, hero-worshipping the Pankhursts and the other leaders of the movement. When Sir Edward Grey, the Foreign Secretary, visited Edinburgh and Leith in December 1909 to address a series of public meetings violence broke out among the crowds outside and for the first time in her life she witnessed a baton charge. Cissie was then 17: a militant radical, a socialist and a passionate supporter of women's rights. Meanwhile her home and school situation were becoming increasingly uncomfortable. Her two older sisters were both working away from home – Winnie as a schoolteacher in France and Lettie as a clinical assistant in Birmingham – and her mother's health was again causing anxiety. Isabella's eyesight had been defective for many years and goitre was now diagnosed. When she became so ill that hospital treatment became necessary Cissie was left on her own. To aggravate matters Isabella strongly disapproved of her daughter's feminist views and made it clear that Cissie's father would have been outraged had he known. In polite society at that time militant suffragettes were regarded with abhorrence, and respectable Edinburgh was no exception. From Isabella's point of view Cissie had become involved with a band of revolutionary extremists. She had also antagonised her strait-laced headmistress, Miss Ainslie, who also frowned on her political views and regarded her as a rebel. It was with few misgivings that Cissie left College in April 1910, at the age of 17, to travel to London. She had decided to try for an audition at the Academy of Dramatic Art (later, with the addition of the prefix 'Royal', known as RADA) and to make her living on the stage.

Since childhood she had been fascinated and enthralled by the stage. At the age of 10 she had seen the great Sarah Bernhardt perform, and as a teenager had watched Ellen Terry and Mrs Patrick Campbell. She made a point of going to the theatre in Edinburgh as frequently as she could and for some years was a member of a local amateur dramatic society. She loved Christmas pantomimes and liked to go backstage to observe the actors and actresses at close quarters. Through her adolescence drama rivalled music as an enthusiasm, though she became frustrated at the limited opportunities to display her love of the stage. She possessed a number of histrionic attributes which may have encouraged her to believe that she could make a career as an actress: she was headstrong, highly strung, inclined to melodramatic gestures and intensely emotional in times of crisis. She liked being the centre of attention.

The Academy of Dramatic Art was then a new and comparatively untried institution (it was founded in 1904) and she cannot have been at all sure what to expect when she made the journey to Gower Street for her audition. Nervous though she was she passed the audition with flying colours and was accepted as a full-time student to commence later in the same month. Cissie remained at RADA from April 1910 to March 1911. With her move to London the remainder of the family followed suit. Winnie and Lettie had both meanwhile obtained posts in London and Isabella Fairfield was glad to move the whole household to a small house in Chatham Close, Hampstead Garden Suburb, which they named Fairliehope. It was a quiet, cottagey house in a semi-rural setting remote from the noise and bustle of the city. From here the girls set off on their long daily journey by horse bus and tube to their city occupations. For Cissie the year she spent at RADA was one of active growth intellectually and emotionally, and one in which she found herself as a person and acknowledged her true vocation in life. For she came to see that she could fulfil herself not as an actress but as a writer.

She had gone to the Academy with a recommendation from the well-
known actress Rosina Filippi who had heard her recite poetry and
sensed that she had potential. Unfortunately Cissie felt ill at ease
compared with the other students, partly because she could not afford
stylish clothes and partly because she was unable to overcome her
nervous mannerisms. But the training at the Academy helped her to
project her voice, to soften her Scottish accent and to learn the nuances
of expression and voice control. It also taught her to develop a stage
'presence' and to acquire the poise and command necessary for a stage
career. These qualities proved of considerable value to her in her later
public life. Though she left the Academy after only three terms she
acquired sufficient self-confidence to seek employment in the theatrical
world. She was offered the part of Regine in a production of Ibsen's
Ghosts and also accepted a number of minor roles with a touring
dramatic company. But the urge to express herself continued to niggle
at her subconscious. While still at the Academy her first piece of paid
journalism had been published: a review of Gorky's *Lower Depths* in the
London *Evening Standard*. This had whetted her appetite for more but her
attempts to follow up this beginning with further drama criticism came
to nothing. In the end it was her feminism which provided the avenue
for literary expression.

Lettie, a keen socialist, joined the Fabian Society (and its offshoot the
Fabian Women's Group) as soon as the family moved back to London
and her two younger sisters soon followed her example. Cissie began to
dabble in socialist meetings, just as Wells had done a generation earlier,
listening to Bernard Shaw and other luminaries of the movement. She
began to hear Wells's name mentioned more and more frequently in
these circles and to listen to discussions about his novels. She had not at
this time read *Ann Veronica* but must have heard it discussed for it was
then a *cause célèbre* and remained so for some years. When a new feminist
weekly, *The Freewoman*, was launched in November 1911, Cissie at once
became a subscriber and by the second issue had begun to write for it.
Her first piece was a book review published under her own name, a
review written in a forthright style she was to make her own. It was
ostensibly an appraisal of a book discussing the role of women in India
but she took the opportunity to lambast the indifference of the authors
to the secondary status of women and to articulate a passionate
restatement of the feminist case. The idea that middle-class housewives
are ignorant incompetents 'is one of the most cherished beliefs of the
wholly undomesticated women of the aristocratic classes', she declared.
'It is of course a device to cheat poor girls out of their education.'
Turning her attention to the large numbers of poorly paid clerks and
governesses she claimed roundly:

It is obvious that this glut of worthless labour is partly due to the desire of parents to absorb their daughters into unprofitable domestic labour, partly to the lack of first-rate educational facilities, and partly to the fact that a woman knows that her labour capital – her education, her talent, her experience – is confiscated on her entrance into marriage.[16]

The review, though brief, is a remarkable piece of writing for an unknown 19-year-old with no previous experience of this kind of journalism. Its tone – fearless, iconoclastic, radical – was entirely characteristic of her work throughout her long life and set the theme for all her subsequent contributions to the journal. She became a member of *The Freewoman*'s fortnightly discussion circle which brought her into a new ambit of ardent intellectuals and radicals. These regular discussions on social questions, current affairs, literature and politics fired her enthusiasm for polemics and fuelled her regular articles and book reviews for the paper. *The Freewoman* came to an abrupt demise in September 1912 through lack of funds, but not before it had launched Rebecca West on her literary career. Its early issues included reviews by her of books by Mrs Humphrey Ward, Rose Macaulay, Arnold Bennett and D. H. Lawrence, and plays by Granville-Barker and August Strindberg. These are characterised by an astringent style and a total lack of inhibition in attacking sacred cows or prominent writers of the day.

Her articles are notable not simply for their daring and wit but for their evidence of wide reading and avid curiosity. It was a courageous thing in those days to defend Oscar Wilde – then still regarded by many as the ultimate in despicability – and perceptive of her to praise D. H. Lawrence, in 1912 a new and comparatively little-known novelist. She was not afraid to attack widely respected shibboleths nor to commend talent wherever she found it. The pieces are brimming with energy and filled with aphorisms which must have made them talking points in many middle-class households. 'When a socialist takes to being dull, he is much duller than anybody else'; 'I find it impossible to argue with a person who holds the doctrine of original sin'; 'Writers on the subject of August Strindberg have hitherto omitted to mention that he could not write'; 'Mrs Ward reveals to us the psychology of the clergyman class – the class which throughout the Victorian era peopled the church and the universities to the exclusion of any other' – these and other shafts poured from her pen in a brilliant series of articles which established her as a name to be reckoned with.[17] Taking on targets of the eminence of Mrs Humphrey Ward was, in the eyes of many, a foolhardy thing to do but it was completely in character and is consistent with her lifelong candour in speaking out against hypocrisy and pretentiousness. Her reviews became pegs on which she hung the flags of her faith:

impatience with confused thinking, intolerance of writers with no appreciation of the lot of women, outspoken advocacy of socialism and an impassioned defence of equal rights. It was these which became her hallmark as she gained growing self-confidence in expressing her ideas and in fashioning a distinctive polemical style. Increasingly her articles came to be recognised as the voice of a new and penetrating writer who knew her mind and had fresh and stimulating things to say. It was in the spring of 1912 that she opened a new chapter in her life by adopting the pseudonym Rebecca West.

III

It is worth pausing at this juncture to examine the significance of her assumption of a pen-name, since the name itself and her adoption of it have been the subject of much critical speculation. Ostensibly she decided to write under a pseudonym in order to placate her mother, who would have been embarrassed by Cissie's increasingly outspoken journalism. Cissie felt that her real name, Cicely Fairfield, was an impossible name for a serious writer, suggesting someone soft and effeminate. In contrast to this she wished to adopt a pseudonym which would suggest a fearless regard for the truth and a total outspokenness in discussing social and political issues. Yet the adoption of the name Rebecca West was much more than the assumption of a *nom de plume*. It was a deliberate decision to assume a second self.

The character of that name in *Rosmersholm* is a strong-willed, forth-right heroine who defies the conventions of her time and commits suicide rather than succumb to the prevailing code of morality. Though in later life Rebecca became disenchanted with Ibsen's ideas there can be no question that for her the character exercised a deep appeal. In her eyes the character embodied all those elements which were anathema to respectable society: outspokenness, defiance, unconventionality, fearlessness. Her adoption of the name as a mantle gave her a persona that she grew into and one which proved exactly right for one of her temperament and beliefs. In assuming the name she *became* Rebecca West: vigorous, iconoclastic and forthright. Though the family contin-ued to call her Cissie she increasingly used her adopted name both for private and professional use. To her the name and its associations summed up all that she stood for: a fearless quest for the truth, a refusal to bow down to convention and a passionate defence of liberty. From 1912 onwards 'Rebecca West' was increasingly a force to be reckoned with in English literature.

In September 1912 she wrote a review of a novel by Ford Madox Ford, *The New Humpty Dumpty*. Her article was published in *The English Review*, a leading critical journal which had serialised novels by Wells, Hardy and James. Ford was so intrigued by the review that he and his mistress Violet Hunt invited her to meet them at their London home at 80 Campden Hill Road. This house, known as South Lodge, was something of a mecca for artists and writers; Violet made a practice of organising literary soirées to which she invited up-and-coming writers and poets. With her burning literary ambitions Rebecca found this menage interesting and congenial. It was at South Lodge over the following months that she met such figures as Wyndham Lewis, Compton Mackenzie, Somerset Maugham and May Sinclair. Through Ford and his circle she widened her range of friendships and enjoyed the stimulus of discussions on topics of the day.

After the collapse of *The Freewoman* she fought hard to get it re-established and tried to raise money in a vain attempt to revive it. Meanwhile she found an outlet for her outspoken journalism in *The Clarion*, a socialist newspaper edited by Robert Blatchford. *The Clarion*, founded in 1891, had steadily increased its circulation until by 1910 it had established itself as the leading radical journal of the day. In addition to articles on social and political questions it published short stories, verse, jokes and criticism; it sought to be readable and popular rather than highbrow. Blatchford invited her to become a political writer for the paper after reading her attack on a notorious anti-feminist in *The Freewoman*: 'I wouldn't have missed it for a pension', he told her, 'It's like a ride on an aeroplane; so exhilarating, so breezy; it is also irresistibly funny.'[18] From September 1912 to December 1913 she contributed regularly to the paper, writing on the role of women in society, the Labour party, racial prejudice, the future of the middle classes, the House of Commons, the suffragette movement and the relationship between socialism and feminism. These pieces brought her name before a wide audience and greatly enhanced her reputation as a fearless exponent of the rights of women. Trenchant, passionate and forthright, her articles and book reviews vigorously defend the entitlement of women to an equal place in society, plead for an end to bigotry in religion and politics and castigate politicians for their blindness in refusing to grant female suffrage. Her targets ranged from Lloyd George to bishops, from Parliament to the police. She earned herself the nickname 'a Bernard Shaw in petticoats'.[19] Tireless in their exposure of cant and pusillanimity, her articles possess a freshness and individuality which make them fascinating reading even eighty years later. For many contemporary readers her page was the first they turned to each week. Increasingly the name Rebecca West came to be synonymous with radical journalism at its most astringent: lampooning pomposity and hypocrisy, exposing intolerance and speaking up boldly for the rights of women.

Throughout these months she was seeing Wells with increasing frequency, visiting him at Easton Glebe, at his London home in Hampstead and at his new flat in St James's Court. It is perhaps difficult for a reader at the end of the twentieth century to understand the powerful attraction Wells exercised for her. It is important to grasp, firstly, that in Edwardian England writers enjoyed the kind of popular status accorded to pop stars and television personalities today. Wells, Shaw, Chesterton and Bennett were famous public figures, enjoying an income and a social cachet comparable to that of a wealthy entrepreneur. For Rebecca and her generation, moreover, Wells exercised an irresistible appeal because of his socialist and feminist views and the persuasive idealism of his novels and prophecies. Through her adolescence and the beginnings of her literary career his name was revered in socialist and radical circles and his books were eagerly sought after and discussed in the Fabian and feminist groups she attended. In such works as *In the Days of the Comet, A Modern Utopia, This Misery of Boots* and *New Worlds for Old* he was gaining new adherents for socialism and in his prolific journalism he was adding a warm humanitarian voice in defence of feminist and radical thought. His novels *Tono-Bungay* and *The New Machiavelli* were widely read, particularly by the young, while the furore caused by the publication of *Ann Veronica* brought his name before a new audience of eager and youthful readers. As Rebecca's name came more and more to be identified as that of a distinctive original voice in the world of political journalism, so Wells's was synonymous with imaginative writing of unforgettable eloquence and power.

In the influential journal *Fortnightly Review* in November 1911 Wells had published his essay 'The contemporary novel', a revised version of a lecture he had delivered earlier that year to the Times Book Club. In this paper he struck a note of defiance which must have appealed powerfully to Rebecca:

> We are going to write, subject only to our limitations, about the whole of human life. We are going to deal with political questions and religious questions and social questions. We cannot present people unless we have this free hand, this unrestricted field . . . What is the good of pretending to write about love, and the loyalties and treacheries and quarrels of men and women, if one must not glance at those varieties of physical temperament and organic quality, those deeply passionate needs and distresses from which half the storms of human life are brewed? . . . We are going to write about it all. We are going to write about business and finance and politics and precedence and pretentiousness and decorum and indecorum, until a thousand pretences and ten thousand impostures

shrivel in the cold, clear air of our elucidations. We are going to write of wasted opportunities and latent beauties until a thousand new ways of living open to men and women. We are going to appeal to the young and the hopeful and the curious, against the established, the dignified, and the defensive.[20]

It was this aspect of Wells which intrigued large numbers of young socialists and feminists, inspiring them to read and re-read his novels and stories, discuss them eagerly with their friends and argue passionately about his ideas. For a generation of young people H. G. Wells was their champion, representing all that was new and progressive against all that was stuffy and hidebound. For one of Rebecca's views and background his appeal was irresistible.

When she came to review *Marriage* for a second time (*Everyman*, 8 November 1912) the waspish tone of her first review is altogether absent. By this time she had had the advantage of meeting Wells personally and discussing the novel with him. *Marriage*, she wrote, represented a

> spiritual dissatisfaction brooding over the dinginess that has come between us and the reality of love . . . With a sharp sense of the values of life, he [Wells] cannot bear the artificial sanction given to gross, destructive, mutual raids on personality which often form marriages.

The review may not have pleased Wells but it was at least an honest attempt on her part to grasp the intrinsic theme of the book and to come to terms with the novel's protagonists, Marjorie and Trafford. It may be seen as a kind of footnote to their lengthy discussions about life and society.

The friendship between Rebecca and Wells began as a literary friendship and continued on that basis for some months, meeting in one another's homes, discussing books and ideas, and exchanging letters. Early in 1913 the scenario changed – it seems clear that it changed on Rebecca's initiative.

There is no need to disbelieve Wells's version of what happened. In an account he included in the posthumously published *Postscript* to his autobiography he wrote:

> I liked her and found her very interesting, but I was on my good behaviour with Little e and we kept the talk bookish and journalistic. Until a visit to Church Row when, face to face with my book-shelves, in the midst of a conversation about style or some such topic, and apropos of nothing, we paused and suddenly kissed each other. Then Rebecca flamed up into open and declared passion.[21]

A surviving letter from Wells to Rebecca, dated February 1913, makes it clear that he is responding to her plea that they should become lovers:

> You're a very compelling person. I suppose I shall have to do what you want me to do. But anyhow I mean to help you all I can in your great adventure.
>
> You consider me an entirely generous and sympathetic brother in all your arrangements.
>
> I'll help you all I can and I'll take the risk of its being known about and misunderstood and I trust you implicitly to do your best that it isn't known about.[22]

His excessive caution is understandable in the light of the scandal surrounding his affair with Amber Reeves and its consequences. The emotional and psychological wounds caused by this episode still rankled deeply and he was in no mood for any repetition of a trauma of this kind. Partly because of this caution, partly because he was uncertain of his real feelings towards Rebecca, and partly because he was reluctant to antagonise Little e, he prevaricated for some months. He was away in Italy for the whole of May and on his return busied himself with a hectic round of entertaining at Easton Glebe and settling into his London flat. He was at this time working on a scientific romance *The World Set Free*, a novel, *The Wife of Sir Isaac Harman*, and also busy with prolific journalism for *The Daily Mail* and other journals.

Simultaneously Rebecca's hopes of a reborn *Freewoman* came to fruition. A wealthy backer had been found in the person of Harriet Shaw Weaver, an enlightened and shrewd Englishwoman – she later became one of the earliest champions of James Joyce – who became treasurer of *The New Freewoman* in June 1913. Dora Marsden became editor and Rebecca was offered the post of assistant editor at a salary of £52 a year. The new journal was described as 'humanist' rather than 'feminist' and from the outset Rebecca sought to make it a forum for the widest possible discussion of literature and politics.

With the launching of *The New Freewoman*, her writing in *The Clarion*, her burgeoning fame as 'Rebecca West' and her growing love for Wells she had clearly reached a turning point in her life. From now onwards innocence and adolescence lay behind her. What lay ahead of her was as yet unknown.

Part II:

The Passionate Friends

Miss Rebecca West, pensive, after writing her well-known opinion of that Great Good Woman-Soul, Miss Ellen Key.

A sketch of Rebecca West drawn by H. G. Wells and included in his novel *Boon* (1915).

Chapter 4

The Woman of My Life

It was his hopeless hope that some time he would have an experience that would act on his life like alchemy, turning to gold all the dark metals of events, and from that revelation he would go on his way rich with an inextinguishable joy.

Rebecca West, *The Return of the Soldier*

Two worlds are altered every time a man and a woman associate. The alterations may vary widely in extent but an alteration is always there. It would indeed be a very remarkable thing if Nature, for all her general looseness and extravagance, had contrived it otherwise.

H. G. Wells, *Experiment in Autobiography*

I

It is plain that in the early months of 1913 Wells was deeply attracted towards Rebecca and flattered by her open declaration of love. At the same time he was hesitant about committing himself too irrevocably to a relationship from which he knew it would be extremely difficult to disentangle himself. He was caught in a classical double bind: he found Rebecca intriguing and appealing but was reluctant to become involved in a repetition of the Amber affair when the repercussions from the latter were still very much alive. He was also not at all sure of her wisdom in becoming involved with a married man twenty-six years her senior who already had a reputation with women and who had been at the centre of an ugly gossip campaign only a few years earlier.

Hurt and puzzled by his prevarication and his frequent absences abroad Rebecca set off in May, accompanied by her mother, for a holiday in Spain. Some indication of her state of mind at the time may be gauged from her short story 'At Valladolid', published in *The New Freewoman* on 1 August 1913. The narrator describes how she visits a doctor at Valladolid (a town in Castile, Northern Spain, where Rebecca stayed) and confides to him that 'though my lover had left my body chaste he seduced my soul: he mingled himself with me till he was more myself than I am and then left me'. The narrator finds life so intolerable that 'death is an urgent need'; she tries unsuccessfully to commit suicide. The story is clearly the reflection of a mood of deep unhappiness and emotional disturbance but the writing of it – against a background of Spanish scenery and new experiences – seems to have purged Rebecca of much of her misery. Through the story she succeeded vicariously in ridding herself of some of her tensions. She continued her journey through Spain, her mother urging her to have nothing more to do with Wells, and returned to England at the end of the month.

On Wells's return from Italy they resumed their meetings at his London flat and began an increasingly agitated correspondence – her letters passionate and headstrong and Wells's trying to maintain a tone of calm detachment. To one of her impassioned appeals, in which she threatened suicide, he replied: 'How can I be your friend to this accompaniment? I don't see that I can be of any use or help to you at all. You have my entire sympathy – but until we can meet on a reasonable basis, good bye.'[1] Meanwhile her regular journalism was continuing to appear in *The Clarion* – on 20 June 1913 she published a moving and eloquent essay on the life of Emily Davison, a suffragette who had killed herself by throwing herself in front of the King's horse at the Derby – and she was writing with coruscating wit on a host of feminist and political issues. Simultaneously, three vividly written semi-fictional pieces appeared in *The New Freewoman*, 'Trees of gold', 'Nana' and 'At Valladolid'. These pieces, inspired by her visit to Spain and imbued with the heat and magic of that country, are written with striking verve and colour. Rebecca was maturing visibly as a literary artist and in writing these descriptive pieces she had clearly found a medium that deeply appealed to her. In depicting foreign scenes and peoples and reflecting on the lives and loves of people outside her normal ambit she was tapping a hitherto unexplored part of her talent. Wells wrote at once to express his admiration:

> You are writing gorgeously again. Please resume being friends . . . Nana was tremendous. You are as wise as God when you write – at times – and then you are tortured, untidy . . . You are like a beautiful voice singing out of a darkened room into which one gropes and finds nothing. Anyhow I read you with unquenchable amazement.[2]

His new novel *The Passionate Friends* was published in September 1913 and she reviewed it in *The New Freewoman* on 1 October. *The Passionate Friends* is a long, discursive work in which he returned to the theme he had explored with such candour in *The New Machiavelli*: that of the man of promise who is deflected by an intense romantic passion. In the story of Stephen Stratton and his doomed love for Lady Mary Christian he was clearly working out of his system some of the deep frustrations arising from his enforced separation from Amber Reeves. The narrative is told with great skill: the boyhood and adolescence of the narrator, his naïve love for Mary Christian, his adventures in the South African war, his burgeoning love for the now married Mary, their deeply emotional affair and her suicide consequent on her husband's discovery of her infidelity. Interwoven with the story of Stephen Stratton's life and loves is an account of his social and political ideals and his dawning realisation of the need for an open conspiracy of intelligent men and women who would take the initiative in reshaping the world. Stratton emerges as a sensitive, thoughtful man who is driven by moods of self-doubt and is haunted by a vision of loveliness he had known as a child:

> I wonder if you dream as I dreamt. I wonder whether indeed I dreamt as now I think I did. Have I, in these latter years, given form and substance and a name to things as vague in themselves as the urgencies of instinct? Did I really go into those woods and waving green places as one keeps a tryst, expectant of a fellowship more free and delicate and delightful than any I knew? Did I know in those days of nymphs and dryads and fauns and all those happy soulless beings with which the desire of man's heart has animated the wilderness? Once certainly I crawled slowly through the tall bracken and at last lay still for an interminable while, convinced that so I should see those shadows populous with fairies, with green little people. How patiently I lay! But the stems creaked and stirred, and my heart would keep on beating like a drum in my throat.
>
> It is incredible that once a furry whispering half-human creature with bright brown eyes came and for a time played with me near where the tall ferns foam in a broad torrent from between the chestnuts down to the upper mere. That must have been real dreaming, and yet now with all my sanities and scepticisms, I could half believe it real.[3]

Wells poured into the novel all his idealism, his discontent with the prevailing code of sexual morality and his deep unease concerning the drift of civilisation. Henry James wrote to him at once to praise it: 'I bare my head before the immense ability of it – before the high intensity with which your talent keeps itself interesting and which has made me absorb the so full-bodied thing in deep and prolonged gustatory draughts.'[4] The reviewers were less kind. Robert Lynd in the *Daily News* and A. R. Orage in the *New Age* both savaged the book, the latter declaring that 'What Mr Wells calls passion is nothing but lust. All the chief characters are as promiscuous as they can hang together. There is neither charm nor virtue in one of them.'

In her review, published in *The New Freewoman* on 1 October 1913, Rebecca began by saying that the novel 'is infinitely nobler than

Mr Wells's last book, *Marriage*' and went on to praise 'the finest thoughts, the bravest speculations that bridge possibilities as steel bridges span dark rivers, the most delicate dreams' which permeate the book. But she then drew attention to some of the novel's weaknesses, commenting in particular on the solemnity with which Wells discussed the theme of jealousy and raising the question whether the solution to the problem might not be to treat sex with less seriousness:

> Surely the only way to medicine the ravages of this fever of life is to treat sex lightly, to recognise that in this as in philosophy the one is not more excellent than the many, to think no more hardly of two lovers who part soon than we do of spring for leaving the earth at the coming of June.

Her review concluded with an observation of noteworthy perception:

> But the question arises as one finishes *The Passionate Friends* whether Mr Wells's attitude to life does not create an atmosphere that is favourable to that poisoned growth. This perpetual deprecation of rash defiances, this tolerance of flinching and weakness, this constant subordination of the quick personal wisdom to the slow collective wisdom, makes for selflessness. And jealously is the complaint of the incomplete self. The woman who is acting the principal part in her own ambitious play is unlikely to weep because she is not playing the part in some man's no more ambitious play.

The comment that 'jealousy is the complaint of the incomplete self' is a barb worthy of Rebecca at her most direct. In making the observation and linking it with the claim that a woman is unlikely to weep 'because she is not playing the part in some man's play' she was highlighting a fundamental weakness in the novel and (by implication) in Wells's own make-up. The story of Stephen Stratton and Mary Christian, elegantly written though it is, is seen almost entirely from Stratton's point of view: the missing element in the book is an account of the same events from Mary's perspective. Though Wells goes to some lengths to try to redress this imbalance – for example by devoting a whole chapter to quotations from lengthy letters written by her – the impression of the novel as a whole is that it is written from an exclusively male standpoint. Stratton is both judge and jury in his own cause. James made much the same point when he commented: 'I don't think you *get* her, or at any rate give her, and all through one hears your remarkable – your wonderful! – reporting manner and voice . . . and not, by my persuasion, hers.'[5]

Implicit in her review and in her earlier appraisal of *Marriage* is a shrewd suspicion that Wells was being disingenuous in arguing for the equality of the sexes: that, despite all his protestations, he did not really

mean what he said. Years later when he came to write his autobiography he acknowledged the justice of her criticisms without
mentioning her by name:

> The spreading knowledge of birth control . . . seemed to justify my
> contention that love was now to be taken more lightly than it had been in
> the past. It was to be refreshment and invigoration, as I set out quite
> plainly in my *Modern Utopia*, and I could preach these doctrines with no
> thought of how I would react if presently my wife were to carry them
> into effect . . .[6]

What Rebecca found distasteful and intellectually dishonest was that
in novel after novel he appeared to be pleading for the equality of men
and women when in reality, she suspected, he wanted nothing of the
kind. She felt he had not thought through the implications of what he
was preaching and that equality of the sexes on the lines he was
advocating would lead to greater freedom for men unaccompanied by
any corresponding enlargement of freedom for women. In her eyes 'the
endowment of motherhood' was an empty phrase which would fail to
have any currency until women were fully equal in law and in practice.

Rebecca, with her unerring ability to detect the thin ice in an
argument, had pointed her finger at a loophole in an otherwise
masterly and impressive novel and she must have waited with some
trepidation for his reaction. He had a reputation for responding angrily
to derogatory reviews of his works and was prone to firing off sarcastic
and wounding letters to editors who published them. To her relief he
wrote on 4 October thanking her for the review and saying it was 'first
rate criticism'. He was becoming more and more impressed with her
literary prowess and urged her to collect her early journalism together
in a book; the title he suggested was *From the Junior School*. As an
alternative he suggested that she should collect all her articles and book
reviews, including the most recent, under the title *The Taste of Life*.

When he returned to England from another holiday in Italy in
November 1913 he had quarrelled finally with Little e and was ready to
embark on a lasting partnership with Rebecca. In the months between
her first overture to him in February of that year and their mutual
decision in November to become loving friends his perception of her
and of her role in his life had shifted fundamentally. His original
impression had been of a rather gauche young woman 'with a curious
mixture of maturity and infantilism about her'.[7] Her early letters to
him – in which she seemed to him to be throwing herself at his feet –
had struck him as immature and unwise. He had questioned in his own
mind whether he wished to become involved with yet another young
woman; and whether she for her part was fully aware of what she was

proposing. He thought his attraction for her might prove to be a nine-day wonder which would soon fizzle out. With the passage of time he was compelled to acknowledge that his original estimate of her had been profoundly mistaken. Though she was only 20 she displayed a remarkable maturity for her years. Her feelings towards him had remained constant despite his rebuffs and his seeming discouragement. She had shown that she possessed a mind of her own and was not to be deflected by changes of mood. Above all, in her book reviews, her political journalism and short stories she was displaying convincing evidence of real literary power and a formidable creative intelligence. He was forced to acknowledge that in Rebecca West he had met someone quite unlike his previous encounters and that for the first time in his life he was faced with a determination and an intellectual power equalling his own. The central quest of his life which he defined as 'the mixture of sexual need and the hunger for a dear companion'[8] had hitherto only been partially fulfilled. Jane had met abundantly his hunger for companionship; Amber had temporarily assuaged his emotional needs; but his quest for both needs combined in one person had always eluded him. Now in the person of Rebecca he had found someone who held out the promise of both. He had found a young writer of extraordinary gifts and immense potential who seemed to embody within herself all the attributes he craved: physical attractiveness, mental acumen and impressive creative energy. It seemed to him that at last he had found the partner of his dreams.

II

For a time his excessive caution meant that their relationship had to be conducted with the greatest secrecy. Rebecca left the family home in Hampstead Garden Suburb and went to live at 28 Clifton Gardens, Maida Vale; she and Wells contrived to see each other frequently in London, either at Maida Vale or at apartments lent by sympathetic friends. 'You are the sweetest of company', he wrote to her in December 1913, 'the best of friends, the most wonderful of lovers. Thank you for 10,000 things.' It was agreed between them from the beginning that theirs was not merely a passing affair but a partnership of equals – they were to be two writers working and loving together in a creative unity. As he expressed it in his novel *The Research Magnificent*, which was commenced at this time: 'He had fallen in love with her, and that being so whatever he needed that instantly she was. He needed a companion, clean and brave and understanding . . . He thought always of the two of them as being side by side.'[9]

As a symbol of their equal partnership they adopted as their pet names for one another Panther and Jaguar; throughout their relationship she was Panther and Wells was Jaguar. These were not simply the intimate names chosen by two lovers. The names embodied a shared attitude to life: defiance of established law and convention, withdrawal from society, and a recognition that each had found a soul mate quite separate from the common herd. The names implied a delight in lovemaking and an acceptance of the need to meet in secret to express their affection for one another. But for both Wells and Rebecca feline imagery had a special significance apart from its suggestion of independence and animality. 'I should love to be a cat', she had written earlier that year, 'and lie in a basket by the fire all day and go on the tiles at night. And the life of a tiger seems attractive; even in captivity. It must be great fun to escape from a menagerie and liven up a rural district.'[10] From childhood onwards she loved cats and was fascinated by their air of mystery and aloofness. For her they embodied all that need for affection, companionship and solace she had experienced at times of loneliness. They represented the warmth and comfort she associated with home and her lost childhood. For Wells cats and the cat family held an equal fascination. Feline imagery frequently recurs in his fiction and as early as *The Island of Doctor Moreau* (1896) it occupies a dominant place. Moreau, a vivisector living on a remote Pacific island, transforms animals into men through a process of surgery. The island is peopled with his failed experiments but it is a puma which proves to be his undoing. Deprived of its freedom, fettered and tortured, the puma succeeds in escaping from Moreau's laboratory and finally kills him. The reader has a keen sense of the cruelty of imprisoning such a beautiful wild animal and the grace of such creatures in their natural state. Moreau with his indifference to pain, his inhumanity, his obsession with his research to the exclusion of all other considerations, symbolises the emptiness of knowledge without compassion. He is the steely man of science: stoical, unemotional, obdurate. The puma represents the opposite values: wildness, feeling, energy, animality. In the end Moreau is destroyed by the creature he has imprisoned; the feline triumphs over inhumanity.

In the short story 'The door in the wall' the narrator relates how as a child he wandered into an enchanted garden:

'You see', he said, with the doubtful inflection of a man who pauses at incredible things, 'there were two great panthers there. Yes, spotted panthers. And I was not afraid. There was a long wide path with marble-edged flower borders on either side, and these two huge velvety beasts were playing there with a ball . . . And before me ran this long wide path, invitingly, with weedless beds on either side, rich with untended flowers, and these two great panthers. I put my little hands fearlessly on their soft fur, and caressed their round ears and the sensitive corners under their

ears, and played with them, and it was as though they welcomed me
home. There was a keen sense of homecoming in my mind . . .'

The use of such adjectives as 'velvety', 'soft', 'caress' and 'sensitive' is
interesting and suggests that for Wells a panther represented the
feminine aspects of life, all that is soft, receptive and affectionate. That
the panthers are associated with homecoming is also a reminder that, as
with Rebecca, cats suggested the home-like qualities of warmth and
security. The names Panther and Jaguar were therefore symbolic not
only of their deep love for one another but of their joint resolve to
withdraw from the society around them, to pursue their partnership
regardless of the judgement of others and to derive the greatest
possible fulfilment from their friendship.

By the end of 1913 Rebecca had decided to sever her connection with
The Clarion. For some time she had been aware that her interests were
changing and that writing polemical journalism no longer satisfied her
as it had in former years. Her inclinations were becoming more and
more literary and she longed to express herself in reviewing and in the
writing of fiction. At the same time she discovered she was pregnant.
The scenario which she and Wells had planned together had not
included motherhood. Theirs was to be a loving partnership in which
each would be free to pursue their creative work. His account of what
occurred is quite candid and matter of fact:

> She came to see me at my flat in St James's Court one afternoon when we
> were in danger of being interrupted by a valet; it was our second
> encounter and she became pregnant. It was entirely unpremeditated.
> Nothing of the sort was in our intention. She wanted to write. It should
> not have happened, and since I was the experienced person, the blame is
> wholly mine.[11]

Whatever the truth of the matter – and it seems to the present writer
that Wells's account has the ring of veracity about it – it is clear that
parenthood formed no part of their original plan and that both were
compelled to readjust to the new situation. Wells set off on a long
planned visit to Russia but wrote to her daily, assuring her of his love
and devotion. The plan he now evolved was that she should install
herself in a quiet location off the beaten track, a haven where she could
lie low until the baby was born and where he could visit her frequently.
At first Llandudno was suggested as a possible retreat but this idea was
abandoned in favour of Hunstanton on the Norfolk coast. Hunstanton
had the advantage that it was accessible by train from Easton Glebe and
was so completely unfashionable that it was extremely unlikely he
would meet anyone there whom he knew. He found suitable lodgings

for her on Victoria Avenue, a quiet road of Victorian villas, and – attended by her sister Lettie and one or two close friends – she moved there in February 1914. There she remained until September of the same year. He was still nervous of the possibility of discovery and urged her to tell no one except her most intimate friends. The rooms were booked in the name of Mr and Mrs West. As far as her landlady was concerned she was Mrs West, the wife of a writer who had to spend long periods away from home. 'We have to settle down and work there and love there and live there, and you have to see that it is all right . . . You are going to be my wife', he wrote to her.[12] During the six months Rebecca spent at Hunstanton he spent all the time with her he could, staying with her for a few days each week and occasionally for longer stretches. Nevertheless she was frequently alone. At Hunstanton she was cut off from all her usual circle and also had to contend with the implacable hostility of her mother who from the outset had strongly opposed her relationship with Wells. She did her utmost to compensate for her enforced loneliness by making the most of moments of intense happiness in his company. Together they went for walks, went motoring in a hired car, boated and bathed, talked and wrote. He was now deeply immersed in *The Research Magnificent*; she was writing book reviews for the *Daily News* and also working on a critical study of Henry James. It was pleasant to spend part of each day writing. These were among their happiest moments: each preoccupied with their own work, separate yet united in silent companionship.

The Research Magnificent, though almost completely forgotten today, is an extremely interesting novel from many points of view, not least because it was the first of Wells's novels to be written during his creative partnership with Rebecca West. From this standpoint it offers a fascinating insight into his attitude towards Rebecca during the first year of their friendship and an intriguing commentary on his outlook and personality at a crucial stage of his intellectual and emotional development. It is a long and ambitious novel in which Wells tried the experiment of 'making the ostensible writer speculate about the chief character in the story he is telling. The ostensible writer becomes a sort of enveloping character, himself in discussion with the reader.'[13] The novel relates the life story of William Benham, an idealistic, rather priggish young man who is obsessed by his quest to live nobly and thoroughly. Instead of telling the story in conventional first-person or third-person narration Wells adopts the unusual device of presenting it as if it has been shaped by an editor, White, a novelist who was a friend of Benham's and who goes through Benham's diaries and writings after the latter's death. White (a surrogate for Wells) is referred to throughout as 'he', so that both he and Benham are seen from the outside; this gives a distancing effect to the narrative as a whole and enables the reader to see both the hero and the storyteller from the perspective of an impartial observer.

After two introductory chapters describing Benham's boyhood and adolescence – chapters which many readers would find tiresome because of their long windedness and excessive solemnity – the novel suddenly comes to life when Benham embarks on a walking tour of Surrey and Sussex and meets and falls in love with Amanda Morris. Amanda is a carefully drawn portrait of Rebecca as she was when Wells first became enchanted with her, and she is depicted in glowing colours:

> She had an eyebrow like a quick stroke of a camel's-hair brush, she had a glowing face, half childish imp, half woman, she had honest hazel eyes, a voice all music, a manifest decision of character . . . she was the freest, finest, bravest spirit that he had ever encountered.[14]

The fact that Benham and Amanda first meet near Uppark strongly suggests that Wells links her in his mind with his earliest romantic imaginings, a link made explicit when the novel continues: 'She had brought back to his memory the fancies that had been aroused in his first reading of Plato's *Republic*; she made him think of those women Guardians, who were the friends and mates of men.' The two fall deeply in love and embark on a passionate courtship and marriage; presently she is 'Leopard' and he is 'Cheetah'. Amanda laces their journeys 'with a fantastic monologue telling in the third person what the Leopard and the Cheetah were thinking and seeing and doing'. For a time the lovers are extremely happy together. The account of their delight in each other's company, their lyrical discovery of new found happinesses, their love of travel and adventure, clearly echo aspects of Wells and Rebecca during the early months of their partnership. These chapters are written with a felicity and conviction he rarely equalled. They are filled with a sense of Amanda as someone 'wonderful, beautiful, glowing, life-giving, confident, clear-eyed'; the lovers are 'ardently delighted with the discovery of one another'. But even before their honeymoon is over Benham is aware of a growing conflict between them:

> For days and weeks together it did not seem to Benham that there was anything that mattered in life but Amanda and the elemental joys of living. And then the Research Magnificent began to stir in him again . . . Moods began in which he seemed to forget Amanda altogether.[15]

In this passage can be discerned the plainest possible statement of the friction which came to disturb Wells and Rebecca increasingly as their friendship progressed. When they were together nothing seemed to matter but their love for one another and the sheer delight each found in the other's companionship and affection. But then things would begin to niggle. There would be trouble with servants (Rebecca seemed to have an uncanny knack of choosing incompetent or interfering staff), or he would complain they had too little time alone, or he would find her continual ill health an irritation. Even when none of these things niggled him he would begin to be impatient to return to Easton Glebe or to London; constantly his work beckoned him – the novel he was currently writing, his prolific journalism, his ventures into sociology and prophecy, his voluminous correspondence. At the centre of his life was Jane, his family and his home. Rebecca was always conscious that, whatever joy he found in their love and friendship he would continually need to return to that centre for reassurance and stability.

Benham's awareness that 'the Research Magnificent began to stir in him again' – his recognition that he is torn between his love for Amanda and his need to make something positive of his life – is a point of fulcrum in the narrative in which Wells, consciously or unconsciously, is echoing his ambivalent feelings towards Rebecca. Benham asks himself the question 'whether he wasn't catching glimpses of reality through a veil of delusion that grew thinner and thinner and might leave him disillusioned'. With the passage of time he becomes more and more aware of Amanda's limitations. He realises that she does not share his lofty ideals, that she is 'a miscellany bound in a body', 'an animated discursiveness'. Gradually the two lovers drift apart. Benham sets off on his travels without her; in his absence she is unfaithful to him. The remainder of the novel consists of an account of his journeyings in Asia and South Africa, ending abruptly with his death by gunfire during a riot in Johannesburg.

Despite many fine descriptive passages and moments of spirited dialogue it is not difficult to understand why *The Research Magnificent* has never gained the popularity of *Tono-Bungay* or *The New Machiavelli* or why it has received so little critical attention. The novel contains Wells's strengths and weaknesses in abundance. Its great strength lies in the central story of the deep love between two extraordinarily interesting and gifted people who find great happiness in each other's company and embark on a love affair which brings to both of them some of life's profoundest joys. The story of their encounter, their discovery of their feelings for one another and their determination to extract the utmost richness and meaning from their partnership is told with consummate skill. So too is the account of Benham's gradual discovery of the 'conflict of intellectual temperaments', the 'fundamental antagonism of their quality' which divides and exasperates them. The story of their growing disillusionment, the slow recognition of a gulf of incompatibilities is unfolded with genuine conviction. Benham and Amanda are believable characters caught up in a believable and all too realistic situation.

The weakness of the book lies in its irritating prolixity, its tendency to indulge in long passages of introspective soliloquy when Benham meditates on his purposes in life or White speculates about Benham. In later years Wells described the novels of his middle period as his 'Prig Novels': by this term he meant the fiction from *The New Machiavelli* to *The Research Magnificent* inclusive, fiction in which a solipsistic hero is obsessed with the quest for a purpose in life. *The Research Magnificent* is perhaps the least vital and most insular of all this group and possesses the defects of the genre more obviously than most; its almost total absence of humour, its tendency to self-pity, the hero's preoccupation with ideas which many readers must have found incomprehensible – all militate against its acceptance as an enduring work of art. Strangest of all is the woodenness of some of the conversations between the lovers, as if this most passionate of men was incapable of conveying the wonder and magic of adult love. What redeems it as a novel and makes it worth reading and re-reading today is the character of Amanda, who is so obviously drawn from life. 'Amanda is alive', Wells wrote years later, 'and Benham has his moments of vitality.'[16] It is Amanda Morris who transforms the book from an otherwise pedestrian story into a vital and memorable picture of love and friendship in the years immediately before the First World War. It is her character – vigorous, questioning and brimming with life – that breathes through the novel and many readers found her his most attractive heroine since Ann Veronica. Rebecca liked the book when she read it both in proof form and as a published work, praising it in reviews in the *Daily News* and in the *New Republic*. One cannot help speculating whether even then, at this early stage in their relationship, it caused her to rethink her attitude towards him or to have any doubt about the long-term durability of their association.

Meanwhile she was finding her own feet as a writer, not only in book reviews and polemical essays but in creative work. Her short story 'Indissoluble matrimony' was published in the first number of Wyndham Lewis's *Blast* on 20 June 1914, having been originally written four years earlier and rejected by the *English Review*. Now revised for publication, 'Indissoluble matrimony' remains an immature though powerfully written study of sexual antagonism. It is the story of a married couple, George and Evadne Silverton, whose ten-year relationship is foundering in a series of misunderstandings and arguments. George suspects that his wife is being unfaithful to him when in reality her absences from home are perfectly innocent. Enraged by her apparent infidelity he tries twice to kill her, but each attempt fails. The story ends with George seemingly reconciled to making the most of an empty marriage, caught in the humdrum routines of office and home. Overwritten though it is and heavily influenced in style by D. H. Lawrence, it contains some perceptive moments in which Rebecca seeks to understand differing perspectives towards marriage. There is a particularly sharp moment when the husband reflects on the differences between his conception of love and that of his wife:

> Almost from the first she had meant to marry him . . . And it was time she married. She was ripe for adult things. This was the real wound in his soul. He had tasted of a divine thing created in his time for dreams out of her rich beauty, her loneliness, her romantic poverty, her immaculate youth. He had known love. And Evadne had never known anything more than a magnificent physical adventure . . .

It would be misleading to read too much into this concerning the love between Wells and Rebecca for most of the story was written before she met him, but 'Indissoluble matrimony' is to say the least a shrewd commentary on marriage and reveals a keen understanding of the forces that can lead to the disintegration of a loving relationship. In writing the story of George and Evadne she was, as it were, thinking aloud about the conflicting drives and emotions within her own personality; she was trying to understand herself and what she wanted from life. The story is a trial sketch of themes she was later to explore on a much fuller canvas in *The Return of the Soldier* and *The Judge*.

III

Rebecca's position was now unenviable to say the least. She was on the brink of a promising literary career, was at last finding her authentic voice in the writing of vivid short stories and impressionistic sketches, and – at the moment when the world seemed to be opening before her – found herself committed to pregnancy and motherhood, both of which would inevitably interrupt and hamper her creative life. As an unmarried mother she knew she was risking the reproach of her relatives and friends, particularly of her mother (who disliked and mistrusted Wells) and also of landladies and servants wherever she chose to live. To be an unmarried mother in 1913 was to be 'a fallen woman' and to run a gauntlet of derogatory comments and accusing stares from every quarter. She had no alternative therefore but to make the best of a difficult situation, and in facing up to her predicament she displayed considerable courage. Apart from her deep love for Wells she saw him as a source of security and dependability: he would not let her down. 'I think of that happy thing cuddled up in your soft flesh and your dear warm blood', he wrote to her, 'I'm so glad we've made it.'[17] She fell in with his suggestion that from now onwards in order to avoid wagging tongues she would have to keep up a pretence that she was married. From now on her role was to be 'Mrs West'. But she was under no illusions about the implications of this decision for her social and creative life. Her forthcoming confinement would mean that for some months she would have to cut herself off from her London circle of friends and acquaintances and confide her secret to as few people as possible. The fact that Wells was a public figure meant that he was likely to be recognised and he was understandably reluctant for them to be seen together for fear of starting gossip.

When he could not join her at Hunstanton he wrote to her daily, assuring her of his love and devotion. 'Dear little Mate', ran a typical letter (April 1914):

> Person that it's pleasant to be against
> Dear, dusky, dear-eyed Panther
>   Warm kind Companion
> The world bores me to death
>   (Or rather *my* world does)
> It bores me and irritates me
> When I am away from you.

Throughout her confinement Rebecca was sustained by her knowledge of his love and need for her and by his frequent visits and letters. She was also comforted by the steadfast support of her sister Lettie and one or two close friends, in particular Mrs Townshend – a mutual friend of long standing – and Wilma Meikle, a colleague from her suffragette days. At the same time she was deeply troubled by the attitude of her mother, who expected her to abandon Wells and return home as a penitent, and by the gathering war clouds. As July passed into August it seemed that all the countries of Europe were at each other's throats; nation after nation was mobilising, serving ultimatums or declaring war. The final days of her pregnancy were spent against a background of mounting tension. On 1 August Germany declared war on Russia; on the 2nd, Russian troops invaded Prussia; on the 3rd, Germany declared war on France and invaded Belgium; on the 4th, Britain declared war on Germany; on the 5th, Austria–Hungary declared war on Russia. Rebecca's baby son was born in the early hours of August 5th. He was named Anthony Panther West. The birth certificate names his mother as 'Cicely Isabel Fairfield, journalist'.

To both Rebecca and Wells it must have seemed as if the world they had known and taken for granted since childhood was collapsing about them. There had been no European war since the conflict between France and Germany came to an end in 1871; almost all of Wells's life and the whole of Rebecca's had been lived in a world at peace. This backcloth of security and calm had endured for so long it seemed in the order of things. Wells had written fantasies in which he had vividly described imaginary warfare – most notably *The War in the Air* (1908) which concludes with a haunting account of a civilisation devastated by aerial bombardment, and *The World Set Free* (1914), a striking forecast of world war fought with nuclear weapons – but never in his wildest moments had he dreamed that war would actually happen. In common with most Englishmen of his generation he accepted peace as a fact of life: war was something which occurred infrequently in places utterly remote from Europe. 'Never, it would seem, has man been so various and busy and persistent', he wrote in a 1914 essay, 'and there is no intimation of any check to the expansion of his energies.'[18] Like millions of English men and women he and Rebecca were taken completely by surprise by the outbreak of the war. When the Austrian Archduke Francis Ferdinand was assassinated at Sarajevo on 28 June it must have seemed to them both an event totally removed from their concerns and one which could not possibly impinge on them. Now every day brought grimmer and grimmer tidings of fighting, tension and conflict. The whole of Europe was in the melting pot.

August 5th found Rebecca and Wells in totally different situations. Rebecca was at Hunstanton with her newly born baby, attended by a small circle of intimate friends. She felt cut off from the man she loved, severed from her literary aspirations and acquaintances, and alarmed at the swift disintegration into war. Wells was at Easton Glebe, having returned there after a hasty visit to Hunstanton. He was buoyed up by the news of Anthony's birth and tremendously excited by the outbreak of war. 'I am radiant this morning', he wrote to her on the same day, 'I am so delighted I have a manchild in the world – of yours. I will get the world tidy for him . . .' To him, the German invasion of Belgium seemed an intolerable affront to civilised values and for a time his newspaper articles reflected the popular mood of intense patriotism. 'Every sword that is drawn against Germany now is a sword drawn for peace', he wrote in the first of a series of articles subsequently printed as a book entitled *The War That Will End War*. He was genuinely concerned at the prospect of a German invasion of England and felt that such an attack would endanger all that he held most dear. His articles in the London dailies during the first weeks of the war caught the mood of the nation. In them he sought to clarify the issues at stake, to define what he saw as the evil of aggressive imperialism and to forecast the shape of a new and saner Europe rising from the ashes of the conflict. In these articles can be discerned a sensitive mind trying to come to terms with the nature of modern warfare and to face the fact that the world could never be the same again. The articles were widely syndicated in Britain and the United States and earned him a popular reputation as a prophet and sage. Already in these early pieces another note is evident: behind the patriotism and the accusations against Germany there is a real desire for peace, a recognition of the fact that a European war must end in a world conference followed by a peace settlement and disarmament.

Meanwhile they were both becoming increasingly dissatisfied with lodging-house life and decided to look around for a home of their own. What they wanted was a furnished house or cottage within a reasonable distance of Easton Glebe; a place where Rebecca and Anthony could live and where Wells could visit or stay whenever he wished. After some searching they found what seemed the ideal place in a farmhouse called Quinbury, situated on the edge of the picture postcard village of Braughing (pronounced Braffin) in Hertfordshire. Braughing was within easy cycling or motoring distance of Easton Glebe – Wells would have had a journey of twelve miles along a straight Roman road – yet was well off the beaten track. The village could be reached by rail from London, Liverpool Street, but at the same time seemed remote from the twentieth century. It was (and still is) picturesque, tranquil and altogether charming. Quinbury was a substantial house standing on its own just outside the adjacent hamlet of Hay Street. Today the house is completely bare but in 1914 it was covered in creeper and surrounded by hedges; from it one looks across open fields to the spire of Braughing church and a landscape unchanged for centuries. When Rebecca first set eyes on it in September 1914 it must have seemed idyllic after her six months incarceration on the Norfolk coast. Wells wrote enthusiastically: 'It seems almost too good to be true that we shall walk and talk in our own garden, eat at our own table, entertain visitors in our own house.'[19] She moved into the house as 'Mrs West' and remained there from September 1914 until July 1915.

Looking back on these months she remembered them as a time when she could 'stand at her porch under the white creeper and finger the rough sun-crumbled brick and look down the valley of green water-meadows and cherish once more the illusion of stability'.[20] For her they were months of great happiness and great sorrow. The happy times were when she and Wells explored the countryside together in his new car, 'Gladys', or when he came to stay with her, or when she was free to resume her writing. The much loved child in her novel *The Fountain Overflows* is named Richard Quinbury, as if as a reminder of those moments of fulfilment in her rural idyll. The disagreeable times were when she had trouble with servants (she was, after all, only 21 and unused to running a household), or when she heard gossip about herself in the village, or when Wells was moody and wrote her a cross letter. Despite the distractions of motherhood and the difficulties of trying to live a normal life in wartime she was gradually picking up the threads of her literary career. From November onwards she became a regular contributor to the *New Republic* and continued to write book reviews for the *Daily News* as well as work sporadically on her critical study of Henry James. Through the winter of 1914–15 this remained the pattern of their lives. For Wells Quinbury was a welcome refuge from the mounting pressures of the war. The war with its terrible casualty lists, its daily toll of destruction and cruelty, its all-pervasive background of falsehood and treachery, became the dominant fact of his life. By March 1915, in *The Peace of the World*, he was writing eloquently of the need for 'a permanent World Congress for the enforcement of international law and the maintenance of the peace of mankind'. The escalating carnage sickened and distressed him. Early in 1915 he began work on *Mr Britling Sees It Through*, the novel in which he chronicled the impact of the war on a representative English household, and put the finishing touches to *Boon*, a conversational novel on which he had been intermittently at work for some years. In *Boon* he expressed as never before his anguish at the war, at 'this dreadful outbreak of brutish violence which has darkened all our lives':

> The struggle began to assume in our minds its true proportions, its true extent, in time, in space, in historical consequence. We had thought of a dramatic three months' conflict and a redrawn map of Europe; we perceived we were in the beginnings of a far vaster conflict; the end of an age; the slow, murderous testing and condemnation of whole systems of ideas that had bound men uneasily in communities for all our lives.[21]

Boon purports to be the 'literary remains' of a famous writer, George Boon, whose unpublished writings are posthumously edited by his friend Reginald Bliss. Much of the book consists of conversations between Boon and his literary friends, conversations in which Boon is continually obliged to clarify his views on life and literature. The result is a work of unusual intimacy, as if Wells is thinking aloud on the fundamental issues facing the creative artist at a time of war and forcing himself to define and sharpen his attitudes by having them discussed by characters opposed to his own views. Running through the book as a whole is a debate, echoing the ambivalence in Wells's own mind, between optimism and pessimism – between the notion that the war was a chastening opportunity to make a fresh start and recast international relations on saner lines, and the idea that it was the inevitable resurgence of man's animality, a bestial outbreak of hatred and violence which could never be contained.

The various chapters of the book consist of a number of parodies in which Wells lampoons literary personalities of the day and gently deflates the idea that to be a man of letters is a dignified or gentlemanly profession. At the heart of the novel is a lengthy section entitled 'Of art, of literature, of Mr Henry James', containing a devastating pastiche of James's ponderous style of conversation and a critique of his attitude towards literature:

> But if the novel is to follow life it must be various and discursive [says Boon]. Life is diversity and entertainment, not completeness and satisfaction. All actions are half-hearted, shot delightfully with wandering thoughts – about something else. All true stories are a felt of irrelevancies. But James sets out to make his novels with the presupposition that they can be made continuously relevant. And perceiving the discordant things, he tries to get rid of them. He sets himself to pick the straws out of the hair of Life before he paints her. But without the straws she is no longer the mad woman we love.[22]

In thus defining the differences between James and himself Wells was highlighting a polarisation of attitudes towards the novel that not only divided him irrevocably from the Master but became increasingly a bone of contention between him and Rebecca. His favourite novelists since boyhood had been Dickens, Fielding and Sterne – all writers who favoured a discursive approach in which the author was free to comment and digress, omitting nothing he felt to be of interest. To James, on the other hand, the novel was an art form, the noblest of all art forms, and the task of the novelist was to render a distillation of life and incident in a wholly symmetrical and structured unity. Rebecca's conception of the novel leaned far more towards James than Wells. Her heroes were not Dickens and Sterne but Lawrence and Bennett. To her art was of supreme importance and since childhood she had imbibed from her mother the significance of art in all its forms. When she reviewed Ford Madox Ford's *The Good Soldier* only a few weeks before *Boon* was published she praised 'the light of its extreme beauty', 'the obvious loveliness of the colour and cadence of its language', 'the delight of a noble and ambitious design', 'the finest technique'.[23] These are Jamesian rather than Wellsian values. In her fundamental assumptions concerning the means and ends of literature she was poles apart from Wells's view that all art was provisional and that beauty was incidental. This dichotomy of attitudes towards the novel was to be a source of friction between them in the years that lay ahead.

On its publication in July 1915 Wells sent a copy of *Boon* to James, who not surprisingly found it distasteful. The deliberate mockery of his convoluted style, the imaginary conversations between himself and

George Moore, the parody of *The Spoils of Poynton* as 'The spoils of Mr Blandish', were all calculated to annoy him and he was hurt and puzzled at what he regarded as Wells's rudeness. Wells found his pained attitude rather hypocritical, for James in his essay 'The younger generation' (*Times Literary Supplement*, 19 March and 2 April 1914) had been frankly critical of Wells, castigating *The New Machiavelli* and *Marriage* as 'so very much more attestations of the presence of material than of an interest in the use of it' and querying apropos of *The Passionate Friends* 'what that composition is specifically about and where, for treatment of this interest, it undertakes to find its centre'. From Wells's point of view *Boon* was simply a good natured reply to James's strictures and should be taken for what it was: a light-hearted attempt to define their differences in which a variety of styles (including Wells's own) were gently satirised. James declared that he found much of the book unreadable and that the destruction of the common ground between them meant 'the collapse of a bridge which made communication possible'. Wells replied with an apologetic letter in which he sought to make amends for his apparent bad manners, saying that 'To you literature like painting is an end, to me literature like architecture is a means, it has a use.' James replied at once with a dictated letter refuting Wells's arguments and asserting that this distinction was 'wholly null and void'.[24] James seemed determined to regard the breach as marking the end of their friendship but Wells continued the correspondence in an attempt to keep the dialogue going. Whether James replied again is not known. He died less than a year later, in February 1916, having been in deteriorating health for the last months of his life.

IV

Quinbury and its surrounding countryside had seemed attractive and welcoming in summer but with the onset of winter the house seemed bleak and cold. Wells could not visit Rebecca as frequently as she wished – he was extremely busy with journalism and was working hard each day on *Mr Britling* – and when he did come he resented the fact that they were rarely alone. There was also trouble with servants; war conditions meant that reliable domestic staff was hard to come by, especially in an isolated spot like Braughing. Though theoretically Rebecca was not so cut off from her friends as she had been at Hunstanton, in practice she received few visitors apart from Wells and close associates such as Violet Hunt and Ford Madox Ford. She began more and more to pine for London or at least for somewhere within easy striking distance of theatres, concerts and all that the capital could offer. During one of her depressed moods Wells wrote her a letter of reassurance:

> You know it's as clear as daylight to me that you are my love. Mentally, temperamentally, physically, I've never been so warm and close with anyone as with you. And we have been ragging it all to pieces and spoiling it with detailed bothers for which we are both indisposed and naturally not very capable.[25]

She found a temporary solution to her difficulties at the end of July 1915 when she vacated Quinbury and moved into a large furnished villa at Hatch End, Pinner. This house, called Alderton, remained her home until September 1916. Here she adopted the pretence that she was 'Miss West' and that Anthony was her nephew. The advantage of the Hatch End house from Rebecca's point of view was that she could travel to London easily for her *Daily News* and *New Republic* articles, and it was also much more convenient when visiting her mother, her sisters and her friends. Wells came to see her as often as his commitments permitted and they were able to meet discreetly in London. He began to discuss his work with her and invite her to comment on his manuscripts. When she praised the draft of *Mr Britling* he wrote a warm letter of thanks: 'It does me no end of good to get you into my work', he confided.[26] Like many writers Wells was prone to moods of self-doubt and he greatly valued the encouragement and reassurance she gave him. When the American critic Van Wyck Brooks wrote a study of his work under the title *The World of H. G. Wells* she reviewed it in the *Daily News* (14 August 1915), praising *The History of Mr Polly* as 'one of the great books of the world' and expressing surprise that Brooks had not been impressed 'by the epic quality of *Tono-Bungay*'. In her review she takes the American writer to task for failing to appreciate the wide range of Wells's characters and for accepting 'the current vulgarism that books which aim at the expression of ideas are not art'. The review is a powerful defence of Wells as a novelist and as a man of ideas. But it is not without its characteristic barbs: *The Passionate Friends* is 'the worst book written since *Robert Elsmere*', whilst *A Modern Utopia*, she remarks perceptively, was 'the last frenzied attempt of Mr Wells to set his steed at the Fabian fence'. Already she was keenly aware of his strengths and his defects: quick to praise his work where she felt praise was due but intolerant of pretentiousness or intellectual dishonesty, either in Wells himself or his critics.

Rebecca's critical study of James, published in the year of his death, is totally different in conception and approach from Wells's parody. *Henry James* is a strange book – part gushing eulogy, part penetrating criticism and part hard-hitting deflation. Many of her comments on James are

9. Monkey Island, Bray, a favourite retreat for Wells and Rebecca during the troubled years of the First World War. The island figures prominently in West's novel, *The Return of the Soldier.*

10. Quinbury, Braughing, in 1988. This was Rebecca West's home from September 1914 to July 1915.

11. H. G. Wells outside Quinbury. Wells was a frequent visitor to the house, motoring from his home at Easton Glebe.

12. Ford Madox Ford and Rebecca West at Quinbury, 1914. Her review of his novel *The New Humpty-Dumpty* in 1912 brought her into his literary circle.

13. Rebecca West and Anthony, about 1916.

14. Jane Wells (Amy Catherine Robbins) Wells's wife from 1895 until her death in 1927.

15. 17 Church Row, Hampstead, Wells's home from 1909–12. Rebecca visited him here as well as at Easton Glebe and his flat in St James's Court.

16. Southcliffe, Marine Parade, Leigh-on-Sea, Rebecca West's home from March 1917 to the autumn of 1919. Leigh-on-Sea figures prominently in her novel, *The Judge*.

candid to the point of waspishness: his early novels, she wrote, were 'spoilt by technical blemishes of a sort that the most giftless modern miss with a subscription to Mudie's would never commit in her first literary experiment'; the sentences in his later novels were like 'a delicate creature swathed in relative clauses as an invalid in shawls'; *The Bostonians* 'reminds one of a foolish song set to a good tune'. Most frank of all is a shaft that might have been lifted from the pages of *Boon*: 'With sentences vast as the granite blocks of the Pyramids and a scene that would have made a site for a capital he set about constructing a story the size of a hen-house.'

Despite the candour of her criticism the tone of the book as a whole is one of reverential praise; it is clear that for her James is a genius and that the values which animate her study are utterly removed from Wells's. Thus, the novels of his middle years are likened to 'exquisite vessels that swaggeringly hold and clearly show the contained draught of truth, like tall-stemmed goblets of Venetian glass'. Or again, his story *The Altar of the Dead* is of 'so perfect a beauty that one can read every separate paragraph every day of one's life for the music of the sentences and the loveliness of the presented images'. When discussing *The Turn of the Screw* and *In the Cage*, which she describes as 'these masterpieces', Rebecca's commentary bursts into a passionate declaration of her fundamental attitude to art:

> Criticism must break down when it comes to masterpieces. For if one is creative one wants to go away and spend oneself utterly on this sacred business of creation, wring out of oneself every drop of this inestimable thing art; and if one is not creative one can only put out a tremulous finger to touch the marvellous shining crystal, and be silent with wonder.[27]

References of this kind must have irritated Wells extremely, for in truth James stood for all that he found most alien in literary endeavour. Rebecca made it abundantly clear in her book that she admired and endorsed James's assumptions concerning the novel and that for her the most enduring elements in his work were the novels in which he strived consciously to achieve wholly symmetrical and intricate works of art. Her continual use of such terms as 'exquisite', 'perfect', 'sacred', 'precious', 'miraculous' and 'eternal' apropos of his novels is an indication of her deep conviction that for the creative artist what mattered was the attainment of perfection: the writing of works of fiction in which language, structure, narrative and imagery were consummately wrought. This conception of the role of the artist was diametrically opposed to Wells's as expressed in his critical writings and in his letters to James, and Rebecca cannot have been unaware of this fact. Such sentences as 'Once at least Henry James poured into his crystal goblet the red wine that nourishes the soul', or the claim that James's death left 'the white light of his genius to shine out for the eternal comfort of the mind of man' would have left Wells utterly cold. He regarded James as a man who, over a period of many years, had pretended to give him encouragement and praise whilst secretly despising his work (James had made his real attitude all too clear in 'The younger generation') and not unnaturally resented her adulation of him.

Henry James sold only 600 copies – and consequently has become an extremely rare book. It was grudgingly reviewed by the critics who felt it was an effrontery for a woman of 24, who had at that time published no fiction herself, to dare to criticise such a respected man of letters. When the *Times Literary Supplement* declined to review the book Wells, despite his disagreement with her fundamental position, was instinctively on her side. Later he wrote angrily to Hugh Walpole: 'My blood still boils at the thought of those pretentious academic greasers conspiring to down a friendless girl (who can write any of them out of sight) in the name of loyalty to literature.'[28] Rebecca at this time could hardly be described as 'a friendless girl' but both she and Wells saw the situation in these terms; she was an underdog, a nobody who had dared to antagonise the establishment. In the eyes of the establishment she had no right to criticise the Master; in Wells's eyes she had every right. Even more significant is his reference to her as a girl 'who can write any of them out of sight'. He was already aware of her as a formidable literary talent, as a writer with great stylistic and imaginative gifts. He knew in his bones that, though he disagreed profoundly with her attitude to art and deplored her preoccupation with aesthetic values, she was indispensable to him. He could not do without her fresh vision, her ability to see everyday things from a different perspective and to render the commonplace memorable.

Their relationship was now falling into a stable pattern. At Alderton she rebuilt a life of her own, steadfastly supported by her sisters and friends, and resumed contact with her mother. She was happily occupied with book reviewing although this alone could not satisfy her creative instincts: during the winter of 1915–16 she commenced work on her first novel, *The Return of the Soldier*. Wells was now permanently settled at Easton Glebe, having greatly enlarged and improved the house to make it more suitable for his requirements, and seemed content to live the life of a successful author so vividly evoked in the opening chapters of *Mr Britling*. He was happy in his home, his wife and his sons and saw no reason to uproot this side of his life.

When he and Rebecca could not meet in London or at Alderton their treasured retreat was Monkey Island, a tiny island on the Thames at

Bray, a few miles up river from Windsor and close to his childhood haunts at Surly Hall. Today Monkey Island is connected to the mainland with a bridge but in 1916 it could only be reached by boat. It was covered in trees and shrubs and wild mystery, and its only building was a small inn converted from a fishing lodge built by the Duke of Marlborough. Rebecca recalled the place with affection:

> In front were the dark green glassy waters of an unvisited backwater; and beyond them a bright lawn set with many walnut trees and a few great chestnuts, well lit with their candles, and to the left of that a low white house with a green dome rising in its middle and a veranda whose roof of hammered iron had gone verdigris colour with age and the Thames weather . . . I suppose that a thing that one has looked at with somebody one loves acquires for ever after a special significance . . . So they went to Monkey Island, whose utter difference was a healing, and settled down happily in its green silence.[29]

Here they could be alone, revelling in the peace and quietness of the island, the Thames-side scenery and the blessed solitude. The only other guests at the inn were fishermen or retiring people in search of tranquillity; here the two lovers could be at peace, remote from servants, newspapers, the war, and all the bothers of the outside world. For both of them it became a haven they remembered with nostalgia: Wells because it recalled childhood happinesses, and Rebecca because she was fascinated by country inns and loved its pastoral calm. On moonlit nights and at sunset the reflections in the water were a delight to see and on summer days the island with its trees and birds was a rustic paradise.

Mr Britling Sees It Through, published in September 1916, was an immediate success and Wells was gratified to find himself a best-selling novelist after several years in the doldrums. The leisurely opening section, 'Matching's easy at ease', describes the unhurried, cultured life he and his menage had enjoyed at Easton Glebe in the months leading up to August 1914. These chapters, with their vivid picture of a country railway station, a country house weekend, tea on the lawn, a hockey match, and the innocent pleasures enjoyed by the English in a world at peace are a precisely drawn vignette of an England which – in a world of casualty lists, the Somme, mutilation and death – seemed increasingly remote. During these chapters Wells skilfully builds up an atmosphere of suspense, contrasting the peaceful events in Essex with the assassination in Sarajevo and its consequences. The next group of chapters, 'Matching's easy at war', record the day-by-day impact of the war upon Mr Britling and his circle, chronicling his fluctuations of mood from patriotism to anger to mounting disillusionment. These chapters are given verisimilitude by their acute mirroring of Wells's shifting attitudes to the war and his frustration at his inability to make any practical contribution to the war effort. The most memorable part of the novel is a moving description of the death of Mr Britling's son, Hugh, and the account of Mr Britling desperately attempting to come to terms with this void in his world and finding consolation in a renewal of religious faith. (In fact this was an entirely imaginary loss. Wells's sons Gip and Frank were too young to fight in the war – in 1914 they were 13 and 11 respectively – but Hugh's death is so vividly rendered that many readers took it to be a description of an actual event.) The final section, 'The testament of Matching's Easy', is a picture of Mr Britling seeking to find some meaning in the terrible catalogue of death and destruction. It is a haunting portrayal of a sensitive and thoughtful man reluctant to admit that all these deaths have been in vain, that 'the war, even by the standards of adventure and conquest, had long since become a monstrous absurdity'.

The novel is not only of considerable intrinsic interest as a contemporary account of reactions to the war but also as a picture of Wells and Rebecca as they were at this early stage in their friendship. Some impulse made him include a character named Cecily Corner, a vivacious young girl with 'an extraordinarily pretty smile, and there was something in her soft bright brown eye – like the movement of some quick little bird'. The fact that her name is Cissie, that she has a sister called Letty, that her father is a journalist and that she possesses many of Rebecca's mannerisms makes it very clear whom he had in mind. Cissie is a thoughtful, eager young woman who is uncertain in her own mind whether or not she is in love with an American visitor, Mr Direck. She is 'but a year or so out of the stage of melodrama' and 'growing up now to a subtler wisdom'. But in the description of her attitude towards Mr Direck there are ominous hints of deeper sources of conflict:

> When Cissie had dreamt of the lover that fate had in store for her in her old romantic days, he was to be *perfect* always, he and she were always to be absolutely in the right (and, if the story needed it, the world in the wrong). She had never expected to find herself tied by her affections to a man with whom she disagreed, and who went contrary to her standards. . . .[30]

Were this passage to be found in a novel by Rebecca it would still be revealing but in a novel by Wells it becomes doubly so. In describing Cecily Corner, her serious but naïve outlook on life, her romantic conception of love, her colourful imagination and her troubled sense that human relationships are far more complex than she had realised, Wells is presenting aspects of Rebecca's personality from a sympathetic though acutely perceptive standpoint. Although the portrait is not as fully rounded as that of Amanda in *The Research Magnificent* – by comparison Cecily is a minor character and much more lightly sketched – she is still interesting as a reflection of his conception of Rebecca during the first phase of their partnership. In presenting her as a beautiful young woman who is divided and perplexed within herself, haunted by a romantic dream of a perfect love, he is making an acute comment on Rebecca herself and on his image of her as an embodiment of his own longings. He himself, in the guise of Mr Britling, is described as a man who could imagine

> as existing, as waiting for him, he knew not where, a completeness of understanding, a perfection of response, that would reach all the gamut of his feelings and sensations from the most poetical to the most entirely physical . . . In her presence there could be no self-reproaches, no lapses, no limitations, nothing but happiness and the happiest activities . . .[31]

Mr Britling dismisses this vision as an impossible dream but throughout the novel he is depicted as a man in quest of fulfilment, a writer who is profoundly dissatisfied with the routines of his life and searching for a relationship that will give meaning and purpose to his existence.

From a strictly literary point of view neither *The Research Magnificent* nor *Mr Britling Sees It Through* are outstanding novels though both occupy an important place in the canon of his writings and both contain examples of fine writing. If one asks the question 'what effect was his friendship with Rebecca West having upon his novels?' the answer lies not simply in his portrayals of her as Amanda Morris and Cecily Corner but, of almost equal significance, in the evidence of a sharpened perception of familiar sights and sounds. Rebecca possessed the rare ability of looking at the world afresh and obliging all who knew her to observe their surroundings with a keener insight. She quickly communicated this gift to Wells who said of her: 'I never knew anyone else who could so light up and colour and intensify an impression.'[32] One has only to look at the description of the hockey match or the dance at Matching's Easy to see the skilful manner in which ordinary events can seem memorable, as if they have been preserved in amber, a moment preserved in time; or, in the later chapters, the description of Mr Britling walking in the garden after receiving the news of his son's death, or the brilliant concluding paragraphs with their unforgettable word-picture of sunrise over the Essex countryside. Discernible in these passages is a fresh voice, a fresh way of looking at everyday things. It is as if he is perceiving his surroundings with new vision, with keener eyesight. A different pair of eyes is observing the world over his shoulder and saying 'Look'.

V

Rebecca's war novel *The Return of the Soldier* is a beautifully written story on a much smaller canvas. Its central character, Christopher Baldry, returns to England from the battlefields of France severely shell-shocked. He is suffering from loss of memory and cannot remember that he is happily married to Kitty, his selfish and attractive wife; he can only recall his first love, Margaret, the compassionate and motherly girl with whom he had enjoyed an idyllic affair in the distant past. The substance of the story is Kitty's attempts to bring Christopher to his senses, to make him see that his longing for Margaret is an illusion which can only bring unhappiness. Ostensibly neither the story nor the characters bear any relation to Rebecca's situation yet it is apparent that below the threshold of the surface narrative she is brooding intensely on her relationship with Wells and that in writing the novel she is expressing in fictional form some of her deepest innermost feelings about the man she loved.

On the face of it Christopher is totally unlike Wells – he is described as a tall and soldierly figure – though he possesses some of Wells's charcteristics, in particular his tendency to seek refuge in daydreams and flights of the imagination. After describing his childhood love of games about enchanted princesses and make-believe forests (a passage containing unmistakable echoes of Stephen Stratton daydreaming about fairyland in *The Passionate Friends*) the narrator adds:

> And from a thousand intimations, from his occasional clear fixity of gaze on good things as though they were about to dissolve into better, from the passionate anticipation with which he went to new countries or met new people, I was aware that this faith had persisted into his adult life.[33]

Christopher, in common with Wells, is a man who seeks escape from the world of everyday in dreams of lost happiness. He is a man of imagination, haunted by the idea that, inaccessible and beckoning, there are possibilities of delight and completion only just beyond his present reach. But it is in the characters of the two women, Margaret and Kitty, that we find the clearest indication of Rebecca's thoughts. For behind the story of a soft and glowing first love and an unsympathetic marriage can be seen a personification of Wells's first wife Isabel and his second wife Jane: not as they actually were but as Rebecca perceived them to be. Margaret – loving, unselfish, warm, steadfast – corresponds to all that Rebecca had heard about Isabel Mary Wells. Deep inside herself she sensed that Isabel was the only woman he had ever really loved, that Isabel was the 'primary fixation' of his dreams and that no other woman could embody his youthful desires as she had done. In perceiving this Rebecca was making a very shrewd judgement about Wells and one which he would have hotly denied had he known of it. The memory of Isabel continued to haunt him for many years after their separation and it was only after her death in 1931 that he felt able to come to terms with all that she had meant to him. Kitty, on the other hand – spoilt, demanding, hard, exquisitely dressed – corresponds to Rebecca's image of Jane as the shallow and unfeeling wife. It is a portrait that neither Wells nor Jane would have recognised and one that many who knew Jane would have seen as a travesty of the truth, yet it is undoubtedly a representation of facets of her character *as seen from Rebecca's point of view*. From Rebecca's standpoint Jane was unemotional, a non-sexual woman who was standing in the way of her happiness. Contrasting their respective situations it seemed to Rebecca that Jane lived a comfortable life in a gracious country house and had all the kudos of being Mrs H. G. Wells while she, his mistress, had to live a hole-in-a-corner existence on a limited income. Not unnaturally she deeply resented Jane and failed to understand the powerful bonds of affection and respect that held Wells and Jane together. 'She developed much the same resentment at Jane's letters that Little e had felt', Wells recalled later. 'She could not understand our mutual good-will nor our unconcealed liking.'[34]

Whatever the unconscious drives behind the novel, *The Return of the Soldier* remains a tender and haunting portrayal of love and a book which marked a striking debut as a creative artist. Many first novels are marred by being overwritten or obsessed with self-pity but *The Return of the Soldier* suffers from none of these weaknesses. Written in prose of refreshing simplicity (in the sharpest contrast to the overelaborate prolixity of 'Indissoluble matrimony') it conveys in a moving and convincing narrative a portrait of a sensitive man obsessed by the memory of a perfect love. Perhaps its most haunting chapter is the beautiful evocation of the summer idyll between Christopher and margaret on Monkey Island: 'It was strange that both Chris and she spoke of it as though it were not a place, but a magic state which largely explained the actions performed in it.'[35] In telling the story of the two lovers on their magic island Rebecca was looking back with a hint of wistfulness on memories of almost unbearable poignancy. At the same time she was expressing in the form of a myth her profoundest emotions concerning life and love.

During August and early September 1916 Wells was in France making a tour of the battle fronts which he later described in his book *War and the Future*. He was becoming increasingly frustrated by the seeming endlessness of the war and his failure to do anything effective to arrest the carnage. Like Mr Britling he was anxious to be 'part of it', to make some contribution – however modest – to the Allied cause. But he could not for the life of him see what he could do. He hammered away at newspaper articles seeking to clarify the issues at stake and turning his mind more and more to the nature of the peace settlement and the shape of the world after the conflict was ended. In such books as *What is Coming?* and *The Elements of Reconstruction* and in his prolific journalism he sought to clarify in his own mind the causes of the war and the political and social changes that would be needed before a stable peace could be secured.

His absence abroad meant that he was parted from Rebecca for a month and on his return they both determined that their present life was unsatisfactory. Somehow they must find a way to be together more often. 'There is no life for us separately', she wrote to him sadly, 'just a few nice hours over our books and articles and then when we can't write any longer an empty feeling.'[36] What they both wanted was a London base, a place where they could be alone without housekeepers or servants or anyone else. Wells could not stand Wilma Meikle, who was living with Rebecca as a companion, and told Rebecca so in unmistakable terms. His next move was to rent an apartment at 51 Claverton Street, Pimlico, as a London retreat where they could meet whenever they wished. Claverton Street runs down to the Thames near Vauxhall Bridge; he remembered the district in his novel *The Dream* as filled with 'a great wilderness of streets of dingy grey houses in which people lived and let lodgings'. But he also recalled the reflecting lights in the river, the magical effects of light and shadow, and the beautiful patterns on the pavements caused by lamps shining on the leaves of plane trees. For him Pimlico was 'altogether mysterious and romantic', a district of ships, jetties, huge buildings, bridges, and kindly sunshine.[37] For the next two or three years the Pimlico apartment remained their hideaway. It was scantily furnished but at least they could call it their own. Here they could meet in private and find in each other the solace and fulfilment they both needed.

In the early spring of 1917 Rebecca and Anthony moved from Alderton to a pleasant modern house on Marine Parade, Leigh-on-Sea, Essex. She was no longer accompanied by Wilma but by Gladys Stern – later known as G. B. Stern, the popular novelist – who took her place. The house, called Southcliffe, was semi-detached and decorated with ornamental woodwork in the mock-Tudor style. It commanded a superb view of the Thames estuary which she recalled with affection in *The Judge*: 'She had turned and looked down, as she always did when human complexities made her seek reassurance as to the worth of this world, on the shiny mud-flats, blue-veined with the running tides, and green marshes where the redshanks choired.'[38] Leigh-on-Sea was a town of cobbled roads and old world cottages, totally different from her previous abodes in London or Edinburgh. It was a landscape of marshes, boats, quays and shingle, with wonderful sunsets and spectacular effects of light on water and sand. Rebecca and Anthony took to the place at once and both remembered their stay there as a happy interlude.

Anthony, now aged 2-and-a-half, was still unaware of his true parentage. He had been brought up to call his mother Auntie Panther; to the outside world she was 'Miss West' and Anthony was her nephew. Wells deplored this subterfuge but Rebecca insisted on it. 'Nobody was more conscious than I that this was not a very good arrangement', she wrote many years later, 'but it was the best I could do.'[39] Wells felt that the real reason for her pretence that she was not Anthony's mother was the implacable disapproval of her family, particularly of her mother Isabella Fairfield. Isabella's attitude was that Wells was a wicked seducer, that Rebecca should never have become involved with him and that she should now totally renounce him. She was never allowed to forget that this was her mother's attitude; she was forcibly reminded of it in letters and confrontations at every opportunity. In spite of this disapproval and the stigma of illegitimacy all the available evidence suggests that Anthony was dearly loved by both his parents. He was a delightful child, intelligent, sensitive and affectionate. Rebecca doted on him, recalling later that his babyhood 'was the playful disguise in which he came into the world in order that they might get on easy terms with one another and be perfect companions'.[40] She loved his precocious ways and amusing sayings, his endearing habit of following her about and his joy in discovering the world around him. When she described the love of Marion Yaverland for her son Richard in *The Judge* she poured into the account all her feelings towards her own infant. Children like him, she wrote, 'had been conceived more intensely than other children, of love so passionate that it had drawn together men and women separated by social prohibitions'. She felt that in bringing Anthony into the world she had assumed a great responsibility and that she must surround him with warmth and love. She could not give him a normal upbringing but she would do her utmost to see that he was given a promising start in life.

During these years Wells was passing through a phase of religious belief which seems to have been engendered by the emotional and psychological stress of the war. The closing pages of *Mr Britling* are saturated with references to God – the central character, desperately seeking reassurance at a time of profound distress, finds consolation in the idea of God as the captain of mankind. *Mr Britling* was quickly followed by a theological work, *God the Invisible King*, and a novel, *The Soul of a Bishop*, in which he expanded his religious ideas and sought to justify his belief in a personal and finite God. The phase was only temporary and he later bitterly regretted that he had ever fallen into it; he realised that it represented an intellectual cul-de-sac and had misled many of his readers. The God he professed in these works was simply the Mind of the Race, the undying body of thought examplified by books, ideas and science. He wrote later:

> it was plain to me that this God the Invisible King of his was not so much God, in the sense in which people understand that word, as Prometheus; it was a titanic and not a divine being . . . God the Invisible King was merely the Humanity of Comte with a crown on.[42]

This religious phase can be seen as a symptom of the deep malaise which affected him in the middle years of the war as he took up and abandoned project after project in his quest for a purpose in life. Proportional representation, republicanism, free trade, the idea of a League of Nations – all came under the microscope as he cast about for a leading idea to which he could devote his energy and enthusiasm. In a series of articles published in 1917 and later collected in book form under the title *In the Fourth Year: Anticipations of a world peace* he outlined his proposals for a League of Free Nations which would enforce peace in the world after the war. It is clear that the League he envisaged would not be a mere assembly of sovereign states but a world authority possessing a monopoly of armed force:

> The League of Free Nations must, in fact, if it is to be a working reality, have power to define and limit the military and naval and aerial equipment of every country in the world . . . Disarmament is a necessary factor of any League of Free Nations, and you cannot have disarmament unless you are prepared to see the powers of the council of the League extend thus far. The very existence of the League presupposes that it and it alone is to have and to exercise military force.

In these far-seeing articles he was advocating a generous not a punitive peace, to be followed by a lasting settlement involving world control of the armaments industry and the creation of a world community. He recognised that the invention of the aeroplane meant that national sovereignty was now obsolete, and that to prevent a recurrence of war there was no alternative but the establishment of a world order in which no one nation would be predominant and where history would be taught not on a national or partisan basis but as the history of mankind. To Wells the war had come as an immense shock. It had meant the destruction of the safe, familiar, stable world he had known and accepted as the background of his life since 1866 and its replacement by a Europe of warring nations. It had meant the dissolution of the Victorian age and its replacement by a world in which death, violence and hatred were commonplace. Frustrated, tired and disillusioned, he began work on a long, ambitious novel which occupied him for many months during 1917 and 1918, *Joan and Peter*. 'Many oversensitive people were suffering', he wrote, 'from a sense of cruelty, wickedness and disaster that staggered their minds. They had lived securely in a secure world; they could not readjust.'[43]

As the war dragged on both he and Rebecca were conscious of a growing restlessness in which the tensions inherent in their partnership came more and more to the surface. The truth of the matter was that both of them were being compelled to lead a double life. For her part she was on the one hand Rebecca West the writer and critic, a young woman of letters who had made a promising debut with her critical study of Henry James and was now anxious to make her reputation as a novelist. She was writing regular book reviews in the *Daily News* and other journals, appraising new fiction by Violet Hunt, D. H. Lawrence and Arnold Bennett and books on social and political questions by Havelock Ellis, Ellen Key and others. These reviews were written with all the verve and outspokenness of the *Freewoman* pieces but her enthusiasm for this kind of work was waning. In her heart of hearts she knew that she wished to write novels and she yearned for the peace and solitude that would enable her to create a sustained work of art. Both *Henry James* and *The Return of the Soldier* had to be written in circumstances which were less than ideal. For she was on the other hand the mother of a small boy and the mistress of a famous writer with whom she was obliged by necessity to conduct a clandestine relationship. What she wanted above all was security and peace. But in the nature of things these objectives were unattainable in the England of 1917. Wartime conditions meant that many foods were scarce, travel by public transport was slow and crowded, it was increasingly difficult to find reliable staff who could be trusted to be discreet. Above all she had to contend with the near hysterical opposition of her mother. Her restlessness meant that she was often out of sorts and suffered from a wide variety of minor ailments: illnesses with which Wells had little patience. He wanted a loving and welcoming partner not a tired young woman obsessed with worries and petty complaints.

Wells, for his part, was also leading a dual life. At Easton Glebe he was a husband and father married to a woman he had loved for twenty-five years. 'I love you very warmly', he told Jane in one of his letters to her, 'you are in so many things, bone of my bone, and flesh of my flesh and my making. I must keep you.'[44] He was also H. G. Wells the renowned novelist and prophet whose writings commanded a world audience and whose pronouncements on issues of war and peace were listened to with respect wherever they appeared. At Leigh-on-Sea and Claverton Street he abandoned these roles and became a lover eager for distraction and stimulus. He needed Rebecca for her beauty, her youth, her vitality and invigoration. She occupied an irreplaceable role in his life and he knew that without her an essential element to his happiness would be missing. Without her there would be a void no one else could fill. To Jane he looked for dependability, order, harmony, companionship: all the things he valued in the making of an environment conducive to creative work. To Rebecca he looked for his emotional needs, for that bodily and spiritual completion without which he would be unfulfilled. The double life he was compelled to lead resembled one of the *doppelgänger* situations he described so vividly in his stories. In such tales as 'The story of the late Mr Elvesham', 'The crystal egg' and 'The door in the wall' he had depicted characters who led a dual existence, individuals whose inward lives for one reason or another were utterly different from their outward lives. Since the end of 1913 his own life had followed this pattern. His world was divided into two halves; much of his time and energy was spent in sustaining the two parts in equilibrium and in the metamorphosis from one to another. His dilemma was that both were essential to his wellbeing. He could no more do without Rebecca than he could do without Jane.

In all this it is easy to lose sight of the fact that beneath all the tensions and frustrations inseparable from their relationship there was much happiness for them both. Looking back on their friendship towards the end of his life he recalled that during their happiest moments hers was 'the warmest, liveliest and most irreplaceable of fellowships'.[45] Both had a rich sense of fun which in his case took the form of drawing 'picshuas' – droll illustrations of people and incidents – and the invention of amusing nicknames for their friends and acquaintances. Thus, Robertson Nicholl became Dr Tomlinson Keyhole, Marie Belloc-Lowndes became The Tea Cosy, Anthony's nurse became Googoo, and so on. For her part Rebecca loved indulging in fantasies in which she kept an imaginary country inn and Wells drove a gig, or they were two eccentric animals called 'the Pussteads'. They took a genuine delight in one another, revelling in each other's fantasies and inventing humorous names for people and places. They went for long walks along the sea walls and the coast around Leigh-on-Sea, finding contentment in walking, laughter and observing the interesting world around them. Their happiness was heightened by the fact that both of them liked Leigh and found the house and the town itself congenial. Leigh, with its fishing boats, winkle sellers and tarred huts had a quaint charm reminiscent of the Peggotty's home in *David Copperfield* and reminded Wells of Sandgate as he had known it at the beginning of the century. For all his reputation as a prophet and a man of the future he had a deep affection for the simple, unspoilt life of the rural past: for country lanes, wild flowers, thatched cottages and wayside inns. Leigh in the spring and early summer of 1917 was as yet untouched by the twentieth century. It was a microcosm of an English coastal town, a place where fishermen and boat builders went about their business as their forefathers had done, a million miles away from the mud and blood of France. Here for a while they were extremely happy. Here they could take stock of their situation, looking back on three years and more of warm companionship in which each had given much to the other and had gained friendship of an intensity rare in human experience. Then the German bombing raids began.

Chapter 5

Discords

Women *make* life for me. Whatever they touch or see or desire becomes worthwhile and otherwise it is not worthwhile. Whatever is lovely in my world, whatever is delightful, has been so conveyed to me by some woman. Without the vision they give me, I should be a hard dry industry in the world, a worker ant, a soulless rage, making much, valuing nothing.

H. G. Wells, The Secret Places of the Heart

He looked peevishly past all these offers of satisfaction to a future that was to be reformed half for its own sake and half as an insult to the hated present. That was the fault of his greatness; it was because he had to roll in such fierce grips with his times in his effort to dominate them that he loathed them. It was the fault of his greatness too that he minded it all so much.

Rebecca West, Sunflower

I

As spring turned to summer the German Gotha bombers intensified their raids on London. The planes followed the Thames estuary and Leigh became a frequent target, Rebecca and Anthony having several narrow escapes from daytime raids. In the late summer night raids began. Rebecca realised that Leigh was no longer safe and sent Anthony away to a school in London. Since London too was unsafe she worried about him more than ever. The combination of anxiety, sleeplessness and her own poor health led to her first major quarrel with Wells (September 1917) culminating in a long letter from him in which he sought to define their differences. The air raids terrified her and during a bombing attack of particular ferocity she had been unable to conceal her fear. He wrote to her on 13 September:

My instinct is to alter or avoid disagreeable things if that can be done and to sit tight and jeer if it can't. You behaved like a different sort of animal altogether . . . I am constantly dismissing evil realisations from my mind. The world and everything may be damned but I *won't believe it*. The whole

world may be against me, *the world is wrong*. That's my temperament, my
habit of mind. You are – otherwise. You go out to get the fullest
impression of any old black thing. Every disagreeable impression is
welcome to your mind, it grows there. All the past four years which
might have been a love-adventure in our memories, your peculiar genius
has made into an utterly disagreeable story – which has become the basis
for an entire hopelessness about anything yet to come . . . It is your
nature to darken your world and blacken every memory. So long as I love
you you will darken mine.

This letter – harsh, irritable and wounding – clearly marks a turning
point in their relationship and brought to a head a number of issues
that had been simmering between them for some time. In the first place
was the specific bone of contention which Wells highlighted: the fact
that their attitudes to evil differed fundamentally. In common with his
father, Joseph Wells, 'a large part of his waking energy was spent in
evading disagreeable realisations'.[1] It was his fundamental habit of
mind to dismiss evil from his thoughts. (This statement has to be
qualified by the acknowledgement that he was not always successful in
doing so. In such works as *The Island of Doctor Moreau*, 'The wild asses of
the devil', *Mr Blettsworthy on Rampole Island* and *The Croquet Player* his sense
of the deep fountains of evil in the human make-up overwhelmed him
with irresistible force.) Rebecca's conception of the human dilemma, on
the other hand, was basically Manichean: that our lives are dominated
by the powers of light and darkness and that there is no escaping one's
destiny. She had imbibed from her parents a view of life and fate that
was almost Calvinistic in its intensity, an awareness of destiny that
pervades all her writings from her early short stories to her final works
on treason and judgment.

Behind this dichotomy in their respective attitudes to good and evil
lay other differences of equal significance. There was the 26-year age
gap: in 1917 Wells was 51, an established novelist who was now
renowned throughout the world as a prophet and sage; Rebecca by
contrast was 25, a young woman at the dawn of her literary career.
Inevitably their interests and attitudes differed. She resented the fact
that whilst her interests and aptitudes were turning her more and more
towards the art of fiction, Wells, under the stimulus of the war, seemed
to be losing interest in writing novels and becoming obsessed with
education and politics. In both *The Research Magnificent* and *Mr Britling Sees
It Through* there was evidence of an increasing tendency to hector the
reader in long passages of commentary, a tendency repeated in much of
his wartime journalism. She had read and admired these novels but
regretted the loss of the 'Uncle Wells' who had written so magically in
Tono-Bungay and *The History of Mr Polly* and felt his preoccupation with
history and sociology was a misuse of his creative powers. The age

difference also meant that their social and emotional needs were difficult to reconcile. Rebecca needed and enjoyed the company of young men and women of her own generation but Wells seemed to resent this. To make matters worse he disliked most of her friends and took her to task when she wanted to spend time with them. He seemed, in fact, to want the best of both worlds: to have a comfortable home where he could write and enjoy the company of his wife and sons, and at the same time to be able to visit and monopolise her whenever he wished or when the demands of his work would permit. Above all she felt emotionally insecure. Whereas Jane was the anchor, the kingpin of his life who could be depended on to stick to him through thick and thin, she had no such security. Though she was bound to Wells with ties of love, affection and companionship she knew that these ties could be severed at any time; he could simply walk out of her life, leaving her with Anthony to bring up on her own. She came increasingly to resent Jane's central role in his life and could not understand why, if he loved her as much as he professed to do, he did not divorce Jane and marry her. This issue gnawed in Rebecca's mind until it became her *idée fixe*. Linked with it was her resentment at her own secondary position by comparison with Jane's. She felt that by now she should have been building up a promising position in the London literary scene instead of having to live a clandestine existence in places like Hunstanton, Quinbury and Leigh-on-Sea. She wanted her position *regularised* – if Wells would not marry her then let him at least provide her with financial security so that Anthony's future was assured.

Wells's angry letter brought all these matters to the forefront of her mind and she was stung into an equally hard-hitting reply. This in turn led to a further exchange of letters in which each did their best to heal their differences. By late September he pronounced the quarrel at an end: 'Never in the whole world has there been anyone so sweet, so adorable, so various, so wonderful, so consistently dear and beautiful as my Panther.' But in the course of the exchange each had been provoked into making harsh statements which could not be retracted. Each had tried to define what they wanted from the relationship and what they felt was wrong with the situation as it stood. For all their earnest desire to restore the relationship to the beauty and harmony they had known in the beginning it was too late to put the clock back. Things could never be quite the same again.

II

Early in 1918 Wells was invited by Lord Northcliffe, director of propaganda in enemy countries, to join the Enemy Propaganda Committee based at Crewe House, London. He accepted the invitation and early in May became director of propaganda policy against Germany. He was still determined that, despite all the calls for Germany to be punished, there should be a generous peace settlement followed by the establishment of a League of Nations to enforce and monitor world peace. Invited by the Committee to draft a *Memorandum on Propaganda Policy* to define the war aims of the Allies he set to work to frame a document which would embody his vision of world order. The *Memorandum* insisted that 'the real war aim of the Allies is not only to beat the enemy, but to establish a world peace that shall preclude the resumption of war.' It postulated a League of Nations (including a Germany purged of her military ambitions), a Congress with the powers of a federal world authority and a process of disarmament and reconstruction. Wells asserted that an essential element within any declaration of war aims must be a definition of what the Allies were fighting for and an outline of the kind of Europe envisaged after the peace settlement. There must be no annexations 'or any military interference with any peoples whatever' without a mandate from the League. The memorandum foresaw the ultimate creation of international forces under the control of the League to maintain order in unsettled regions, and warned that the alternative to the establishment of a world authority would be a steady descent towards fragmentation 'such as the world has not seen since the fall of the Roman Empire'. It was a far-seeing and eloquent document, concluding with the recognition of an absolute necessity for a peace settlement that would permit 'a world-wide concentration upon reconstruction, in good faith and without any complications of enmity and hostility'.[2]

The memorandum was accepted by Northcliffe and by the Enemy Propaganda Committee and for a time Wells played an active part in urging the need for a clear statement of war aims and for a League of Nations to be set up as an integral part of the post-war settlement. In July 1918 he became one of the founder members of the League of Free Nations Association, a pressure group advocating the creation of a world organisation, and kept in close touch with kindred bodies in other European countries. It soon became apparent, however, that Wells had been misled by Northcliffe and that the latter had no intention of toning down the virulent anti-German campaign being conducted in his newspapers. What so disheartened Wells was not only Northcliffe's duplicity but the disingenuousness of the Government which claimed to agree with the *Memorandum* but in reality had no intention of honouring the document's implicit promises to Germany. It seemed to him to be hypocritical to offer, on the other hand, a generous peace with no secret treaties or annexations, the creation of a League including Germany, and a programme of disarmament in which all would take part, when simultaneously politicians were scheming to impose a punitive settlement in which Germany would be made to pay for the war. He wrote bitterly that his *Memorandum* had been used as the basis for a campaign of promises by which Germany was 'bilked into an armistice that placed her, without better security than English good faith, at the feet of her enemies'.[3] In mid-July he resigned as director of propaganda policy but continued his advocacy of a League of Nations. His experience as a member of the Enemy Propaganda Committee, working closely with politicians and professional soldiers, affected him almost as profoundly as the Fabian affray had done. It convinced him that there could be no enduring peace until there was a firm basis of historical realities and that there was an imperative need for the teaching of history as a world process, the story of the human adventure, instead of the history of individual states. He turned his mind more and more to the idea of writing a history of the world. He felt that as a writer and popular educator he could make a contribution of far greater effectiveness than as a member of a committee.

Despite his preoccupation with political and historical questions he was not neglecting the writing of fiction and September 1918 saw the publication of his new novel *Joan and Peter*. This is a long, rambling, ambitious novel in which he sought 'to reflect upon the types of educated youngster that the period round and about the war years was giving the British world'.[4] It is the story of two orphan children, Joan Debenham and Peter Stubland, from birth to maturity, and gives a detailed picture of their childhood, schooling and adolescence under the tutelage of two guardians competing for their attention, Lady Charlotte Sydenham and her nephew Oswald. Joan and Peter are brought up as if they are brother and sister, though in fact they are unrelated. As the novel proceeds their love for one another deepens and they finally marry. The story is set against a richly depicted background of the closing years of the Victorian age, the Edwardian years, the capsize of Europe into war and the changing attitudes of the English intelligentsia as the war moves towards its end. As a picture of two young people growing up in this era it is an impressive achievement and Wells set great store by it. He wrote later that 'it remains to this day one of the least known and, considering its aims and scope, the least regarded' of his books.[5] He intended it to be a novel on the grand scale and to complement *Mr Britling Sees It Through* 'as a study of the English spirit at war and in the face of the problems of reconstruction arising out of the war'. It is a vivid panorama of England during the years 1893–1918 in which all his powers as a novelist are brought to play to create a moving and convincing narrative. It has great strengths and great weaknesses but within its pages can be discerned a major writer striving to get a grip on his world and to see his personal and social situation in perspective.

The most memorable feature of the novel is the portrayal of the two central characters, Joan and Peter. In the whole gallery of Wells's characters – and some of them are as living and vital as those created by Dickens – it would be hard to find two figures so carefully and convincingly drawn. The description of their childhood, their touching innocence, their relationship with one another and with their guardians, their gradual realisation of their feelings towards each other and slow emergence from adolescence to adulthood is beautifully crafted and amply justifies Wells's estimation of the novel. Joan, with her steadfastness, her high spirits, her delight in fantasy and her infectious ability to transform gloom into happiness is one of his most delightful heroines and clearly owes much to Rebecca as he knew her in the closing years of the war. 'Joan', he wrote, 'the author fell in love with himself as she grew; and she is still his favourite and, he thinks, in many ways his best done heroine.'[6] In her knack of seeing the world with fresh eyes, her moods of exaltation and moments of leaping vivacity she embodies many of Rebecca's characteristics:

> In these new phases of expansion she had the most perfect conviction that life, and particularly her life, was wonderful and beautiful and destined to be more and more so. She began to experience a strange new happiness in mere existence, a happiness that came with an effect of revelation. It is hard to convey the peculiar delight that invaded her during these phases. It was almost as if the earth had just been created for her and given to her as a present. There were moments when the world was a crystal globe of loveliness about her, moments of ecstatic realization of a universal beauty. The slightest things would suffice to release this sunshine in her soul. She would discover the intensest delight in little, hitherto disregarded details, in the colour of a leaf held up to the light, or the rhythms of ripples on a pond, or the touch of a bird's feather. There were moments when she wanted to kiss the sunset, and times when she would clamber over the end wall of the garden at Pelham Ford in order to lie hidden and still, with every sense awake, in the big clump of bracken in the corner by the wood beyond.[7]

Joan is one of the most living of his heroines partly because the reader has a tangible sense of her as a physical presence. Consider, for example, the moment when she and Oswald are engaged in conversation in his study:

> He seemed preoccupied as if he did not feel how close she was about him, how close her beauty came to him. She sat now on the arm of his chair behind him, with her face over his shoulder. Her body touched his shoulders, by imperceptible degrees she brought her cheek against his crisp hair, where it pressed no heavier than a shadow. She had no suspicion how vividly he was aware of her nearness.[8]

In some of his earlier novels the reader is aware of a lack of solidity about the female characters, as if they are composed largely of literary materials. But Joan Debenham is flesh and blood. She lives and breathes, irradiating the book with her presence so that the reader yearns to meet her in real life. She brings the book to life in the same way that Amanda transforms *The Research Magnificent* from a dry treatise to a pulsating reality.

Joan and Peter is an extremely long novel – it contains 225,000 words, about three times the length of an average work of fiction – and he clearly intended it to be a comprehensive picture of England in a phase of transition. Reading it today one is struck by its discursiveness, by the narrator's irritating tendency to comment on everything and everybody. What could have been a great novel, worthy to stand comparison with *Tono-Bungay* and *The New Machiavelli*, is marred by this tendency to *talk at* the reader, to pontificate on the war, on education, on the Northern Ireland problem, on Africa, on women's rights, and on every subject under the sun. The real nobility of Wells's overall design is obscured by these digressions which many readers would regard as a distraction from the main thread of the story. At one point Wells brings himself up with a start, as if he too has suddenly realised he is wandering from his main purpose:

> But it is high time Joan and Peter came back into this narrative. For this is their story, it bears their names on its covers and on its back and on its title-page and at the head of each left-hand page.[9]

This habit of lecturing the reader had been evident in his fiction from *Marriage* onwards and as early as 1905 Arnold Bennett had warned him about it:

> And the mischief is that, though you will undoubtedly do a vast amount of good in the world, you will get worse and worse, more and more specialised, more and more scornful. All this is not an explanation of you; but an explanation of me. It 'connotes' the difference between our minds.[10]

Joan and Peter, in fact, can be taken as a case study illustrating Wells's powers and defects as a novelist, for it exemplifies many of the points Bennett is raising in his letter and which Rebecca had drawn his attention to on many occasions. She felt that all of his 'Prig' novels plus those written during the war years had been spoilt by excessive philosophising and that he was in danger of dissipating his genuine gifts as a creative artist in the writing of journalism of only contemporary relevance. Much of *Joan and Peter* has *dated*, simply because he could not resist the temptation to comment on the contemporary political scene. Yet there is so much in the book that is of permanent value as to amply repay the reading of it. The sensitive account of Joan and Peter's early years (which clearly owes much to Anthony's infancy), the hilarious description of their christening at the instigation of Lady Charlotte, their developing awareness of the world around them, their widening social and emotional horizons, the earnest discussions of adolescence: all are described with a skilfulness he had rarely excelled. Much of the dialogue has the ring of truth about it, as if he is recording his impressions of conversations actually heard. Above all his characters – including the minor ones – are solid, believable people, in the sharpest contrast to the ciphers of some of his earlier fiction.

When *Joan and Peter* was being written in the dark months of 1917–18 his feelings towards Rebecca were undergoing violent changes of mood in which his attitude veered from passionate declarations of love to angry statements of indifference. One of the most interesting aspects of the novel is the way in which Peter's attitudes towards Joan change as the story proceeds, till at last he can no longer conceal from himself the fact that he loves her. When he finally takes her in his arms 'the magic barrier' which has hitherto kept them apart is destroyed. 'there are two sorts of love between men and women, and only two', says Peter: 'love like the love of big carnivores who know their mates and stick to them, or love like some man who follows a woman home because he's never seen anything like her before. I've done with that sort of love for ever.'[11] Peter has sampled promiscuous love in the shape of Hetty Reinhart, a loose-living girl with whom he has a brief affair, but abandons her when he recognises Joan's true worth. In relating the story of Peter, a thoughtful young man who comes to discern the difference between false and true love – 'Making love happens, but love endures' – Wells was expressing in fictional form some of his deepest intuitions concerning himself and Rebecca. Their quarrel had led him to think afresh about their partnership and to assess her role in his life. He knew that he could not do without her, that a world without her as his companion and lover would be unthinkable. The story of two young people who imagine they are brother and sister but realise they are drawn together by a mysterious affinity and finally acknowledge that theirs is a love 'like the love of big carnivores who know their mates and stick to them' can be read as a metaphor for Wells's conception of his love for Rebecca. The fact that the novel is dedicated 'To P & J' (Panther and Jaguar) strongly reinforces this interpretation. In this sense the novel is a kind of stocktaking: a summation of his state of mind in the closing months of the war. Within its pages he reviews his world. The novel's sub-title, 'The story of an education', suggests that he intended to place his main emphasis on an account of Joan and Peter's schooling, but the most enduring pages in the book are those describing their slow awakening to the fact of their love and their realisation that henceforward their lives must be spent in partnership. As the war dragged on Wells was feeling tired and irritable. He was at odds with the world; he was overworking and casting about for a project to which he could devote his energies. Rebecca was indispensable to him as a source of renewal, of laughter, wit and fantasy.

III

During 1918 and 1919 their life together continued on much the same pattern. They met regularly in Leigh and London and went on motoring excursions together, happy in exploring the Essex countryside or making longer journeys to the West of England. During these years Rebecca was re-establishing her contacts with literary friends including Bernard Shaw and Apsley Cherry-Garrard, the author of *The Worst Journey in the World*. She was extremely busy with journalism, writing book reviews for the London dailies and the *New Statesman* and drama criticism for *Outlook*. She began to mix more in society, meeting such figures as Max Beaverbrook and Joseph Kenworthy, a popular sportsman. Anthony was now 5 and already at boarding school, first at Minster (Kent) and later at Wokingham.

Beaverbrook, whom she first met in 1918, was thirteen years older than Rebecca and had recently been appointed Minister of Information in the Coalition Government of David Lloyd George. He was a small, stocky, handsome man with a broad forehead, penetrating eyes, and an alert, intelligent expression. He had a keen sense of humour, driving energy, and shrewd ability to assess other people's worth. He was born William Maxwell Aitken, the son of a Scottish clergyman who had emigrated to Canada. Max made his fortune in Canada as a financier and by the time he came to England in 1910 was already a millionaire. He entered Parliament as Conservative member for Ashton-under-Lyne and became a friend of Andrew Bonar Law, the leader of the Conservative party. He was given a knighthood in 1911 and in 1915 acquired control of the *Daily Express*. In the following year he was given a peerage and became Lord Beaverbrook, living in a country mansion and enjoying an expansive lifestyle. At first sight it seems difficult to understand how Rebecca, with her fiercely radical and independent views, could have been so attracted towards a. man whose political views were so alien to her own. What fascinated her about Beaverbrook was his manliness, his air of dynamism and thrusting achievement.

Here was a man of 39 who was already a figure in national affairs, a man who enjoyed power and knew how to use it. Although he was a Cabinet minister his heart was not really in politics; his real interests lay in business and in the cut and thrust of running a thriving organisation. His ambition was to be a newspaper magnate on a grand scale and to make his mark in British affairs as a force to be reckoned with. He possessed qualities which Rebecca immediately responded to: decisiveness, energy, virility, leadership. At the same time he had the look of a man who is seeking something in life that he has not yet found. When she came to portray aspects of his character in the figure of Richard Yaverland in her novel *The Judge* she defined his expression in these terms:

> his face was marked with an expression that it vexed her she could not put a name to, for if at her age she could not read human nature like a book she never would. It was not hunger, for it was serene, and it was not greed, for it was austere, and yet it certainly signified that he habitually made upon life some urgent demand that was not wholly intellectual and that had not been wholly satisfied.[12]

Rebecca found Beaverbrook intriguing, not least because he was a type largely outside her previous worldly experience. She had met writers, dramatists, actors and feminists, but the man of action who could wield executive power was a new thing in her experience. Moreover, Beaverbrook possessed great charm and charisma; women found him attractive and sought his company. She was by no means alone in finding him appealing. After their first meeting she continued to look out for further opportunites of deepening their acquaintance.

Meanwhile Wells was busy with another novel, *The Undying Fire*, and by the autumn of 1918 had commenced work on his most ambitious project to date, *The Outline of History*, a survey of human history from the earliest dawn of civilisation to the world war. *The Undying Fire* is the work of a tired, embittered man, and reflects Wells's mood of uncertainty in the immediate aftermath of the war. It is a modern reworking of the Book of Job. Its central character, Job Huss, is a schoolmaster about to have an operation for the removal of a morbid growth; the substance of the book is the conversations between Job and his associates on the eve of the operation in which they discuss the spirit of man and whether *Homo sapiens* is fundamentally good or evil. Essentially the book is a continuation of the debate begun in *Boon*: that between optimism and pessimism. The fluctuation of Job's moods between an invincible faith in human goodness and a conviction of man's bestiality mirrors Wells's ambivalence as his own attitudes changed. As the novel draws towards its close Job, tired and ill, veers towards pessimism: 'I talk . . . And then a desolating sense of reality blows like a destroying gust through my mind, and my little lamp of hope goes out.' The novel concludes with a description of Job's dream under the anaesthetic, a dream in which God speaks to him and urges him not to lose faith in the human spirit or to be ungrateful for so much in life that gives happiness. Despite much eloquent dialogue the tone of the book as a whole is almost unrelievedly grim. There is a jaundiced version of Southcliffe, Leigh-on-Sea, as 'Sea View, Sundering-on-Sea' which makes it sound as unattractive as possible, and a veiled reference to his emotional situation at this time in the picture of Job's wife as a harassed woman towards whom Job feels guilty: 'He was helpless and perplexed; he had not meant to quarrel. He had hurt this poor thing who had been his love and companion; he had bullied her. His clogged brain could think of nothing to set matters right.'[13] Clearly *The Undying Fire* is the reflection of a phase. As he worked with mounting enthusiasm on *The Outline of History* and his vision of human destiny broadened, his natural ebullience came to the fore. The pessimism of *Boon* and *The Undying Fire* receded as he came to see himself more and more in the role of educationalist, as a man who could make a significant contribution to international understanding and hence to world peace.

The writing of *The Outline of History* occupied him from the autumn of 1918 until November 1919 when it began to be published in fortnightly parts. The intervening twelve months were a period of unremitting toil as he worked away on draft after draft, collating, revising, reading and checking until he was satisfied with each chapter as the book progressed. Throughout this work Jane Wells acted as his secretary and assistant, looking up references, checking proofs, and helping in the hundred and one tasks involved in such a mammoth undertaking. What he was aiming at, as the sub-title of the *Outline* suggested, was 'A plain history of life and mankind': a clear, readable summary of human history written not for academics or professional historians but for the ordinary reader. He envisaged it as being used in schools and colleges as a source of reference and hoped it would serve a useful purpose as a general overview of history before embarking on a study of a particular period or region. The result exceeded all his expectations though not in the way he had imagined. The book was virtually ignored by the educational world but widely read by the general public. The serial instalments sold more than 100,000 copies of each part and brought his name before an even wider audience. When it appeared as a book in 1920 it was a sell-out and was immediately translated into many foreign languages. 'One went to bed educational reformer', he commented, 'and woke up to find oneself best-seller.'[14] The success of the *Outline* greatly encouraged him in his belief that he had a role to fill as a popular educator and he devoted much time in the ensuing years to the preparation of revised and updated versions. He had tapped a huge demand for popular summaries of knowledge and felt that his background, his scientific training and knack of writing in a clear, readable style equipped him for the task. But Rebecca was not so sure. She resented the amount of time and energy he spent on writing nonfiction – in her view a waste of his talents – and the fact that working on the *Outline* had brought him even closer to Jane and Easton Glebe. She sensed that from now on she would have to come to terms with the realisation that he was not only a novelist and journalist but a world figure and educationalist whose name was a household word.

Towards the end of 1919 Rebecca decided to take her destiny in her own hands and move to London. She had had enough of obscure seaside resorts and provincial lodging-houses and wanted to be back in the mainstream of the social and literary world. She moved into a fine modern flat at 36 Queen's Gate Terrace, South Kensington, an address of impeccable respectability where all the conveniences of twentieth-century living were at her elbow. Wells, who contributed towards her expenses, could easily visit her from his flat in St James's Court or whisk her off elsewhere when the mood took him. The stigma associated with their relationship in the stuffy world of pre-war London was now subsiding. They began to travel about together with increasing frequency, dining out, going to theatres, or setting off on car excursions to Dorset, Cornwall, or Virginia Water. When Anthony came to write his autobiographical novel *Heritage* many years later he remembered South Kensington as a district that was 'regularly laid out to express the importance and respectability of its residents, people who knew how to live with dignity'.[15] Rebecca's decision to move to London and to take up her abode in such a fashionable quarter marked a new stage in her partnership, one in which she intended to exercise a greater share of responsibility for her own affairs. Under pressure from her mother she continued to badger Wells either to marry her or let her go her own way, but he regarded both these alternatives as unthinkable. He wished matters to remain as they were. As he put it: 'I ought to have liberated her; I realise I got much the best of our relationship; but there was no one to take her place with me, and she was fond of me as well as resentful and there was no one ready to take my place with her.'[16] So matters remained. But she was now more determined than ever to make a name for herself as a novelist. Simmering at the back of her mind was an idea for a novel, *The Judge*, a work in which she could express her thoughts and feelings about motherhood, life and love and pour out all her pent-up emotions concerning the past and the present. This finally appeared in 1922 after three years of travail.

In the spring of 1920 Rebecca sustained a painful accident which necessitated a convalescence of six months. She fell into an open cistern while she and Wells were staying with friends in Cornwall and badly injured her hand; the wound turned septic and the infection eventually spread to her face. During her convalescence in a nursing home, ill and feverish, she suffered from sleeplessness for long periods and had ample opportunity to think over her life and her relationship with Wells. When sleep overcame her she had terrifying Poesque nightmares about death and decay. Wells's comment in his autobiography that 'she had a splendid *disturbed* brain'[17] is derived partly from this propensity to nightmares and to the ease with which she passed from the world of reality to a subliminal world of dreams and fantasies. Through much of her life she believed she had the gift of second sight and that in her dreams she sometimes glimpsed the realms of the supernatural. One of Wells's least attractive characteristics was his impatience with illness. When he was ill himself he was tetchy and bored, but when Rebecca was ill his attitude was that it was somehow her own fault. Instead of sympathising with her during her long convalescence he bombarded her with letters urging her to get well soon and making excuses why he could not come to Cornwall to see her. He was busy with plans for a visit to Czechoslovakia and Russia and did not seem to grasp the fact that she was going through a serious mental and physical trauma. She found his lack of concern for her at this crucial phase of her life hurtful and inconsiderate, and was more determined than ever to get on with writing *The Judge* as a means of working her frustrations out of her system.

During September and October 1920 he was visiting Russia, accompanied by his eldest son, and gathering material for his book *Russia in the Shadows*. He visited Petersburg and Moscow and met Maxim Gorky and the Bolshevik leaders Lenin and Zinoviev. He was deeply impressed by Lenin and admired his obvious determination to rebuild the Soviet Union from the ruins of war and civil war and transform it into a modern industrialised state. While in Russia he had an amorous encounter with Gorky's secretary, Moura Benckendorff, a vivacious girl whom he had first met on his previous visit to Moscow in 1914. On his return to England he admitted to Rebecca that he had been unfaithful to her, an admission which Rebecca found unforgivable. His infidelity, occurring at the very time when she was in low spirits through tiredness and anxiety, was deeply wounding. When she expressed her feelings in no uncertain terms he wrote begging forgiveness: 'I am horribly afraid now of losing you. It will be a disaster for both of us. It will cut the heart out of my life. I don't think it will leave much in yours.'[18] Despite every provocation to leave him she could not bring herself to take the decisive step; to do so would have caused a wrench she could not contemplate. Besides her genuine love for him she liked him as a friend and companion and took real delight in his company. She was well aware that when he was in good health and spirits he could be the most agreeable partner in the world and the most engaging of allies.

The problem was that by the end of 1920 both of them were out of sorts and depressed. She had recovered from her carbuncle but was still anaemic, overtired and worried about Anthony's future. Wells was suffering from congestion of the lungs and was moreover tired and overworked. The plain fact is that the war and its aftermath had taken its toll of them both and each was now feeling the stress. The war had aged them, though in markedly different ways. For Wells it had meant the destruction of the stability and security he had known and taken for granted since childhood; the 1890s, when his literary career had been launched, now seemed utterly remote. But it also meant for him a new lease of life as an educator and sage. From now on he felt that his mission in life was to propagate the idea of mankind as a single community with common origins, and to do his utmost to popularise the concept of world history and citizenship. He sensed that his 'boom' years as a novelist were now over though he had no intention of abandoning fiction as a medium of expression. For Rebecca the years 1914–20 were those in which she was transformed from a gushing ingenue to a writer of immense promise, a penetrating critic and a novelist in embryo. She was a mother with decided views on the upbringing of children and all that concerned the welfare of her child. They were both very different people from when they had first met in 1912; both felt they had reached a watershed in their friendship. It was against this background that Wells wrote to her plaintively in November:

> You are probably the only person who can really give me love and make me love back. And because you've been ill I've treated you so's I've got no right to you any more . . . *Dear* Panfer. I wonder how much this is just being cut off from you. I don't know, but of the unexampled misery of my mind there is no doubt whatever.[19]

He cancelled a lecture tour of the United States planned for December 1920 to January 1921 because of poor health (the lectures were published in book form under the title *The Salvaging of Civilisation*) and arranged to join her in January at Amalfi, on the Italian coast, for an extended holiday. They remained in Amalfi for a month and then travelled through Italy together before he returned to England in April. Wells enjoyed the vacation and found solace in her companionship, writing to thank her for 'two months and a half of almost unbroken happiness'. Rebecca did not recall their time together so warmly. She found him tired and irascible and prone to sudden fits of jealousy. While she remained in Florence alone for a further month working on *The Judge* he wrote to her frequently from London, assuring her of his love and devotion. 'I love you more than any other human being', he wrote on 30 April, 'You are my dearest companion. I love and admire you. If I did not love you I should still think you one of the wisest and sweetest of human beings.'

On her return to London they resumed their life together, Wells visiting her frequently at South Kensington and taking her and Anthony on motoring excursions to the Norfolk coast and to Bath. He was taking a growing interest in Anthony, now a bright 7-year-old, and making plans for his education. He was anxious to be consulted about Rebecca's plans for his schooling and to be responsible for school fees. Anthony, then as always, thought the world of his father and found great joy in these excursions. It is clear from Anthony's autobiographical writings that he was still ignorant of his true parentage; Rebecca was still 'Auntie Panther' and his father was 'Wellsie'. This led to difficulties at school for he was inevitably quizzed about his parents by the other boys. Since he genuinely did not know who his mother and father were but was reluctant to admit this he invented details about his parents. When these fabrications were exposed as untruths he had to tell further lies to get him out of the difficulty. His life would have been made much easier if he had been told the simple truth but Rebecca declined to take this step. It was not until he was 8 that she told him the truth, and only then on the strict understanding that he must not share his knowledge with anyone. He wrote later that to be sent away to boarding school at such an early age and with no knowledge of his true parenthood was 'a classic set-up for inducing emotional malnutrition, and all the distortions and hallucinations that go with it'.[20] He was now a pupil at a preparatory school for boys – St Piran's at Maidenhead – but found the pledge of secrecy he was under placed him in an even worse position than before. For some years he was deeply unhappy at school, and it says much for his natural resilience that he grew up to be a sensitive, intelligent, affectionate boy. The evidence of his novels *Heritage* and *David Rees Among Others* is that he was a quiet, thoughtful boy who took a keen interest in the world around him and was devoted to his parents. The fact that he possessed a brilliant, histrionic mother and a wayward genius of a father only became clearer to him as he grew older.

Both Wells and Rebecca were now extremely busy with literary work. He had begun writing a new novel, *The Secret Places of the Heart*, and was planning a shorter version of *The Outline of History* under the title *A Short History of the World*. In October 1921 he travelled to the United

States alone to attend the Washington Disarmament Conference and to write a series of articles for the *New York World*. These articles, syndicated throughout the world and published as a book under the title *Washington and the Hope of Peace*, expressed his growing fears for world peace as the opportunity for an imaginative post-war settlement seemed to be receding in a welter of diplomatic haggling. Rebecca was deeply immersed in the writing of *The Judge*, a project which grew in scope as her ambitions for it heightened. The death of her mother in the summer of 1921, while the book was in progress, strengthened her in her determination to make the novel a fitting tribute to Isabella's memory. PEN, the international association of writers, was founded at this time and Rebecca attended the inaugural meeting in London. She became a member of its executive committee under the presidency of John Galsworthy.

Following Wells's return from the United States he and Rebecca met in Spain in January 1922 and spent some weeks together on vacation. The reunion was not a success. She found him tired and conceited and expecting to be waited on hand and foot. In one of their arguments she accused him of being 'a nagging schoolmaster', a charge which rankled with him not least because he recognised its truth. What she failed to acknowledge was that behind his nagging and scolding he had great respect for her prowess as a writer and was genuinely concerned for her literary reputation. She had published no work of fiction since *The Return of the Soldier* in 1918 and he was constantly urging her to finish *The Judge* and thus consolidate her growing reputation with the critics and the reading public. It also irritated him that she refused to make a 'scheme' for the novel but wrote it as the spirit moved her. All his own novels were written to a plan; he would first write out a list of chapter headings and then write the book within that framework. Her method of working was the reverse of this. She simply wrote and wrote as inspiration came, so that by the time she completed *The Judge* early in 1922 its overall scheme bore little relation to her original conception. Nor was this the only source of contention between them. In her regular literary column in the *New Statesman* she continued to praise authors such as D. H. Lawrence whom Wells regarded as pretentious and obsessed with aestheticism. He felt that her espousal of Lawrence and his circle was 'in defiance' of himself and all that he stood for – 'in despite of Jane and everything trim, cool and deliberate in the world'.[21] While he was aiming for clarity and conciseness in all his work, it seemed to him that she was pursuing the opposite values: prolixity and elaboration. The truth was that they were both right and wrong in about equal measure and whilst she did not accept the justice of his criticisms she felt it ill became him, after the long windedness of *Joan and Peter*, to take her to task for the length of her own novel. When he came to reflect on this phase of their friendship in later years he commented wryly: 'Neither of us, I suspect, is absolutely wrong about the other.'[22]

Behind their disagreements over the writing of *The Judge* lay profound temperamental differences. Wells, with his scientific training and background as a teacher, valued order and precision; he could not stand what he regarded as loose thinking and he disliked histrionics. Rebecca, with her training as an actress and her deep love of drama tended to see life in terms of scenes and confrontations. As he put it: 'Rebecca could produce voluminous imaginative interpretations of action and situation that dwarfed my own fairly considerable imaginative fluctuations altogether.'[23] This tendency to overdramatise their disagreements – a tendency which she felt to be perfectly normal and natural – exasperated him more and more as their friendship proceeded. From his point of view she was melodramatic, intense and temperamental; from her point of view he was moody, withdrawn and self-centred. But the genuine affection that held them together triumphed again and again over these divergences. As soon as they were apart each began to fret for the other and to miss the reassurance, humour, companionship and happiness both derived from their partnership.

Despite their disastrous Spanish holiday they soon patched up their quarrel and, back in England once again, resumed their relationship as if nothing was wrong. The car excursions with Anthony were resumed and for a time all seemed well. The publication of *The Judge* and *The Secret Places of the Heart* within a few months of each other in the spring and summer of 1922 brought to the surface disagreements and tensions which had been latent in their friendship for some years. The two novels, utterly different in scope, intent and theme, encapsulated the tensions that divided them and the values which dominated their lives.

IV

The Judge is an extraordinary personal document, a tour de force of impressive truthfulness and power. It is animated by an elemental vision of good and evil which dominates the writing from beginning to end and gives it a thematic affinity with such works as *Wuthering Heights* and *Precious Bane*. The first two-thirds of the book is a fascinating if wordy account of the adolescence of Ellen Melville, an intensely idealistic young feminist who is Rebecca in all but name. The Edinburgh setting of Rebecca's girlhood is vividly recreated, with memorable evocations of her mother and her unconventional home background. What emerges from these chapters is a striking portrait of a fiercely independent young woman who knows her own mind and is not afraid to express her opinions at home or at the workplace. The rather overelaborate prose has a florid texture, as if one is reading Lawrence heavily laced with James. When this impasto is peeled away and the occasional purple passage is discarded a style of vigorous individuality is revealed, with vivid word pictures which linger in the mind: the rock of Edinburgh castle is 'menacing as the rattle of spears'; the houses in Hume Park Square (Hope Park Square) 'sat closely with a quarrelling air'; the cries of birds 'did but drill little holes in the clear hemisphere of silence' that lay over the Pentland hills; at a family meal there are 'unspoken comments on her position hanging from each face like stalactites'; Ellen's sharpness reminds Richard Yaverland of 'the taste of fresh celery'. Rebecca's skill in recreating her 17-year-old self is remarkable when one reflects how utterly distanced she was from the gushing *ingénue* of her Edinburgh years. The author of *The Judge* was a mature woman with practical experience of motherhood and love; the heroine of her novel possesses all the innocence and gaucheness of youth. We follow Ellen through her suffragette activities, her home life, her relationship with her mother, her gradual awakening to romance with the handsome and manly Richard Yaverland. These chapters, though distended beyond their natural length, possess a conviction and energy that Rebecca rarely excelled. She succeeds in reaching inside the mind of both Ellen Melville and Marion Yaverland and conveying an intensely feminine vision of life. Ellen's relationships with her mother, her employer and Richard are handled with great skill and a novelist's eye for detail.

Pervading the book as a whole is an almost Calvinistic awareness of predestination. A sense of the past, of the powerful unspoken influences that affect our lives, broods over the story, shaping and inhibiting the characters. Ellen is deeply affected by her mother and by the emphasis on thrift and independence of thought characteristic of her Scottish background. Richard is dominated by the influence of his mother Marion and by the fact of his illegitimacy. Again and again these influences from the past affect the present, obliging Richard and Ellen to be continually aware of the forces that shaped their attitudes to life. Neither Richard nor Ellen can escape from the consequences of their own past; each is following out their inevitable fate. It is this awareness of fate, this emphasis on events in the past determining our destiny, which is the leading idea of the novel. When Marion Yaverland proclaims: 'Every mother is a judge who sentences the children for the sins of the father' she is expressing an attitude to life which held a powerful appeal for Rebecca: that our fates are determined by the actions and beliefs of our forebears and that life is a perpetual struggle against intangible influences. What Ellen terms the 'human conspiracy of malevolence' is a very real factor throughout the story.[24]

The final section of the novel, interspersed with flashbacks recounting Richard's illegitimate birth and the traumas experienced by his mother, are less successful. The episodes describing Marion Yaverland as a young woman are overly dramatic and lack the conviction of the Edinburgh chapters. Moreover the narrative tends to move from past to present with insufficient clarity so that at times the reader is unsure whether the events described are happening to Marion or Ellen. When the story mounts to a climax with the description of Richard's murder of his brother, Roger, the plot slides from melodrama to bathos:

> What was Richard's hand searching for on the breakfast-table? She bent forward to see, so that she might give it to him.
>
> Richard had found what he wanted. His fingers tightened on the handle of the breadknife.
>
> 'Let's put an end to this,' he said.
>
> He drove the knife into Roger's heart.
>
> 'Mummie!' breathed Roger. Meekly, but with no sign that he had any other quarrel with the proceedings save that they were peremptory, he sank down on the chair beside him and fell forward, his head lying untidily among the tea-cups.[25]

It would also not have escaped Wells's notice that in the love scenes between Richard and Ellen, Rebecca is guilty of the very thing she was accusing him of. There is a curious woodenness about these scenes, as if she hesitates to find words to describe their affection for one another. In the stilted love passage at the end of Chapter 8 culminating in 'their lips met in a long kiss, and they travelled far into a new sphere of love' she descends into the language of a novelette, oddly at variance with the consciously 'literary' tone of the remainder.

Despite the tailing off of the final chapters *The Judge* remains a novel of extraordinary vitality. Virginia Woolf praised it as a 'stout, generous, lively, voluminous novel', and James Stephens wrote in *The New Age* that Rebecca was 'as close to genius as the critical mind can get'.[26] Rebecca poured into the book her deep love for her mother, her love of Edinburgh and the Essex sea marshes, her passionate feelings towards Anthony and her determination to cherish him in his journey through life. It is a passage spoken by Marion Yaverland which provides a clue to the novel as a whole:

> Women are such dependent things. They're dependent on their weak frames and their personal relationships. Illness can make a women's sun go out so easily. And then, since personal relationships are the most imperfect things in the world, she is so liable to be unhappy. These are handicaps most women don't get over. And then, since men don't love us nearly as much as we love them, that leaves them much more spare vitality to be wonderful with.[27]

It is this sense of the *dependence* and vulnerability of women that Rebecca conveys to the reader throughout the narrative; a sense of women as prone to illness and subject to the selfishness of a predominantly male world. She felt strongly that the dice were heavily loaded against women and that men in general and Wells in particular failed to appreciate this central truth. Behind the story of Marion's guilt at her son's illegitimacy can be discerned Rebecca's deep sense of life's unfairness and her knowledge that men were cushioned against many of the troubles that afflicted her. Marion's feelings of guilt, of being smirched, are echoed by Rebecca's deep sense of inadequacy in coping with life's crises and her view that – especially in the first few years of Anthony's life – she had been compelled to occupy a secondary position. The assertion that 'These are handicaps most women don't get over' is spoken from the heart. Marion Yaverland is a *wronged* woman who has had a raw deal from life; her sense of wrongdoing is visited upon her son, for she feels he will have to suffer because of her waywardness. The real happiness of the Edinburgh chapters and the beautiful descriptions of Leigh-on-Sea are counterbalanced by this darker vision, a sombreness reminiscent of Gissing. 'Personal relationships are the most imperfect things in the world', states Marion. Both Wells and Rebecca would have agreed with this statement but from very different points of view. Wells, because his moods fluctuated so much and because the fulfilment he sought from his relationships continually eluded him. Rebecca, because she felt passionately that women were disadvantaged by being so dependent upon men and were circumscribed by law and convention.

The Judge is such an idiosyncratic work and possesses so many insights into Rebecca's mind and emotions that one turns to it again and again when seeking to understand her personality. It is indispensable to an appreciation of her character and her outlook on the world, for in this novel she expressed so much of her personal self. It also has a central place in her development as a writer because in the turmoil of its composition she matured as a woman and as an artist, coming to terms with her own emotions in the process. Although it was not her first novel it is the workshop in which she found herself as a literary craftsman and defined her fundamental attitudes to life and art. One cannot fully understand H. G. Wells without reading *Tono-Bungay* because it is such a personal statement of his attitude to life. By the same token, one cannot grasp Rebecca West's extraordinary personality without reading *The Judge*. It is in a real sense her testament, and to read it – with all its exuberance, emotional force, drama and tendency to digress – is to enter the mind of an original and deeply serious novelist.

The Secret Places of the Heart is a much more compact novel, telling the story of eight days in the life of Sir Richmond Hardy, an arms manufacturer and expert on fuel who is a surrogate for Wells. The title is a quotation from *Madame Bovary* and refers to the innermost secrets of the emotional self: the core that lies at the heart of the personality. Sir Richmond, tired and overworked, decides to embark on a holiday accompanied by a psychologist, Dr Martineau, and permit the doctor to probe the secrets of his mind. His hope is that during the holiday he will unburden his emotional dissatisfaction to the doctor and thus regain his equilibrium. The experiment is only a partial success. Sir Richmond does confide much of his emotional history to the doctor – including the admission that he has a mistress, Martin Leeds (a recognisable portrait of Rebecca) and that she has had a child by him. The holiday has reached its half-way point and all seems to be going well when, much to Martineau's annoyance, they encounter a young American woman at Stonehenge, Miss Grammont, to whom Sir Richmond is at once deeply attracted. Sir Richmond decides to spend the remainder of the holiday in her company and Martineau, in a huff, goes off on his own. Miss Grammont and Sir Richmond fall in love with one another but, realising that marriage is impossible, decide to part and keep in touch as friends. The story ends with Sir Richmond dying of pneumonia and his wife and mistress mourning over his body and his wasted life.

The novel bears all the hallmarks of having been hastily produced: the characterisation is sketchy and Sir Richmond and Miss Grammont indulge in interminable (and highly unreal) conversations which read as if they are extracts from a sociology textbook. Despite this, the book is of more than passing interest as a commentary on Wells and Rebecca at a crucial stage of their partnership, and as a sidelight on how each saw the other. The book is given this three-dimensional effect partly through the device of Dr Martineau, who is a shrewd judge of Sir Richmond's weaknesses, and partly through the fact that in Sir Richmond's dreams a shadow figure of Martin Leeds asks him some penetrating questions about his motives. These twin devices, the candid friend and the critical interlocutor, enable the reader to see the central character *from the outside* and appraise him, warts and all. The result is a novel of surprising honesty, as if Wells is determined to lay his innermost self before the reader. At an early stage in the story, when Martineau is reflecting on Sir Richmond's attitude towards women, the doctor exclaims: 'The amazing selfishness of his attitude! I do not think that once – not once – has he judged any woman except as a contributor to his energy and peace of mind . . . Except in the case of his wife.'[28] The candour of this admission shows that Wells was fully aware of the weakness of his position and that there was a strong element of selfishness in his attitude to Rebecca. Even more candid is the accusation made by Martin's shadow:

'Your love has never been a steadfast thing. It comes and goes – like the wind. You are an extravagantly imperfect lover. But I have learnt to accept you, as people accept the English weather . . . Never in all your life have you loved, wholly, fully, steadfastly – as people deserve to be loved; not your mother nor your father, not your wife nor your children, nor me, nor our child, nor any living thing. Pleasant to all of us at times – at times bitterly disappointing. You do not even love this work of yours steadfastly, this work to which you sacrifice us all in turn. You do not love enough. That is why you have these moods and changes, that is why you have these lassitudes. So it is you are made.'[29]

The acknowledgement that he had never loved wholly, that always he withheld an essential part of himself, is an admission of central importance to an understanding of Wells as a man and of his emotional relationships. Jane Wells was the one person who fully understood him and with her alone he made no attempt to conceal any aspect of his personality. With both Amber Reeves and Rebecca West he presented *facets* of himself: his innermost being remained untouched. The fact that Wells himself recognised this makes *The Secret Places of the Heart* of unusual interest as an insight into his character. When Martin appears to Sir Richmond in his dream and comments: 'You do not even love this work of yours steadfastly, this work to which you sacrifice us all in turn', it is *Rebecca's* voice we hear, perceiving a fundamental truth about Wells – that, despite all his assertions to the contrary, his work as a prophet, historian and sociologist failed to satisfy some deep inner need. The irritability which is so characteristic of *The Undying Fire* and *The Secret Places* is symptomatic of this malaise: a profound discontent with the world and a sense that some vital element is missing from his life. This was a theme to which both Rebecca and Anthony returned in their writings about him.

The Secret Places seems to have amused rather than annoyed Rebecca as a description of their relationship. She had no difficulty in recognising the account of their situation as presented by Sir Richmond Hardy:

'She has a flat in Chelsea and a little cottage in South Cornwall, and we sometimes snatch a few days together, away somewhere in Surrey or up the Thames or at such a place as Southend where one is lost in a crowd of inconspicuous people. When things go well – they usually go well at the start – we are glorious companions. She is happy, she is creative, she will light up a new place with flashes of humour, with a keenness of appreciation . . .'

'But things do not always go well?'

'Things,' said Sir Richmond with the deliberation of a man who measures his words, 'are apt to go wrong . . . At the flat there is constant trouble with the servants; they bully her. A woman is more entangled with servants than a man. Women in that position seem to resent the work and freedom of other women. Her servants won't leave her in peace as they would leave a man; they make trouble for her . . . And when we have had a few days anywhere away, even if nothing in particular has gone wrong –'

Sir Richmond stopped short.

'When they go wrong it is generally her fault?' the doctor sounded.

'Almost always.'

'But if they don't?' said the psychiatrist.

'It is difficult to describe . . . The essential incompatibility of the whole thing comes out.'[30]

The recapitulation of the familiar bones of contention – servants, moods, illnesses, incompatibilities – reveals how intensely these things rankled with him and how the fundamental happiness of their friendship was being eroded by factors neither could control. When Sir Richmond concludes bitterly 'The essential incompatibility of the whole thing comes out' he is putting into words all Wells's frustration at the difficulties of their situation and his sense of being caught in a trap from which there is no escape. Implicit in the novel is the recognition that in the end he and Rebecca wanted fundamentally different things from their partnership. She wanted security, companionship, support; he wanted reassurance, inspiration, emotional fulfilment. The contradictions inherent in this division formed the substance of their quarrels and underlay his fiction of this period.

V

The 1920s was a period of experimentation in the English and the European novel and Wells was by no means immune to the stirrings of modernism all around him. His friendship with Rebecca had made him more aware of a new generation of younger writers who had emerged on the literary scene since 1910 and, whilst he did not always admire their work, he read their novels with keen interest. As early as 1917 he had contributed a perceptive review of James Joyce's *A Portrait of the Artist as a Young Man* to the influential journal *Nation*, praising it as 'great writing' and 'by far the most living and convincing picture that exists of an Irish Catholic upbringing'. His review, published in the issue of 24 February and subsequently reprinted in the *New Republic*, compared Joyce to Swift and Sterne and commended *A Portrait* for its 'quintessential and unfailing reality'. Joyce was then almost completely unknown outside Ireland; *A Portrait* was his first novel and had been privately printed in London in 1916 because, as Wells wrote, 'nobody else will issue it on this side of the Atlantic. It is a book to buy and read and lock up, but it is not a book to miss.' Wells's review was one of the first significant notices Joyce received and the English novelist continued to take a friendly interest in Joyce for many years. He repeated his praise of *A Portrait* in *Joan and Peter* and again in *The Secret Places of the Heart*, and commended the book warmly to Arnold Bennett. Bennett wrote in *Things That Have Interested Me*: 'I read *A Portrait of the Artist as a Young Man* under the hypnotic influence of H. G. Wells. Indeed, he commanded me to read it and to admire it extremely.'[31]

In his 1917 review Wells made a point of stressing that, quite apart from Joyce, 'there is a great amount of fresh and experimental writing that cannot be ignored by anyone still alive to literary interests'. He singled out for special mention Dorothy Richardson, Caradoc Evans and Thomas Burke, each of whom were producing novels or short stories that departed from accepted traditions. Though he did not share Rebecca's enthusiasm for D. H. Lawrence and Virginia Woolf he was well aware that he and Bennett were no longer the giants of the English literary world and that a younger generation was now ousting him from the dominant position he had once held; Lawrence's *Women in Love* was published in 1920, Aldous Huxley's *Crome Yellow* in 1921, and T. S. Eliot's *The Waste Land* and Joyce's *Ulysses* in 1922. An important consequence of his friendship with Rebecca was a greater willingness to experiment in his novels and to permit a greater realism in his descriptions of emotional relationships. He had not forgotten her accusation of 1912 that he was 'the old maid among novelists' who had been 'too long absorbed in airships and colloids'. Each of his major novels from 1915 onwards had been innovative in some degree, as if he was consciously striving to keep abreast of current developments in fiction and testing out alternative approaches in narrative and style. In *The Research Magnificent* he had tried the experiment of looking at both the central character and the narrator from the outside and speculating about their motivations and desires. *Mr Britling Sees It Through* was notable for the intimate way in which the principal character, a surrogate for Wells himself, was discussed by the narrator and for the unusual perspective this gave to the novel as a whole. *Joan and Peter* was an honourable if flawed attempt to describe the childhood and adolescence of two representative English youngsters and their gradual awakening to their love for one another against a background of intellectual ferment. *The Undying Fire*, subtitled 'A contemporary novel', was decidedly unusual in structure and theme and a courageous attempt to discuss social and religious ideas in a realistic contemporary setting.

In each of these novels he was feeling his way towards a new type of fiction – a genre he later termed 'the dialogue novel' – in which the characters were free to discuss social problems without the restraints of the conventional novel form as defined by Henry James. 'I found myself', he wrote,

> and I got to the dialogue novel, through a process of trial and error . . . The merit of my particular contributions may be infinitesimal, but that does not alter the fact that they follow in a great tradition, the tradition of discussing fundamental human problems in dialogue form.[32]

He had long had a deep admiration for the conversational novels of Mallock, Peacock and Sterne, and was aware that his own inclinations lay more and more in this direction. What he was aiming at was a form of novel in which ideas and situations could be looked at from many different angles through the conversations and actions of the characters. He knew full well that many critics objected to the amount of dialogue in his novels and accused him of self-projection. 'But in many cases', he retorted, 'these obtrusive individuals were not saying things I thought, but, what is a very different thing, things I wanted to put into shape by having them said.'[33] In many cases the conversations between his characters echo discussions that had taken place between himself and Rebecca, either verbally or in correspondence. In the dialogues between Amanda Morris and William Benham in *The Research Magnificent*, for example, or between Joan Debenham and Peter Stubland in *Joan and Peter*, it is possible to find themes and ideas which greatly exercised the two writers and which formed the substance of much of their debate. The whole question of the role of women, the importance of female suffrage, the place of marriage within society and attitudes towards conventional morality are all discussed with complete frankness in these novels. The fact that Rebecca was a generation younger than himself and held strong views on these and a host of other issues meant that, through their friendship, he was in close touch with a good deal of new and vibrant thinking. The growing realism of his characters – particularly of his heroines – and the veracity of their conversation owes not a little to her. Since the beginning of their friendship she had been critical of the lovemaking in his novels, finding his descriptions wooden and unconvincing. Under the stimulus of her criticism he had made real efforts to make amends, culminating in the tender scenes in *Joan and Peter* where the two lovers acknowledge their true feelings for one another. The love scenes in his novels from *The Research Magnificent* onwards are a world away from the stiltedness of *The Passionate Friends* and *Marriage*.

What he owed to Rebecca, above all, was her gift of looking at everyday things from a fresh perspective. As a boy he had enjoyed a close friendship with a school chum called Sidney Bowkett and he paid a fulsome tribute to Bowkett in his autobiography. After describing their world of fantasy and adventure he wrote:

> He was one of those who see quickly and vividly and say 'Look', a sort of people to whom I owe much. Later on I was to have a great friendship with Rebecca West who had that quality of saying 'Look' for me, in an even greater degree.[34]

Without her he would undoubtedly have continued to write novels, but a vital element would have been missing. Rebecca brought to him youth, vitality and perception. He well knew that his work would be poorer without the invigoration of her friendship and criticism.

Wells's novel *Men Like Gods*, published in January 1923, appears on first reading to be a Utopian romance on a par with William Morris's *News from Nowhere*. Its principal character, Alfred Barnstaple, is an over-worked editor living at Sydenham who badly needs a holiday. He sets off alone in his car intending to head for the Lake District but takes the wrong road while trying to negotiate the London traffic and finds himself en route for Bath. On the road between Slough and Maidenhead his car skids and he momentarily loses his head. When he comes to his senses he is surrounded by beautiful scenery that bears no relation to his previous surroundings – scenery so wonderful that he realises he is no longer on the earth he knew. He finds himself in Utopia and spends several weeks immersed among Utopian people and institutions, marvelling at all he sees. At the end of the novel he returns to earth and his wife, a wiser and chastened man looking back with longing on the ideal world he has left behind.

Most readers tend to dismiss the book as Wells at his most fanciful and impractical, taking the story at face value as an account of an actual experience. In fact Wells drops numerous clues which make it clear that Mr Barnstaple's sojourn in Utopia is a *dream* rather than a real occurrence; one is meant to infer that he was taken to hospital following his car accident and that he dreams his visit to an ideal world while under the anaesthetic. At various points in the novel Utopia is described as 'dreamland', 'wonderland', 'nowhere', 'happening only in his mind', 'a perfect dream', 'the world of his dreams', 'a dear dream of hope and loveliness' and 'a day dream'. At both the start and finish of the dream Mr Barnstaple hears a sound like the snapping of a violin string, a sound resembling the note 'which one hears at the end – or beginning – of insensibility under anaesthetics'. When he regains consciousness after falling asleep in Utopia all he can remember is that 'He had been knocked over and stunned in some manner too big and violent for his mind to hold as yet.' The supposition that Mr Barnstaple has had a vivid dream is strengthened by the realisation that the people he meets and the incidents that happen to him are all reflections of situations which are on his mind immediately prior to his holiday. Just before setting off he has been haunted by a craving to bring out a special issue of his journal devoted to Utopian speculations. The castle on the crag which plays a prominent part in his Utopian experiences is a dreamland version of Windsor Castle which he sees moments before the accident. The Lake District that has been in his thoughts is paralleled by a Utopian character named Greenlake; Hyde Park, which he passes en route for Slough, is reflected by a character called Serpentine; the name Crystal, another Utopian, is a play on Barnstaple's home town of Sydenham (site of the Crystal Palace); the Golden Hope, his private nickname for his bright yellow car, is paralleled by a man called Sungold; and so on. In believing that he had visited Utopia Mr Barnstaple is plainly the victim of a delusion. When, on his return home, his wife demands an explanation of where he has been, he replies: 'I just wandered and dreamt. Lost in a day-dream.' There is an irony about many of the descriptive passages which strongly suggests they are written tongue in cheek. Utopian civilisation is eulogised in such grossly exaggerated terms as to make it apparent that an ironic rather than a literal interpretation is intended and that Wells is conceding the impossibility of such a society.

The effect of such a sentence as 'Utopia has no parliament, no politics, no private wealth, no business competition, no police nor prisons, no lunatics, no defectives nor cripples', is not to make one believe in an ideal world but to express utter disbelief in such a society. By contrasting the world of 1922 with an imaginary never-never land Wells throws into sharp relief the unreality of the Utopian vision and acknowledges that it can only be a chimera. When Mr Barnstaple awakes on his first morning in Utopia the narrator remarks: 'He had a vague feeling that a very delightful and wonderful dream was slipping from him . . . It was about a great world of beautiful people who had freed themselves from a thousand earthly troubles. But it dissolved and faded from his mind.'[35] When finally Mr Barnstaple is forced to admit that 'That dear world of honesty and health was beyond the utmost boundaries of our space, utterly inaccessible to him now for evermore' it is for both author and reader the moment of truth: a perfect society as depicted in *Men Like Gods* is inherently unattainable.

Men Like Gods can be read as an allegory on the theme of loss of innocence. Mr Barnstaple enters his Utopian dream on the way to Maidenhead (maidenhead = virginity = innocence) and returns to earth with Maidenhead *behind* him. The accident that precipitates him into Utopia shatters two apple trees, clearly a symbol of the apple of the tree of knowledge. The destruction of the apple trees at the moment the dream commences is a metaphor for the corrosive power of knowledge and the loss of innocence consequent on its attainment. Wells's innocence had lain in imagining that the kind of society described in *A Modern Utopia* or the closing pages of *In the Days of the Comet* was possible. The destruction of that naïvety in the light of the world war and its aftermath of short-sightedness and greed is expressed in the fable of *Men Like Gods*: the story of a man who is transported to a fairytale world and then returns to earth convinced he will see Utopia no more. Mr Barnstaple's regret at leaving Utopia behind him is quite genuine, but it is also the regret of a man who is reluctantly forced to acknowledge the impracticality of his own dreams.

The book is a parody not only in the sense that Wells is caricaturing earlier romances such as *News from Nowhere* and *The Coming Race* but his own *A Modern Utopia* of 1905. When Wells commented in his autobiography that '*Men Like Gods* frankly caricatures some prominent contemporaries'[36] he omitted to mention that one of the prominent figures being parodied was himself. The book deliberately guys his own Utopian writings and mocks many of the conventions of the genre both in terms of plot and style. Thus, Barnstaple's doctor is called Dr Pagan; his chief editor on the staff of the *Liberal* is Mr Peeve; one of the Utopian valleys is named the Valley of Rest. These names recall the symbolic terminology employed in such allegorical works as *Pilgrim's Progress* and *Rasselas* and reinforce the metaphorical texture so characteristic of the novel. Mr Barnstaple's arrival in Utopia against a background of brilliantly coloured flowers and benign cattle echoes the arrival of the time traveller in *The Time Machine* and Wallace's first glimpse of the enchanted garden in 'The door in the wall'. Most striking of all in the light of Wells's fascination with feline imagery is the reference to 'a big and beautifully marked leopard which had come very softly out of the flowers and sat down like a great cat in the middle of the glass road at the side of the big car'. The leopard sniffs a human hand then sneezes violently and dies two days later, apparently a victim of earthly bacteria. As with the puma in *The Island of Dr Moreau* and the panthers in 'The door in the wall' the reader is made to see the grace and beauty of the huge animal as it sits 'blinking and moving its head from side to side'. It is with a pang of sadness that the reader learns of its death, as if a living presence has been removed. The demise of the leopard marks Wells's unconscious recognition that – with Rebecca receding further and further away from him – a vital part of his emotional life was coming to an end. His beloved Panther was no more. The image of death recurs at the end of the dream when Mr Barnstaple attempts to bring a red flower back with him from Utopia to earth. When he removes it from his pocket it shrivels and dies: an apt symbol of the transitoriness of beauty. The death of the leopard and the flower symbolise the end of passion and romance. Wells had reached a watershed in his emotional journey and expressed it in the form of an allegory.

Anthony West, always a perceptive critic of his father's writings, was one of the first commentators to grasp the point that the book is an ironic myth. In an essay published ten years after Wells's death he wrote:

> But the idea of a change in human nature itself is the *sine qua non* of his Utopia, and in the end Wells conceded that such a change was not within the realm of possibility. His much parodied *Men Like Gods* is the point of concession, and it is odd that those who have criticised the book as representing the unpracticality and unreality of his idealism in its extreme form have not noticed the fact . . . At best it is a cry of distress, a plea for things to be other than they are. *Men Like Gods* is in reality an altogether pessimistic book.[37]

My own reading of the novel supports his contention that it is an anti-Utopia comparable to his earlier dystopias *The Time Machine* and *When the Sleeper Wakes* and marks Wells's recognition of the impracticability of Utopian dreams. When, at the end of the story, Mr Barnstaple says to himself 'Farewell Utopia' it is both a symbolic and an actual leavetaking. Before embarking on his holiday Barnstaple is deeply depressed by the world situation: it is a climate of famine, drought, strikes and conflict – 'everywhere there was conflict, everywhere unreason; seven-eighths of the world seemed to be sinking down towards chronic disorder and social dissolution'. Faced with this state of anarchy Wells had reluctantly to admit the unreality of his Edwardian dreams. The novel marks the end of innocence in the sense that it represents Wells's farewell to the facile idealism of *A Modern Utopia* and *The World Set Free* and a more pragmatic awareness of realities. It is an ironic fable in the same sense that *Gulliver's Travels* and *Brave New World* are ironic fables. From this point onwards Utopian speculations in the vein of his pre-war writings become increasingly rare. There would be optimism in his work still but his predominant mood was more and more one of stoical realism, culminating in the Swiftian parables of *Mr Blettsworthy on Rampole Island* and *The Croquet Player*.

VI

Apart from his preoccupation with Rebecca the year 1922 saw two events which exercised him enormously. The first was the death of his friend F. W. Sanderson, headmaster of Oundle school. Gip and Frank had both been pupils at Oundle and Wells admired Sanderson immensely. Sanderson impressed him as an innovator, anxious to break away from the classical tradition in public school education and to place growing emphasis on science and modern languages. Wells was in the chair at a lecture given by the headmaster at University College, London, on 15 June when Sanderson suddenly collapsed and died. His death was a profound shock and seemed to mark the end of Wells's hopes for an educational renaissance on the Oundle model. Wells was determined that an official biography of Sanderson should be prepared as a permanent memorial to his friend, and spent much time in the ensuing months gathering material for such a *Life*. The other contributors insisted that there should be no reference to Sanderson's humble origins – he had been born and brought up completely outside the established educational world – and Wells found himself unable to agree with this view. He therefore withdrew from the official volume and prepared instead his own biography, *The Story of a Great Schoolmaster*, an inspiring and eloquent tribute to a man he had greatly admired. 'I think him beyond question the greatest man I have ever known with any degree of intimacy', he wrote: 'He filled me, a mere writer, with envious admiration when I saw how he could control and shape things to his will . . .'[38] Following Sanderson's death he cast about for some way in which he could further his friend's ideas and the search led him into a brief flirtation with the Labour party. Wells had never been a political animal in the sense of wanting an allegiance to a party organisation; fundamentally his antipathy to political parties had remained unchanged since his broadside on 'The life history of democracy' published in *Anticipations* (1901): 'I know of no case for the elective democratic government of modern states that cannot be knocked to pieces in five minutes . . . an electional system simply places power in the hands of the most skilful electioneers . . . .' Despite his dislike of political parties and his theoretical opposition to the electoral process he allowed his name to be put forward as the Labour candidate for London University in the general election of November 1922. He knew full well that this was a safe Conservative seat and he therefore stood no chance of being elected but felt his candidature would be useful for propagandist purposes. He addressed several meetings and wrote pamphlets outlining his views on education in the hope that the resulting newspaper publicity would help to popularise his ideas. In the event he came bottom of the poll with less than one-fifth of the votes. In the general election of December 1923 he stood again with the same result. Thereafter his flirtation with party politics was over. One cannot imagine him as being anything other than extremely uncomfortable in the House of Commons and he was well aware of his limitations as an orator. After 1923 he devoted more and more of his energies to the task of world education in the shape of *The Outline of History* and its successors. Here, he felt, lay his real contribution: he had no patience for the machinations of parties and caucuses.

As his relationship with Rebecca deteriorated Wells sensed increasingly that he had reached a turning point in his emotional and creative life, an awareness expressed in his fiction through a series of metaphors. Thus, in *The Undying Fire* the protagonist undergoes a serious operation which he has been dreading for a long time and emerges from it a changed man. In *The Secret Places of the Heart* Dr Martineau dreams that Sir Richmond is 'going as it were away from him along a narrow path, a path that followed the crest of a ridge, between great darknesses, enormous cloudy darknesses, above him and below'. In *Men Like Gods* Mr Barnstaple, trying to escape from a castle in which he has been imprisoned, finds himself trapped on a mountain ledge: 'There was no way out of this corner into which he had so painfully and laboriously got himself. He could neither go on nor go back. He was caught.'[39] The sense of being poised between alternative choices, of having reached a watershed, is a common theme in his post-war fiction. Clearly he sensed that something was deeply wrong with his life but for a long time was unable to define what it was. 'The huge issues of the War and the Peace held my mind steady and kept it busy for some years', he wrote later, but 'a phase of great restlessness and discontent came upon me' in the 1920s. He added that his work in writing *The Outline of History* and seeking to popularise modern knowledge 'did not fully engage my imagination . . . I was oppressed by a sense of encumbrance in my surroundings and of misapplied energy and time running to waste.'[40] There had always been a powerful element of claustrophobia in his make-up, a fear of entanglement that is evident in his flight from the draper's shop, from Midhurst, from his first marriage, from Spade House. But the discontent which overwhelmed him in 1922–3 was, I believe, much more profound than domestic claustrophobia. It was a troubled sense that he was wasting his energies in causes that were essentially ephemeral. Anthony West defined his father's malaise in these terms:

> But he knew that in the long run all human effort was futile and that man was base. The world was Dr Moreau's Island and the men of goodwill were building on sand with obdurate material which by its essence excluded any possibility of success. Wells' 'progressive' writing represents an attempt to straddle irreconcilable positions, and it involved a perpetual conflict of a wasteful character. In all too much of his work he is engaged in shouting down his own better judgment.[41]

In the early romances from *The Time Machine* onwards he had postulated a fundamentally pessimistic view of the human condition: a vision of life derived from Swift and Huxley. Nature was, at best, indifferent; at worst, hostile. His basic attitude of mind remained that that he had advanced in his essay 'The extinction of man' (*Pall Mall Gazette*, 25 September 1894):

> And in no case does the record of the fossils show a really dominant species succeeded by its own descendants . . . In the case of every other predominant animal the world has ever seen, I repeat, the hour of its complete ascendancy has been the eve of its entire overthrow.

This stark biological vision – a recognition that man is an animal species subject to the normal laws of evolution – permeates all his writings up to *Anticipations*. The novels of 1900–14 veer uneasily between optimism and pessimism as the mood took him, culminating in the facile hopefulness of *The World Set Free*.

The outbreak of war, as we have seen, proved to be an immense dislocation. This is evident in the tone of *Mr Britling Sees It Through*, where the mood changes from fierce patriotism to profound disillusionment as the elation of 1914 fades away in the carnage of the trenches; in the sterility of his religious phase, so obviously a diversion from his fundamental attitudes; and in the hectoring tone of much of *Joan and Peter*. Faced with a world war in which brutality and cruelty lay cheek by jowl with extreme bravery and devotion his moods fluctuated between deep pessimism and buoyant hope. Both *Boon* and *The Undying Fire* can be seen as dialogues in which Wells debates in his own mind the fundamental question of whether man is base, or whether there is a genuine prospect of human improvement. But in *The Outline of History*, *The Salvaging of Civilisation* and *The Secret Places of the Heart* a new note is evident: an assertion that man stands at the dawn of a greater civilisation and that *Homo sapiens* has but to organise itself to achieve unparalleled heights of material advancement. He had concluded *A Short History of the World* (1922) with the ringing assertion that we could not doubt that 'presently our race will more than realise our boldest imaginations, that it will achieve unity and peace . . . going on from strength to strength in an ever-widening circle of adventure and achievement'. In making these confident assertions of progress he was doing violence to his deepest intuitions and contradicting much of his most serious writing from the 1890s onwards. The whole tenor of his work from the time of his student writings was that man was provisional and fallible, a creature of adaptations, and that there could be no certainty of human advancement. Intellectually the prospect of material progress held a powerful appeal; emotionally he knew in his deepest self it was a chimera. It is this contradiction that accounts for his sense of 'misapplied energy and time running to waste' and which lies at the heart of his acute awareness of mental distress during these years. He was a man divided against himself, torn between classical and romantic, optimist and pessimist, reformer and artist. In his own words: 'Temperamentally he is egotistic and romantic, intellectually he is clearly aware that the egotistic and romantic must go.'[42] The tiredness and irritability endemic in his fiction of this period and typical of his behaviour towards Rebecca are the outward signs of an inner conflict. During these years Wells was wrestling in his mind with a conflict dividing him as a man and as a writer. He was faced with a choice of whether to abandon literature altogether and follow a career as popular educator, sociologist and sage; or to follow his instincts in the creation of works of imagination. In attempting to do both he dissipated his energies and did irreparable harm to his literary reputation.

Rebecca, with her acute perception of his strengths and weaknesses as a writer, touched on the heart of the matter when she wrote apropos of his quarrel with the aesthetes that 'Wells was arguing not with James but with himself, and he knew in his heart that he should have been sticking to his proper business of writing traditional novels.'[43] To her such works as *The Outline of History, Russia in the Shadows, The Salvaging of Civilisation* and *Washington and the Hope of Peace* were as dead as a dodo. She knew that, for all his preoccupation with education and sociology, the idea of remaking the world exercised his intellect but not his imagination and could not bring him lasting fulfilment. Through all the years of their friendship he was protesting more and more loudly that he was a journalist, not an artist. But she knew that in the secret places of his heart he was deeply unhappy for reasons he would not admit to himself. Like Chatteris in *The Sea Lady* and Wallace in 'The door in the wall' he was haunted by a vision of beauty. He could only express that vision in the creation of stories and fables in which his imaginative powers were fully harnessed. Rationally he was a prophet of world order, intuitively he was an artist; therein lay his tragedy.

Their relationship continued into 1923 without any fundamental change, Wells's letters veering between warm affection and carping criticism, depending on his moods. The truth of the situation was that each of them, for different reasons, was growing tired of the relationship but neither wished to take the decisive step of breaking it off. Through all the frustrations and irritations inherent in their partnership the basic fact remains that each found great happiness in the other's company and found it almost impossible to contemplate the severance of the bonds holding them together. 'You have the most wonderful brain I have ever met', he had written to her in September

1922, 'the sweetest heart, the most loving and delightful humour, wit abounding, on ten thousand occasions you have been supremely beautiful to me.' And long after his death she recalled that 'Wells was a delightful person to be with, his company was on a level with seeing Nureyev dance or hearing Tito Gobbi sing.'[44] The evidence of their letters and reminiscences confirms time and again that their friendship was one of intense happiness and communion, and each sensed that – despite their disagreements – theirs was a partnership of rare closeness unlikely to be repeated. For his part Wells must have been aware that he was unlikely ever again to capture the love and devotion of a young woman of her vitality and spirit. For her part Rebecca delighted in his company and knew that, beneath his moods and tantrums, his was a mind of genuine greatness.

In the spring of 1923 Rebecca received an invitation to undertake an extended lecture tour in the United States. This seemed to her to present an opportunity of ending Wells's prevarication and she accordingly presented him with an ultimatum: either he should divorce Jane and marry her, or she and Wells should separate permanently. Predictably, his reaction was an angry one. He wrote to her on 21 March: 'For ten years I've shaped my life mainly to repair the carelessness of one moment. It has been no good and I am tired of it.' They continued to meet and correspond through the spring and summer, Wells offering excuses for his past behaviour and reminding her in one letter after another of all the happiness they had shared over the past ten years. He made it clear that he had no intention of bringing his marriage to an end but offered to make generous financial provision for her and to accept responsibility for Anthony's education. They had a last holiday together at Swanage in September and had occasional car excursions but Rebecca was not deflected from her resolve to journey to America. On 20 October she sailed to the United States aboard the *Mauretania*, determined to use the separation as a means of terminating their partnership. Wells pursued her with letters, apparently still not realising that the break was final. When at length he had to accept the inevitable he poured all his desolation into the closing chapters of *The Dream*, the novel he was currently writing. 'Day by day love went westward from me', writes the narrator. 'Day and night I was haunted by a more and more vivid realisation of a great steamship, throbbing and heaving its way across the crests and swelling waves of the Atlantic welter . . . I was full of unappeasable regret, I indulged in endless reveries of a flight across the Atlantic in pursuit . . . .'[45]

The ten-year partnership between H. G. Wells and Rebecca West was over. But the repercussions each exercised on the other's life were very far from over. Each continued to be obsessed by the other and to portray their relationship in fictional form. Each continued to take the closest interest in the other's work and to appreciate one another with renewed respect. Writing to Arnold Bennett after his love affair with Amber Reeves he had written: 'The two principals appear to have underestimated the web of affections and memories that held them together.'[46] The same held true for Wells and Rebecca. Though they were no longer lovers they had the warmest affection and respect for one another and continued to do so until Wells's death twenty-three years later.

Chapter 6

The Aftermath

This impression of wild and surpassing generosity was not in the least one of youth's illusions. One had, in actual fact, the luck to be young just as the most bubbling creative mind that the sun and moon have shone upon since the days of Leonardo da Vinci was showing its form.

Rebecca West, The Strange Necessity

The perennial conflict in my nature between sensuous eroticism and creative passion had come to its ultimate crisis. I had made my last attempt to reconcile them, and it had failed. I had decided for creation and broken my servitude to this romantic love, but at a price.

H. G. Wells, The World of William Clissold

I

The partnership between Rebecca and Wells came to an end because in the last analysis neither could reconcile the tensions inherent within it: between their respective careers, their life together, and his marriage. It was this three-cornered dilemma which ultimately proved irreconcilable.

Both wished to pursue careers as writers and public figures independent from the other; at the same time both derived great happiness and solace from the other's company. Even if this tension could have been resolved the two aims could not be squared with the fact that the centre of Wells's life was his marriage to his wife Jane. Jane was the cornerstone of his world and the maker of his home; he could never leave her and saw no reason why he should do so. Behind this dichotomy lay a widening divergence of approach in their respective attitudes to life and art. Rebecca had long had an admiration for writers whom Wells deplored: Lawrence, James, Ford, Woolf. This admiration was increasingly evident in her own work, both in *The Judge* and in her reviews and critical essays. At the same time Wells – or so it seemed to Rebecca – was inexorably changing from the brilliant novelist she had known to a publicist and commentator on world affairs. It seemed to her that artistically they were moving in opposite directions: she felt drawn more and more to the creation of finely crafted works of fiction, while simultaneously he was abandoning literature in his obsession to save the world through education. For these reasons each felt that the other was pursuing the wrong tack.

Each no doubt had many opportunities of thinking over their situation during the ensuing months. To bring to an end a ten-year partnership cannot have been easy for either of them and one can well imagine their mingled feelings of regret, pain, relief and appreciation as they looked back on their years together. Each had gained much from the partnership. Rebecca had enjoyed the stimulus of Wells's mind and the inspiration of his friendship. She had shared his life during a crucial phase in his creative and emotional development. She was the mother of a fine son. At the same time she could not reconcile the demands of her career with the necessity to be at Wells's beck and call. She wanted to pursue her career as a novelist and critic at the centre of the British and American literary scene and not feel obliged to adopt a secondary or reticent position. For his part Wells had gained the stimulus of a youthful and invigorating friendship that had enabled him to keep in touch with the thinking of a new, vibrant generation. He had been enormously refreshed by her love and this in turn had markedly affected his fiction, especially his descriptions of emotional relationships. He had gained reassurance and happiness in abundance. But in the end the gap between their respective aims and desires could not be bridged. What Wells termed 'the perennial conflict' in his nature between intellectual and emotional drives[1] could not be resolved and he was forced to choose between them. In the last analysis he felt that his work as a writer and educationalist was more important than his love for Rebecca. Equally Rebecca felt that her need to fulfil herself as a creative artist was more important than her love for Wells. In reality both were seeking to impose a rational explanation on a tangle of emotional drives and contradictions for which there was no ideal solution. Both were irreparably harmed by the breach; and both were perplexed and disorientated by the resulting void in their lives. Each in their different ways began to explore in their writings the nature of their quarrel, and in the process to attempt to understand its causes and consequences.

Wells's novel *The Dream*, published in 1924, but written largely in the previous year, is utterly different in tone from the tiredness and irritability of *The Secret Places of the Heart*. It has pace, readability, and genuine literary power. The novel relates the life story of a young Englishman, Harry Mortimer Smith, who is born in Kent in the closing years of the nineteenth century. In describing the narrator's childhood and parents Wells draws on his memories of Bromley in Victorian times; the description of his home, the underground kitchen, his schooling, and the ritual of Sunday morning service all have the ring of truth and are related with a felicity unequalled since *Tono-Bungay*. In these chapters Wells looks back on his boyhood with mingled nostalgia and detachment, incorporating reminiscences of his mother and father and the little shop which had formed the background to so much of his youth. Harry Smith has an attractive elder sister, Fanny, who embodies many of Rebecca's characteristics:

> Her eyes could be as blue as heaven, or darken with anger or excitement so that they seemed black. Her hair had a brave sweep in it always. Her smile made you ready to do anything for her; her laughter made the world clean and brightly clear about her even when it was touched with scorn . . . Fanny you know was one of those people you have to be honest with; she was acute and simple; she cut like a clean sharp knife.[2]

With her beauty, her eagerness for life and experience, her voracious reading and passionate nature Fanny is a vivid portrait of Rebecca as Wells first knew her; it is she who brings the book to life. She recalls Rebecca not simply in her appearance but in her spirit, her defiant attitude towards convention and her ardent desire to sample all that the world has to offer. When still a teenage girl Fanny meets and falls in love with a man much older than herself who is already married. The two become lovers; Fanny elopes with him – much to her mother's horror and disgust – and Fanny is installed in a comfortable flat as his mistress. Here again Fanny's circumstances echo those of Rebecca from 1913 onwards: the decision to leave home, the violent opposition of her mother, the necessity to lead a clandestine life, her intense happiness with her lover, the tensions and drawbacks of leading a double existence. In depicting Fanny's life Wells vividly brings home the loneliness inseparable from her situation as the mistress of a public figure:

> I found out very soon that Fanny's life was divided into two very unequal parts; that she had hours and sometimes days of excitement and happiness with Newberry, who loved her greatly and gave her all the time he could steal away for her and introduced her to such friends as he could trust to respect her and keep their secret, and also she had long stretches of uneventful solitude in which she was terribly left to herself . . . The fact that he was pleasant and delightful and deeply in love with her, the very brightness of being with him, made those great intervals seem darker and duller.[3]

The chapter describing her life as an emancipated woman (appropriately entitled 'Fanny discovers herself') can be seen as Wells reflecting on his years with Rebecca and distilling from his thoughts a moving portrayal of their life together. It is as if a disinterested observer is scrutinising Wells and Rebecca through a microscope and telling their story as a sample of human experience. The reader is left in no doubt that, by the standards of the time, Fanny is in a severely disadvantaged position: as a single woman with a married lover she risks incurring the disapproval of society and has already incurred the wrath of her own mother. She is, in their eyes, a 'kept woman', 'living in sin' in defiance of established codes of behaviour. While Harry does his utmost to maintain contact with his sister, his mother disowns her completely; Harry only contrives to see Fanny by flouting his mother's wishes. Fanny is, in fact, a social outcast and by persisting in seeing her Harry risks the reproach of his family and friends. He takes great delight in her company and loves her curiosity, her enterprise and gift for lighting up familiar scenes.

Through all the vicissitudes of Harry Smith's life – his adolescence, his love affairs, his two marriages, his experiences in the First World War – it is Fanny who breathes vitality into the novel, just as Joan Debenham infuses life into *Joan and Peter*. Written when the breakdown of his partnership with Rebecca was fresh and raw in his mind, *The Dream* is a fascinating commentary on Wells's state of mind at a turning point in his experience and a summation of his feelings about his own past. The characterisation is the finest he had achieved for many years and the first person narration gives the whole work an immediacy and directness recalling the finest of his Edwardian novels. Particularly revealing is the narrator's observation when lamenting the failure of his marriage. Describing the personality of his second wife he remarks:

> she was not for me that particular dear companion for whom the heart of every human being craves, that dear companion with whom you are happy and free and safe. That dear companionship I had met – and I had thrust it from me.[4]

Here again can be discerned the reflective Wells looking back with affection and regret on his ten-year partnership with an extraordinarily vital and attractive young woman. He well knew that he was extremely unlikely to meet anyone else as vivacious and intelligent as Rebecca. In writing *The Dream* he poured out his mature reflections on their partnership and went a long way to seeing himself from her point of view.

At the same time there is an inconsistency in the novel which Rebecca would not have been slow to point out. Wells had been unfaithful to his wife over a period of many years yet still expected (and received) loyalty from her. When Harry Smith's wife Hetty Marcus is unfaithful to him – though she is only unfaithful on one occasion in a moment of weakness – Harry's immediate reaction is one of anger and disgust. He will not listen to her explanation and divorces her in a fit of temper. Had Rebecca read *The Dream* she would certainly have recognised the portrait of herself as Fanny Smith but would have been quick to point out the double standard. Wells seemed to expect the utmost loyalty and devotion from the women he loved but did not apply the same standard to himself; it was this duplicity which Rebecca found hurtful and inconsistent. Harry Smith is a characteristic Wells hero not only in his sensitivity and intellectual curiosity but in his ambivalent attitude towards women.

On its publication *The Dream* sold 15,000 copies within a month and one reviewer hailed it as 'the richest and most generous thing that Mr Wells has given us for years and years and years'. Few readers could have guessed that in the guise of fiction he was exorcising an emotional trauma intensely personal to himself; in doing so he had produced one of the finest novels he had ever written. In writing it he delved into some of his earliest memories in a personal document which anticipates the freshness and honesty of *The World of William Clissold*.

II

Rebecca remained in the United States from October 1923 until May 1924, lecturing in many different cities and being fêted by colleges, women's organisations and literary societies in East and West. Her standard lecture was entitled 'The spirit and tendency of the modern novel'. She delivered this without notes, varying parts of her address to suit the particular interests of her audience. On the whole her tour was a great success and for a time she greatly enjoyed being the centre of attention. At the back of her mind was the idea that if living in America suited her and if she could obtain regular literary employment it might be possible for her and Anthony to make their permanent home there. While she travelled the length and breadth of America Wells continued to pursue her with contrite letters, alternately begging her to come back to him, chiding her for enjoying success without him, and looking back with affection on their years together.

She spent Christmas 1923 in New York, where Beaverbrook joined her. She had been fascinated by Beaverbrook since their first meeting five years earlier and imagined that this reunion in New York would be the beginning of a stable relationship with a man she greatly admired. It soon became clear that this was not to be. What she wanted, after a decade of being in a secondary position with Wells, was a permanent relationship offering security and affection. What Beaverbrook wanted was no more than a casual affair. It became obvious that he had no intention of discarding his other women friends and that he did not regard her as a lifelong partner. When the truth of the situation dawned on Rebecca she was devastated. After years of fantasising about him the realisation that he did not reciprocate her love came as a cruel shock. Recoiling from this blow she fell ill with influenza and bronchitis, enforcing a delay before she could resume her lecture tour. Yet she continued to be obsessed by Beaverbrook for many years. To her he embodied those qualities of manliness and leadership she had so admired in her father and which she glimpsed and lost in the men she knew.

Resuming her tour, she visited California and the West Coast, making new contacts and sounding out the possibilities of literary work. While in the United States she made a number of friendships she greatly valued including Charlie Chaplin, John Gunther, Scott Fitzgerald and the novelist Fannie Hurst. She was greatly sustained by these friendships and those with editors and journalists whom she met, but reluctantly had to admit that her dream of making a new life for herself in New York or one of the other great cities was not to be. America was too brash and materialistic for her tastes, and moreover her status as an unmarried mother was ambiguous, causing gossip and speculation. But in one thing she was successful. The *New York Herald-Tribune*, a highly respected and influential newspaper, offered her a permanent arrangement involving a stay of two months a year in New York, one in the spring and one in the autumn, writing book reviews. She accepted this proposal and continued to write reviews for the paper for many years, strengthening her contacts with American editors and publishers.

Meanwhile Anthony was still installed at St Piran's preparatory school, Maidenhead. The account he wrote later in his novel *David Rees Among Others* (where St Piran's is thinly disguised as St Ennedoc's) reads depressingly like Wells's description of Morley's Academy at Bromley. It is clear that he was subjected to a good deal of bullying. Older children can make life very unpleasant for a quiet, sensitive boy who is not very good at games and has a liking for lonely pursuits such as reading and collecting cigarette cards. Anthony had to put up with a fair amount of ragging from other boys and did his best to cope with the barrage of inquisitive questions about his parents. He was easily reduced to tears which only led to more persecution. At last he found the continual badgering intolerable and sought solace in religion. He wrote later: 'I decided to take refuge from my mounting anxieties by following my Aunt Letty into the Roman Catholic Church.'[5] His Aunt Letty was of course his mother's sister Letitia who had been a Catholic for a long time. Anthony confided his intentions to Rebecca, who in turn wrote to Wells to tell him the news. In view of Wells's lifelong antipathy to the Roman Catholic Church it is hardly surprising that he reacted strongly. He came down to visit Anthony on no fewer than three occasions to outline 'the substance of the rationalist case for treasuring intellectual freedom and steering clear of authoritarian systems of thought that tended to limit or abridge it'.[6] Having outlined his position, without in any way talking down to Anthony or telling him what to think, Wells departed – leaving his son to make up his own mind. In the event, Anthony did not become a Catholic but the brief flirtation with religion was symptomatic of his unsettled state of mind at this time. He was deeply unhappy at the school and confused about his emotions. His mother's violent fluctuations of mood were unnerving – she had an actress's ability to change roles with astonishing speed – and the strained relations between her and Wells inevitably complicated matters. He remained at St Piran's until the summer of 1926 when Rebecca moved him to another preparatory school, The Hall, Hampstead, which proved to be a great improvement. Here there was no bullying and Anthony was happy. He stayed at The Hall until the end of 1928. During these years Wells took an increasing interest in him, inviting him to Easton Glebe on several occasions and introducing him to his half-brothers Gip and Frank.

In 1924 Fisher Unwin in London and Charles Scribner's in New York published a uniform edition of Wells's works in twenty-eight handsomely bound volumes, the Atlantic Edition. The set was prepared with elaborate care. For each volume, whether fiction or non-fiction, Wells revised the text and wrote a special Preface commenting on its genesis and placing each work in its literary and biographical context. He also prepared a lengthy General Introduction to the edition as a whole surveying his literary career and discussing the influences on his intellectual development. The discipline of re-reading and re-appraising all his writings inevitably led him to ponder afresh on his status as a man of letters. Was he a novelist pure and simple? Was he simply a journalist? How did he see himself by comparison with such best-selling writers of the day as Hugh Walpole, Warwick Deeping, Sinclair Lewis and Scott Fitzgerald? Above all, would he 'last', or were his writings of merely transitory interest? Thinking over these issues he confided to his readers that he would 'live and write in rather the same way if he had to live over again. There is, he believes, in the ultimate reckoning something said in these volumes that was not said before, and something shaped that was not shaped before.'[7] Though in public he professed to care little about his literary reputation the evidence of his letters to friends and fellow writers shows that in reality it was a matter of deep concern. As early as 1901, annoyed that Arnold Bennett had omitted any reference to his novels in the critical study *Fame and*

Fiction, he had told Bennett: 'For me you are part of the Great Public, I perceive. I am doomed to write 'scientific' romances and short stories for you creatures of the mob, and my novels must be my private dissipation.' And a few months later, again writing to Bennett, he declared: 'There is something other than either story writing or artistic merit which has emerged through the series of my books, something one might regard as a new system of ideas – "thought".'[8] As he approached his sixtieth year and reflected on his life and output he felt bound to ask himself the question whether he had made a permanent contribution to English literature and thought. 'I perceive', he wrote,

> I have already lived a long, industrious life . . . If I am not actually tucked up in my literary death-bed I am at least sitting on it. Possibly I may yet take a few more airings before I send for the clergyman and the heirs and turn in for good and start blessing and forgiving people from my pillow, but the longer part is finished.[9]

It was this uncomfortable awareness that the longest and most productive part of his life was over, a nagging feeling that life and energy were ebbing away, which accounts for much of Wells's moodiness at this time. In 1924 he still had a good twenty years of creative writing and activity ahead of him, but of course he could not know this at the time. His writings of the mid-1920s are obsessed by a sense of mortality, as if – like Laurence Sterne composing *Tristram Shandy* – he is looking over his shoulder at a pursuing Father Time.

On Rebecca's return to England Wells continued to write to her, mourning the fact that they were now apart. He encountered her by chance in a London theatre and seeing her rekindled his love for her. On 4 June 1924 he wrote to her:

> You are the woman of my life and I've got a great desire to liquidate what is left of our old bankruptcy and get back to terms again. In your own time. I love you very much and I don't want to hamper or distress you any more.

By that summer his nerves were in a terribly jangled state. As he expressed it in *The World of William Clissold*: 'I was left in England with my nerves, my personal pride, and my imagination jangling unendurably . . . I did my utmost to pull myself together, and for a time I could not do so.'[10] Claustrophobia overwhelmed him until at last he felt he must get out of familiar sights altogether. He set off for Geneva, intending to spend some time at the Assembly of the League of Nations as the first stage of a world tour. At Geneva he had a rendezvous with

Odette Keun, a vivacious 36-year-old who had a fanatical admiration for his work and was prepared to throw in her lot with his.

Odette was half Dutch and half Italian, a romantic, spirited young woman who had lived in Paris and Constantinople writing novels and newspaper articles and had also spent some time living in Russia. Her hero worship of Wells culminated in declarations of love and within a few weeks of their meeting they were making plans to live together. Odette had none of Rebecca's beauty or intellectual power but was warm-hearted, passionate, vibrant and zealous. Her devotion to Wells was total. He wrote of her:

> She was sensually gratifying and that was the main link between us. She never *got* me – as Rebecca got me – by any reality of mental wealth; at its best her mind was uncreatively critical; and so she was always struggling passionately against the facts when she sought to put things as if I was indeed her lover.[11]

Odette was volatile and earthy but prepared to sublimate herself to the needs of a temperamental and demanding writer who wanted peace and companionship. Wells was ripe for a fresh start in life in unfamiliar surroundings. His cherished dream was to find a simple house set on a hillside, remote from telephones and distractions, where he would have the time and peace to think out his world and settle down to write a long novel. Together he and Odette travelled to Grasse in the south of France where they rented a farmhouse situated in the hills with a distant view of the Mediterranean. He decided to make this house, Lou Bastidon, his winter home and settled down to realise his dream:

> I began a life in duplicate. The main current of my ostensible life still flowed through my home at Little Easton in Essex; there the mass of my correspondence was dealt with and all my business done, but at the *mas* known as Lou Bastidon near Grasse, I dramatized myself as William Clissold, an industrialist in retreat, – the prophet Hosea could not have been more thorough in his dramatization – and I set this Mr William Clissold to survey and think out how the world looked to him. For three winters I lived intermittently in that pleasant sunlit corner, living very plainly and simply, sitting about in the sun, strolling on the flowery olive terraces about me, going for long walks among the hills behind, seeing hardly anything of the fashionable life of the Riviera that went on so near to me.[12]

III

The World of William Clissold, the long novel that Wells wrote at Grasse during 1924–6, purports to be the autobiography of a successful businessman who settles down in the South of France to record his impressions of life. 'I should say that a description of my world best expresses what I have in view', he writes, 'my world and my will. I want it to be a picture of everything as it is reflected in my brain.'[13] In form it follows the pattern of a *Bildungsroman*: that of a first-person narrative telling the story of the narrator's thoughts and experiences from childhood through adolescence to adulthood. What gives the book its distinctive form are the numerous digressions on every subject under the sun, ranging from the history of advertising to a psychoanalysis of Karl Marx, from the beauty of forget-me-nots to the role of universities. Many readers found these digressions irritating and accused Wells of having written a novel as formless as *Tristram Shandy*. Indeed Wells himself at the end of his life described *William Clissold* as 'a vast three decker, issued in three successive volumes of rigmarole, which broke down the endurance of readers and booksellers alike'.[14] But a careful reading shows that the digressions are an integral part of his overall design and that what he is attempting to do in this novel is to present a comprehensive picture of one man's mind – to survey the mental and emotional world of an intelligent Englishman from the end of the Victorian age to the first quarter of the twentieth century.

The comparison with *Tristram Shandy* is not as bizarre as may appear at first sight, for Wells had a deep admiration for Laurence Sterne and the influence of Sterne on his work is evident at many points, not least in the intimate relationship between author and reader. Just as Tristram Shandy addresses the reader directly throughout his narrative so William Clissold talks directly to the imaginary reader of his book, confiding many of his innermost thoughts and impressions. The result is a text of unusual intimacy, as revealing about Wells as *David Copperfield* is about Dickens. With calmness and detachment Clissold describes his home background, his boyhood, the awakening of his religious and political views, his love for his brother Dickon, his emergence as an entrepreneur and industrialist. The tone of these chapters is of a man who has led a busy and active life and is now anxious to retreat from the world of affairs and distil for his readers the fruits of his experience.

The heart of the novel is a lengthy section entitled 'The story of the Clissolds – tangle of desires' in which, in the guise of descriptions of Clissold's marriage and love affairs, Wells presents his mature reflections on his own emotional life. These chapters include a fictionalised portrait of Jane Wells as Sirrie Evans, an attractive woman whom Clissold deeply loves and who brings him a companionship he has never known before:

It was a friendship, it was a fellowship; it was these things first and foremost. We made love; we had spells of intense happiness of that kind, but our reality was our friendship, based on our unfaltering belief in each other's soundness and goodwill and our common repudiation of the current moral verdict upon us.[15]

Clissold recognises that through his love for Sirrie he is receiving 'the most precious things in life, love, faith, understanding, fellowship, and the reality of home'. After years of happiness together Sirrie dies of tuberculosis (the account of the slow disintegration of her health closely foreshadows Jane Wells' final illness in 1927) and for a time Clissold experiences acute loneliness. He is full of praise for her disinterestedness, for her devotion to his happiness and well-being. He recognises that during his years with her 'I had parted from an earlier, harsher self and become the more tolerant and less intense self I am today.'[16]

The chapter on Sirrie Evans is followed by a chapter headed 'Mirage and moonshine', in which Clissold looks back with tenderness and regret on his passionate friendship with a fearless young woman he names Helen, who is in all essentials Rebecca West. Clissold, in common with Wells, is torn between emotional and intellectual drives; between sexual desire on the one hand and the demands of his work on the other: 'I found my double nature tormenting me . . . I had a mistress without whom, it seemed, I could not live. And, equally, I could not live with her and continue myself.' Helen is a clever and ambitious young actress whom Clissold meets when she is still unknown. (It is interesting that so many fictional portraits of Rebecca are of actresses: Sunflower in Rebecca's novel of that name, Helen in *The World of William Clissold*, and Naomi Savage in Anthony West's *Heritage*. Her background as an actress, coupled with her histrionic temperament, meant that many who knew her saw her in that light.) Clissold and Helen fall in love and become 'lovers, friends, allies and companions'. Lovingly he describes all that Helen meant to him and the debt he owes for her friendship:

What a lovely thing Helen was – and is! She not only evoked and satisfied my sense of beauty in herself, but she had the faculty of creating a kind of victorious beauty in the scene about her. She had a vision that transformed things, annexed them, and made them tributary to her magic ensemble. It was our custom to snatch a day or so and go off together from my business and her career, and I do not remember a single place we ever went to that did not reveal, through her, the most happy and wonderful qualities. It was as if the countryside turned out to salute her.[17]

There are tender descriptions of outings together to Wareham, to

Corfe, to Virginia Water, to Tunbridge Wells – descriptions tinged with nostalgia as he reflects on her loveliness. He acknowledges that there were moments, 'many such moments, with Helen that seemed to be worth all the rest of life put together'. Then Clissold comes to the crucial point of their parting:

> And we quarrelled and parted. We quarrelled and parted because neither of us, when we were put to the test, would consent to regard these moments as worth any interference with our work and the things we wanted to do. We did not really apprehend them as real. We could feel together, but we could make no sacrifices for our feelings. Ours was an intensely sympathetic and an intensely selfish fellowship. We were exacting with each other and grudging.[18]

The use of the word 'selfish' is revealing and provides further evidence of Wells's self-preoccupation.

Essentially the breaking point between Clissold and Helen is identical to that which Wells had rehearsed in so many of his novels: the tension between emotional and rational drives. It is the same breaking-point that wrecks Richard Remington's career in *The New Machiavelli* and destroys the marriage between Benham and Amanda in *The Research Magnificent*. When Clissold and Helen are together they are extremely happy for a while but then he begins to feel restless; he feels the call of his work. This to Helen is unforgivable: 'Because, you see, it was not that I went away to see to tiresome, necessary things; that might be forgiven. But I went away to things because they were more important to me. She was incidental and they were essential!' Clissold vividly evokes the tensions and contradiction which divided them and led to the inexorable deterioration of their love for one another. His love for Helen, he writes, is 'an experience different in kind from any other love affair in which I was ever involved'. It is too recent for him to write about with detachment because 'the scars are fresh and plain' but wonderingly and sadly, as if looking at it from the outside and seeking to understand it, he describes the rise and decline of his passionate love for this fascinating and attractive woman.

The chapter title 'Mirage and moonshine' is significant. At one point Clissold describes himself and Helen looking down on the Thames from a bridge. After watching the moonlit reflections for a time, Helen compares the reflections to thoughts; Clissold 'thrust an oar into the reasoning liquid and turned its argument to quivering ecstasy'. By thrusting his oar into the water he destroys the mirror image of her reflection. In psychological terms mirrors, reflections and shadows are images for the opposing forces within the personality. By destroying her reflection Clissold removes the image of the woman he loves; he destroys his feminine self and is left incomplete. When Clissold writes 'the other half of my androgynous self I had lost and had to find again',[19] he is expressing the longing of a man who knows he is incomplete without the solace, reassurance and companionship which only a woman can give.

The World of William Clissold can be seen as a kind of mental stock-taking. Within its pages Wells is surveying his world with calmness and detachment, allowing his thoughts to range over religion, politics, emotions and attitudes with a freedom greatly facilitated by its first-person autobiographical style. There is a curious sense of detachment about the book, as if the narrator is observing himself *from the outside* and describing events remote in space and time. It is this detachment which makes the novel extraordinarily interesting as a commentary on Wells's state of mind at this time. It is a kind of still photograph of his world as he approached the age of 60.

IV

For some time after her return from America Rebecca felt unable to settle in England. Her relationship with Wells and her unhappiness over Beaverbrook had left her feeling restless and out of sorts. Much of her writing during the next few years was done abroad, either in holiday villas in Italy or the French Riviera, or while staying in New York. Her inability to settle down for long periods and need for a sense of direction led her to seek psychoanalysis from a Freudian specialist. The analysis (which included an examination of her sometimes terrifying dreams) identified a deep-seated obsession with masculinity, probably stemming from her love–hate relationship with her father. According to the analyst Rebecca had masochistic tendencies which had their origin in her fascination with her father's maleness; it was this factor that explained her failure to achieve a satisfactory union since the partnership with Wells had broken down. Whatever the truth of this matter it is certain that she greatly admired the qualities of manliness and leadership possessed by her father and by Beaverbrook and which she portrayed in so many of her fictional heroes – Richard Yaverland in *The Judge*, Francis Pitt in *Sunflower* and Arnold Conderex in *Harriet Hume*. In this sense she and Wells were opposites. In his novel *The Secret Places of the Heart* Wells's surrogate Sir Richmond Hardy confides to a Freudian psychologist, Dr Martineau, that he is haunted by the idea of a 'woman goddess'. Martineau immediately identifies this fixation as 'the mother complex'. It would be too simplistic to assert that Wells had a mother fixation and Rebecca a father fixation, yet there is more than a germ of truth in the generalisation. For much of her life Rebecca was searching for a replacement for her father, a manly dominant figure who would provide her with security and protection. Rebecca West in the mid-1920s was a young woman of immense promise, still unsure of herself but rapidly growing in confidence, feeling her way towards a mature expression of her powers as a novelist. She had learned much from her years of travail in writing *The Judge* and was hard at work on a much more intimate statement drawn directly from life.

Sunflower, begun in 1925 but never completed – it was published posthumously in 1986 – is a powerfully written novel telling the story of an obsessive love for two men. The Sunflower of the title is a 30-year-old actress, rich, famous and attractive, who has reached a turning point in her emotional life. She is the mistress of Essington, a brilliant and temperamental politician (Wells) but simultaneously fascinated by the manly and handsome Francis Pitt (Beaverbrook). The novel is essentially the story of the slow disintegration of her relationship with Essington and her growing love for Pitt, both processes being welded together in a narrative of compulsive readability.

Rebecca skilfully conveys Sunflower's affection for the lovable but volatile Essington and her reluctance to leave him despite his moodiness. She has a genuine regard for him and knows that he can be the most engaging of companions. 'His mind was as large as life'; other men were not like her Essington 'with his honesty, his courage, his wonderful cleverness, and his dear way of looking like a great big lovely cat'; he was 'so dear and wonderful'; he was 'sweet and kind and dependent on her'. Time and again she pays tribute to his kindness, his attentiveness, his endearing mannerisms and gift for friendship. At the same time she is tired of his moodiness, his unpredictability, his increasing tendency to pick quarrels. She senses that their love for one another is gradually deteriorating but has a thousand reasons to be grateful for his generosity and warmth. She senses too that Essington is different from other public men in that he has a private self which only those who knew him intimately had glimpsed. He differs from other men of ambition because he is intensely emotional; he is a man of deep passions who is easily moved. As Sunflower puts it: 'Yet he was not unloving. If you got to know him, you could see that often he had an aching feeling in his heart like anybody else.' This recognition that Essington is capable of deep feelings comes to a head in a powerful scene (the end of Chapter 2) when he throws himself into her arms weeping, begging forgiveness for being such a brute to her. One has the strong persuasion that this can only be taken from life and reflects an incident that actually occurred between herself and Wells. Still more perceptive is Sunflower's recognition that, for all his obsession with ideas, deep in his innermost heart he is unhappy. His preoccupation with ideas and with the future was a violation of his true nature; he was obsessed with a future 'that was to be reformed half for its own sake and half as an insult to the hated present'. It is not simply that he is dominated by politics and economics and world-mending to the exclusion of human values, it is that these things consume his energies yet fail to engage his imagination. Deep inside himself he is unhappy, a man at odds with his world. Sunflower grasps these truths about Essington but realises she cannot alter him. She can only do her utmost to understand him, to surround him with love and affection.

Deeply attracted by Essington and conscious that he would be desolated if she left him, she is magnetised by the virile and masterful figure of Francis Pitt, an ugly pugnacious man who fascinates her by his charisma and charm. She is drawn to Pitt as Jane Eyre is drawn to Rochester; each time she sees him she becomes more and more obsessed by his sense of power and energy. The attraction becomes so consuming it dominates her life until at last she declares her love for him. He tells her he reciprocates her love and asks her to devote her whole life to him. At this point, when the logical progression of the narrative demands the consummation of their feelings for one another, Rebecca abandoned the novel, leaving the story tantalisingly incomplete. The story as we have it today is clearly only a fragment of what she had originally intended. She left the novel unfinished partly because she knew that the portraits of Beaverbrook and Wells would be immediately recognisable, but also because she felt unable to describe the fulfilment of the love between Sunflower and Pitt. Had she done so it would have been at best a wish-fulfilment, an idealisation of a situation which in real life had caused her much unhappiness. She felt inadequate to the task of depicting an imaginary consummation when in truth the love between herself and Beaverbrook had ended in disillusionment.

Unfinished though it is, *Sunflower* remains a fascinating and impressive novel in its own right. The implicit contrast between Francis Pitt – captivating, powerful, earthy, primitive – and Essington, a 'tangle of transmuted sweetness and kindliness and sensitiveness', forms the theme of the story and renders it at once the most personal and revealing of her novels. Rebecca was deeply attracted by many of Wells's qualities: his mind, his vision, his generosity, his gift for irradiating a commonplace scene with a rich tapestry of fantasy and humour. At the same time she had a profound admiration for men of action and for the qualities that Beaverbrook embodied – strength, leadership, decisiveness, vigour. The contrast between Essington and Pitt is not simply a contrast between two different types of men. It is a metaphor for a contradiction in Rebecca's own personality, between competing drives; between the urge to create and the urge to do. This tension between imaginative and practical demands was echoed in the divisions within Wells's make-up and continued to exercise them both in ways that neither fully understood.

Both *Sunflower* and *The World of William Clissold* need to be studied with care for the light each casts upon Wells and Rebecca and their relationship. It is fascinating to contrast Rebecca's portrayal of the crumbling relationship between Sunflower and Essington, and Wells's account of the gradual disenchantment between Helen and Clissold. Each presents facets of the passionate friendship between two gifted and extraordinary people who loved one another and gave happiness and fulfilment to their partner. It is a story of mingled love and exasperation, of intense happiness and deep frustration. When Clissold remarks 'We were not only hurt but perplexed by ourselves' he is trying to convey the sense of pain and unease which affected both Wells and Rebecca in the closing phases of their partnership. Both sensed that the relationship was coming to an end but each felt powerless to prevent its disintegration. It is the slow mutual acknowledgement of a profound contradiction implicit in their partnership which forms the substance of the two novels.

V

In May 1927 Jane Wells, having felt tired and ill for some time, consulted her doctor about a mild abdominal pain which had been troubling her. The doctor sought a second opinion and she learned to her acute shock she was suffering from inoperable cancer. The disease was at an advanced stage and she had only a few months to live. Her son Frank wrote at once to Wells to convey the news and he replied to her immediately:

> Dearest Mother, my dear, dear wife
> I have had Frank's letter today and for the first time I learned how seriously ill you have been & that you may still be very ill. My dear, I love you much more than I have loved anyone else in the world & I am coming back to you to take care of you & to do all I can to make you happy . . .[20]

He signed the letter 'Your loving Bins', her pet name for him which they had used since the early years of their marriage. There can be no doubt that his distress on hearing of her illness was genuine and profound. Jane had sustained him over a period of thirty-three years, looking after all his needs, creating a well ordered and comfortable home, handling much of his correspondence, coping skilfully with his financial affairs and the manifold tasks demanded of a secretary, organiser and helpmate. Beyond all this she had coped with his emotional ups and downs and the moods of a man prone to fits of depression, never faltering in her devotion to him despite every provocation to do so. As Wells expressed it after her death:

> But she managed to sustain her belief that I was worth living for, and that was a harder task, while I made my way through a tangle of moods and impulses that were quite outside her instinctive sympathy. She stuck to me so sturdily that in the end I stuck to myself.[21]

He hastened back to England as soon as he could, determined to spend as much time with her as possible. Both Jane and he knew that her illness was terminal and that all that could be done was to surround her with affection.

Jane and Wells spent the last months of their life together at Easton Glebe. He did his best to make her comfortable, listening to gramophone records together – she was particularly fond of the music of Bach, Mozart and Purcell – sitting with her in the autumn sunshine either talking or in companionable silence. During the long periods when she was asleep he was working fanatically on *The Science of Life*. This was planned as a companion volume to *The Outline of History*, a general summary of biology written for the layman, on which he worked jointly with his son Gip and Julian Huxley, the grandson of the great Thomas Henry Huxley, his former teacher at South Kensington. For relaxation he played bridge or cajoled his guests into playing hectic ball games in the barn. The garden Jane had created at Easton flowered to perfection that year and gave her much pleasure in her last weeks. They went over all their old letters to one another – Jane had carefully preserved their letters since they began corresponding in the early 1890s – reminding each other of old happinesses. They had shared so much over the years: the adventure of their first home in Mornington Place, the excitement of his early literary success, the move to Spade House, the birth of Gip and Frank, the move to Easton Glebe, the war, their work together on *The Outline of History*. It had been an unconventional marriage by the standards of the time but one which had given them both much happiness and had enabled him to produce some of his finest work. Without her it is doubtful if he would have produced novels of the stature of *Love and Mr Lewisham*, *Kipps* and *Tono-Bungay* or written some of the finest short stories in the English language. It was her devotion, loyalty and faith in his abilities that had sustained him throughout his early struggles and the years when he was finding himself as a writer. His debt to her was incalculable. He was fully aware of all that he owed her and that most of the compromises in their marriage had come from her.

Jane died peacefully on 6 October and was cremated at Golders Green a few days later. Many old friends were present including Mr and Mrs Bernard Shaw and Arnold Bennett who had been a devoted friend to them both through thick and thin. Wells was devastated by her passing and her death filled him with a sense of unappeasable loss. Easton Glebe, the scene of innumerable happy memories, now seemed no more than an empty shell. The house had been the centre of so much conviviality over the years; many visitors testified to Jane's hospitality and the unassuming skill with which she presided over a well-ordered and comfortable home.

Rebecca did not share Wells's grief at Jane's death. She had only met Jane on one occasion, during her first visit to Easton Glebe in 1912, and had retained a mental impression of a self-effacing little woman who was rather overawed by her famous husband. But Jane Wells was a much tougher character than she had ever realised. The truth was that Rebecca had never fully understood Jane. In the chapter entitled 'My father' in her book *Family Memories* Rebecca castigated her father for his sexual infidelities and then went on:

> I recall this with anger, for I know enough now to be sure that men's extravagant sexuality is an affectation. Men have nearly all such extra-marital relationships out of hostility to their wives, not that they have any personal hostility to them, but they dislike women in general, and a wife is one woman who has got the law on her side, and they punish her by denying her sexual satisfaction. I say that out of the knowledge I have gained as a mistress – a silly word, it suggests a gaiety not at all relevant – and as a wife, which suggests a stability also not guaranteed.[22]

This seems to me a travesty of the truth and reveals a profound misunderstanding of the relationship between Wells and Jane. There was certainly no hostility between Wells and his wife – quite the reverse – nor did he dislike women in general. All the available evidence suggests that, on the contrary, he immensely enjoyed their company and derived the greatest possible stimulus and completion from his feminine friendships. There is abundant testimony from his novels, his autobiography, his letters and the memories of those who knew him that he had a deep respect and admiration for womankind and well knew that his life was incomplete without them. The suggestion that he 'punished' Jane by 'denying her sexual satisfaction' is grotesque in the light of what is known of their personalities. Wells was a man of deep emotions who possessed an intensely powerful sexual drive. Jane had no such sexual drive and recognised that in this respect she and her husband were fundamentally different. His many infidelities were conducted with her full knowledge and her acceptance that she could not satisfy his emotional needs. When he wrote after her death 'We had two important things in our favour, first that we had a common detestation not only of falsehood but of falsity, and secondly, that we had the sincerest affection and respect for each other'[23] he was simply making a plain statement of their situation. They did not lie to each other, nor did they pretend that their situation was other than it was. For years Rebecca had tended to regard Jane as a wronged woman who was being ill teated by Wells, but Jane did not see herself in that light at all. Nor is there any evidence that Jane was jealous of Rebecca. At the heart of Jane's temperament was a placidity and constancy Rebecca had never grasped. There was also a steadfast devotion to her husband which Rebecca misinterpreted as meekness but which was in reality borne of unshakeable affection.

On his return to Grasse Wells threw himself into literary work once again. His first task was to compile a memorial volume to his wife, *The Book of Catherine Wells*, containing a selection of her short stories and poems and prefaced with a long introduction reviewing their life together. In this introduction he surveyed her life and character, describing the many facets of her personality and praising her qualities of gentleness and kindness. He recalled her love of charades, of mountaineering and music, her love of beauty, her patience as his secretary and proof-reader, her quiet wisdom as a wife and mother. 'She was a noble wife, a happy mother, and the maker of a free and kindly and hospitable home.' *The Book of Catherine Wells* is one of his most carefully written compositions and is indispensable to a full under-standing of all that Jane meant to him. In its pages he did his utmost to convey to the reader the unique charm of her personality and to describe what he owed to her steadfastness, loyalty and support. Her death left a great void in his life which no one else could fill. It was not simply that her illness had taken him by surprise or that he had never imagined he would outlive her. It was that her death meant the end of a vital part of his world. When he referred to her in his autobiography as 'the moral background of half my life'[24] he was acknowledging that henceforth his emotional and imaginative life must be incomplete; that the companion, wife and mother who had sustained him for more than thirty years was no more.

As soon as the memorial volume was completed Wells returned with feverish energy to *The Science of Life* and immersed himself in a novel, *Mr Blettsworthy on Rampole Island*. This was a return to the Swiftian style of his early romances and to a genre he had always admired: the satire written in the form of an allegory. Writing to Julian Huxley on 12 February 1928 (the letter took Huxley to task for the slowness with which *The Science of Life* was proceeding) he told him he was hard at work on *Mr Blettsworthy*, describing it as 'my fantastic pseudo boys adventure story which will be my *Candide*, my *Peer Gynt*, my *Gulliver*'. The novel tells the story of a young Englishman, Arnold Blettsworthy, who embarks on a sea voyage for the sake of his health. A violent storm off the coast of South America wrecks the ship and Blettsworthy is taken prisoner by savages from a remote island. After a sojourn on the island in which he has many opportunities of observing the primitive customs of the natives Blettsworthy returns to civilisation in time to fight in the First World War. The book is clearly allegorical in intent and Wells intended it to be 'a caricature-portrait of the whole human world'.[25] The account of the savage tribes on Rampole Island lampoons many contemporary institutions with a biting wit reminiscent of Voltaire and strongly suggests that the optimism of much of his post-war journalism was now fading from his mind. Perhaps the most interesting aspect of the novel from the standpoint of Wells's personal life is the light it casts upon his emotional outlook in the aftermath of his wife's death.

Blettsworthy describes himself as a man 'divided against myself'. He has 'great disconnected portions' of himself and is a complex mixture of his father's Bohemian temperament and his mother's sensitivity. While on the island he falls foul of Ardam the war leader and wanders through the hills in search of a hiding place. He discovers a huge fissure in a mountain leading to a spacious cavern. It is the womb-like cavern, enclosed and hidden, that he regards as a haven in the event of danger and to this he flees when he is pursued by Ardam. In the cave he is nursed by the motherly and solicitous Rowena, a native girl who has fallen in love with him. He first sees Rowena when he is brooding one day over a deep tarn; he sees her reflection in the water and rescues her from drowning. (It is interesting to note that Weena in *The Time Machine*, Lychnis in *Men Like Gods* and Rowena in *Mr Blettsworthy* are all rescued from drowning. Psychologists identify water as a symbol of the female side of the personality. Beyond this it is clear that for Wells the image of resuscitation after being immersed in water held a powerful imaginative appeal, symbolising regeneration. In Jungian psychology Weena, Lychnis and Rowena are typical Anima figures, symbols of the feminine unconscious.) The fact that Rowena is first seen as a reflection and is associated with images of the womb suggests that unconsciously Wells was deeply aware of the gap left in his emotional world by Rebecca's parting and Jane's death and was still searching for completion. Rowena is a mother-figure, filled with tenderness and gratitude. When Blettsworthy first sees her he remarks: 'Her presence recalled a myriad possibilities not only of delight and excitement, but of companionship and reassurance.'[26] It is these qualities for which Wells longed. Rowena, with her 'possessive love, loyalty and tenderness' is an embodiment of those attributes for which he was searching throughout his life and which beckoned him in all his relationships.

Meanwhile Rebecca had also decided to make a fresh start. In the autumn of 1927 she left Queen's Gate Terrace – it had too many associations with Wells – and moved to 80 Onslow Gardens, South Kensington. This was a larger flat than her previous address and had a wide terrace overlooking gardens. Here Anthony lived with her during the school holidays and she could work on her book reviews and articles. She was now writing regular contributions for *T. P.'s Weekly, Time and Tide* and *John O'London's Weekly* and working on the collection of critical essays published in the following year under the title *The Strange Necessity*. She was making a name for herself as a critic and feminist and becoming a figure of some importance in the world of journalism.

The Strange Necessity, published in the summer of 1928, consists of a selection of her *Herald-Tribune* book reviews together with a long, closely argued essay on the nature and purpose of art. In this essay she argues that art is a 'strange necessity' essential to human happiness and fulfilment and goes on to raise such questions as: Why does art matter? What is the difference between good art and bad art? Can art be defined? It is a highly idiosyncratic argument which is not merely a statement of her intellectual position but of her intense emotional response to literature. For her, she claims, the interweaving of the characters in Joyce's *Ulysses* 'make beauty, beauty of the sort whose recognition is an experience as real as the most intense personal experiences we can have, which gives a sense of reassurance, of exultant confidence in the universe, which no personal experience can give'.[27]

On its publication *The Strange Necessity* caused Wells a good deal of annoyance. His quarrel with the book was not so much with its theoretical content – though he continued to maintain that literary criticism was a misuse of her powers – as the fact that she chose to include a review entitled 'Uncle Bennett' which contained a shrewd appraisal of Arnold Bennett, Bernard Shaw, John Galsworthy and himself. The article begins by praising Wells in fulsome terms. His is 'the most bubbling creative mind that the sun and moon have shone upon since the days of Leonardo da Vinci'; the best of his novels are 'magic crystals . . . that illustrated as well as it has ever been done the relationship between man and his times'. She then goes on to argue that his worst offence is to 'sit down at the piano and have a lovely time warbling in too fruity a tenor, to the accompaniment of chords struck draggingly with the soft pedal held down':

You know perfectly well what I mean: the passages where his prose suddenly loses its firmness and begins to shake like blanc-mange. 'It was then I met Queenie. She was a soft white slip of being, with very still dark eyes, and a quality of . . . Furtive scufflings . . . Waste . . . Modern civilization . . . Waste . . . Parasitic, greedy speculators . . . "Oh, my dear," she said, "my dear . . . darn your socks . . . squaw . . ." ' But take him all in all, Uncle Wells was as magnificent an uncle as one could hope to have.[28]

What irritated Wells so much about this passage is that instead of quoting from one of his novels verbatim she paraphrased extracts from several of his works and in the process invented a character called Queenie, a name he had in fact never used. 'The Strange Necessity is marvellous', he wrote to her on 17 July. 'It ought to have music by Stravinsky.' A few days later he wrote: 'You can go through all my books and list the women characters, not a bad lot from Aunt Ponderevo to Joan and from Ann Pornick to the *Meanwhile* women – and you can't find three pages to justify this spiteful rubbish.'[29] The truth is that Rebecca's criticism had touched a raw nerve. He must have been uncomfortably aware that some of the conversations between the lovers in *Ann Veronica* and between Marjorie and Trafford in *Marriage* bore a close resemblance to the passage she had described. Though she had not used the exact words she had accurately conveyed the *flavour* of some of his love scenes: scenes in which his prose 'suddenly begins to shake like blanc-mange'. She had taken him to task on many occasions for the woodenness of these conversations; that her charge was largely justified did not lessen his anger. The situation was made worse by the fact that when the influential critic Robert Lynd reviewed the book in the *Daily News* he ignored the theoretical discussion of literature and art but seized gleefully on the 'Queenie' reference, quoting it in full. A series of angry letters to Rebecca followed in which he repeated his assertion that the writing of non-fiction was a waste of her talents:

> The Strange Necessity only does for your critical side what The Judge did for your pretensions as a novelist. You have a most elaborate, intricate and elusive style which is admirably adapted for a personal humorous novel. It can convey the finest shades of sympathy, ridicule and laughter. It is no good whatever for a philosophical discourse any more than it was for a great romance about the tragedy and injustice of life. You are ambitious and pretentious and you do not know the quality and measure of your powers.[30]

Unfortunately Rebecca's side of this correspondence does not survive. There can be little doubt that she defended herself vigorously; it must have seemed to her that the accusation that her style was 'no good whatever for a philosophical discourse' was totally unjust coming from the author of *The Way the World is Going* and *The Open Conspiracy*. Just as Wells felt that the writing of polemical works was a waste of her formidable powers as a novelist, so Rebecca felt that his growing preoccupation with politics and ecology was diverting him from his vocation as an imaginative writer.

Early in 1929 she decided to regularise Anthony's legal position by formally adopting him. The necessary procedures were set in motion under the impression that she had Wells's consent to this step. In the event Wells contested the adoption proceedings on the grounds that the legal document drawn up by her solicitor did not grant him adequate access to his son. Following a court hearing the adoption was finally granted subject to the conditions that Rebecca should consult Wells about Anthony's education, that Anthony should spend part of his school holiday each year with his father, and that Wells would become Anthony's guardian in the event of Rebecca's death. These disagreements over Anthony's future did nothing to improve relation- ships between them, nor were matters helped by anxieties over Anthony's health. In 1928 his doctor diagnosed tuberculosis of the right lung and Anthony spent some months in a sanatorium in Norfolk. The diagnosis was in fact mistaken – what he was suffering from was a form of pneumonia – but the experience was none the less a traumatic one for all concerned. Apart from his physical illness Anthony was experiencing a crisis of identity natural to a child in his circumstances. Such questions as: Who am I? What kind of person am I? What do I want to be? – troubled him increasingly as he grew through his teens. It was not until he became a pupil at Stowe that his uncertainties about his parentage and his own personality came to an end. At Stowe he was known and respected as the son of H. G. Wells; he had no need to tell lies any more.

VI

Rebecca's fourth novel *Harriet Hume* was published in the autumn of 1929. It is a highly mannered piece of writing depicting the love story between Arnold Conderex, an aspiring politician, and Harriet Hume, a beautiful young pianist. The essence of the novel is the story of four encounters between the two lovers, spread over a period of several years, and the contrast between the politician's dominance and ambi- tion and the musician's femininity. Harriet and Conderex are not surrogates for Rebecca and Wells in a literal sense – though the extensive use of feline imagery makes it apparent that Panther and Jaguar are never far from the surface of Rebecca's mind. Rather they are symbolic figures dramatising the contradictions inherent in their partnership. By stylising their conversations and setting them against a background divorced from everyday realities Rebecca enables the

reader to see the two lovers as timeless figures embodying a fundamental conflict in human nature: that between masculine and feminine
elements, between the pursuit of ambition and the quest for beauty.
Harriet represents the softer, feminine aspects of the human temperament: whimsicality, intuition, mystery, romance. Conderex stands for
all that is male and domineering: calculation, ruthlessness, logicality,
drive. Seen in these terms *Harriet Hume* is a myth rather than a novel, a
fable highlighting the eternal tension between male and female, animus
and anima.

In telling her story Rebecca makes frequent use of psychological
imagery and the language of dreams. There are, for example, numerous
echoes of Wells's short story 'The door in the wall' and the idea of an
enchanted garden to which only the privileged have access:

> Not till six years afterwards did Arnold Conderex see Harriet Hume
> again. It was nearly otherwise, for within two years from their parting
> his footsteps were led to the door in the wall of Blennerhassett House,
> and it was sheer singularity, of a kind that he blushed to remember, that
> forbade him entering it . . . he was struck by something familiar in the
> aspect of the wall by which he was walking. A pretty green creeper ran
> half the length of it, and at intervals drooped pale waving tendrils a fore-
> arm's length into the street . . . And here, a step or two further on, was
> Harriet's door, which he had often had to pause before in order to
> compose an aspect that he knew to be disordered by the excessive beating
> of his heart. It was newly painted, a tasteful green.[31]

In the interpretation of dreams a door is usually seen as threshold
between conscious and unconscious, inner and outer. By entering the
door, Wallace in Wells's short story (also an ambitious politician) passes
from the masculine into the feminine realm and is immediately
surrounded by beauty and happiness. Conderex, however, does not
enter but hesitates outside it. The door in both 'The door in the wall'
and *Harriet Hume* is painted green, symbolising sympathy and adaptability. The green creeper covering the wall and overflowing into the
street strengthens the feminine, welcoming image; by implication
Condorex is being beckoned to enter and to leave the masculine world
behind him. He resists the implicit invitation, sensing that the door 'has
no license to be a lens through which the unseen can be seen, it has no
permit to tamper with time and exhibit that which has not yet been
encountered'. He has no wish to look into the future, to know what lies
beyond the door, for this would mean the end of his safe, predictable
world.

The contrast between the masculine and feminine worlds forms the
dominant motif of the book. At one point Conderex asks Harriet point
blank what she is. 'Are you love?' he asks, 'Are you poetry?' To which

she replies: 'Write me down as all that Arnold Condorex rejected.' At a later stage he acknowledges that Harriet is his opposite, saying: 'No wonder she can read my thoughts! There is no need to suppose magic there. She need but look in her own mind, record what she sees, imagine its opposite, and she has all of me.'[32] In drawing attention to the fact that the two lovers are opposites – each is a mirror image of the other – Rebecca is making a very perceptive comment on the difference between her own nature and Wells's. In a real sense she *was* all that Wells had rejected. Her qualities of illogicality, fantasy, whimsy, enigma were precisely those which he abandoned when the partnership came to an end and the very qualities he had most admired in her. In rejecting these elements he was turning his back on an essential part of himself. When Harriet likens Conderex to a painting in which a young man is 'stretching out his arms in eternal desire towards a young woman that stands in the recesses of a cave' she is expressing in the form of a metaphor the central dilemma of Wells's life: that for all his pretensions to be a man of science, a thinker and world-mender, he was at heart a man haunted by an elusive vision of loveliness and desire. Twice in *Harriet Hume* Conderex refers to the legend of the Parcae – in Greek mythology the three goddesses who foretell the sequence of life – and recalls 'that these were but figures out of a fairy-tale which had been told him by a woman in a garden; and that the woman was Harriet Hume'.[33] The explicit identification of Harriet with the woman in the garden is a further reminder of 'The door in the wall' and the kindly, welcoming girl who meets Wallace when he enters the enchanted garden. By likening her heroine to this lovely and gentle anima figure Rebecca reinforces the significance of *Harriet Hume* as a myth of far greater import than its surface narrative conveys. Despite its mannered language and the artificiality of its settings the novel embodies many fundamental truths about Wells and Rebecca and is essential reading for all who seek to understand the nature of their personalities. Conderex and Harriet are larger than life figures playing over again the story of Chatteris and the mermaid in *The Sea Lady*: the man of purpose torn by conflicting desires.

Given its recognisably Wellsian theme, its appealing vein of fantasy and frequent use of symbolism it is hardly surprising that Wells liked the novel very much. He wrote to her on 13 September 1929: 'You've got your distinctive fantasy and humour into it, and it gives play for just the peculiar intricate wittiness which is one of your most delightful and intimitable characteristics.' For him *Harriet Hume* was a much finer piece of work than *The Judge* and showed a marked advance in her command of narrative and characterisation. It was also impressive evidence of Rebecca's skill in handling a complex interplay of imagery and weaving this into a coherent story which holds the reader's attention throughout. Above all he recognised the novel as a commentary on their situation and on the web of emotions that had both attracted and repelled them. When Harriet observes that there is 'a mystical confusion of substance' between herself and her lover she is acknowledging a reality which must have dawned many times on both Rebecca and Wells: that, despite their deep differences of temperament and outlook, they shared a love of fantasy and a sense of lost happiness. For both of them the enchanted garden was a sustaining and enduring myth.

Throughout the latter half of the decade there were ominous signs that the flimsy international order enshrined in the Treaty of Versailles was slowly but surely crumbling. *Mein Kampf*, a controversial book by a hitherto unknown young German, Adolf Hitler, was published in 1925. The book highlighted the weaknesses inherent in the Versailles Treaty and drew attention in no uncertain terms to the Germans' genuine grievances. In May 1926 a General Strike paralysed the British economy for nine days and led to unparalleled scenes of violence and tension. Twelve months later, on 'Black Friday' (13 May 1927), the German economy collapsed in a rising tide of bank failures and worthless paper money. In 1928 fighting broke out between China and Japan against a background of rising tensions and mistrust. In March 1929 the Fascists 'won' single-party elections in Italy and on 28 October of that year the US Stock Exchange on Wall Street collapsed, signalling world-wide financial panic. Three days later all American loans to Europe ceased.

Wells could only watch with a sense of helplessness the worsening decline into anarchy and economic depression. Despite the fact that twenty-three nations had signed the Kellogg–Briand Pact renouncing war as an instrument of policy, armaments continued to accumulate at an ever growing rate. In article after article he continued to hammer away at his thesis that war and national sovereignty were now obsolete and that the only way to eliminate war was to establish a federal world authority coupled with a world-wide system of education on cosmopolitan rather than national lines. On 15 April 1929 he addressed the Society for International Discussion at the Reichstag in Berlin on *The Common-Sense of World Peace*. In his speech he made an eloquent plea for the ending of the arms race and for a planetary campaign of peace education. Since 1918, he argued, only the flimsiest of barriers against war had been erected. The race against time before Europe capsized into world war was now extremely urgent. 'Ten years of faith-healing for the sickness of the world are enough. It is time that real work for world peace was begun.' More and more he felt like a lone voice crying in the wilderness.

Meanwhile the relationship between Wells and Odette was steadily deteriorating. Anthony, always a perceptive commentator on his father, wrote many years later: 'Odette Keun had been able to accept her secondary role in my father's life as long as his wife was alive, but she found her position less and less acceptable in the absence of its rationale.'[34] She became increasingly vain and unpredictable, subject to violent storms of emotion and recrimination. She demanded that Wells should sever all his ties with England and settle permanently in Paris with her; this he was totally unwilling to do. He loved his home in Provence (in 1927 he had built a larger, more comfortable house near to Lou Bastidou called Lou Pidou) but equally he loved England and saw no reason why he should uproot his life to satisfy her whim. Some idea of Odette's flamboyant moods at this time can be derived from his novel *Apropos of Dolores* (1938), in which he tried with detachment and good humour to convey the essence of her personality. Vain, melodramatic, egotistic, she was frequently impossible yet when the mood took her could be the most engaging of companions. It was some years before he reluctantly had to face the truth that he and Odette were incompatible and it was not until 1933 that the break between them became final. That it took him so long to accept the fact of their incompatability and to take a firm grip on his life is partly explained by the fact that, unknown to himself, he was suffering from diabetes. For several years he had been aware of diminishing energy and an inability to concentrate his mind. It was not until 1931 that he realised that his symptoms were caused by insulin deficiency, and meanwhile his continual tiredness, aggravated by overwork, meant he was unable to disentangle himself from Odette.

Events were precipitated by the return of Moura into his life – the same Moura who had been Gorky's secretary and whom he had met in Moscow in 1920. In 1929 she visited England and called on him at Easton Glebe. She had now parted from Gorky and she and Wells were overjoyed to see one another again. He wrote of her: 'After my breach with Rebecca I made a real attempt, as I have told, to adjust myself to Odette – and get on with my proper work. But from 1920 onward there was another presence in my imagination, sometimes remote, sometimes near, and at last coming very near.'[35] In 1929 Moura was 36, animated, charming, intelligent and gentle. She was in the completest contrast to the noisy and vociferous Odette, and Wells was deeply attracted. As his feelings for Odette cooled his affection for Moura deepened, until at last he was in no doubt where his real feelings lay. While Wells prevaricated between France and England and tried to sort out his tangled emotional life he was struggling to complete *The Science of Life* (and simultaneously planning a companion volume, *The Work, Wealth and Happiness of Mankind*, an outline of economics), and also working on a film scenario, *The King who was a King*, in addition to a considerable amount of journalism. He felt he had years of good work ahead of him but sensed that his greatest achievements as a novelist now lay in the past. More and more he was aware of a feeling that he was 'yesterday', that a new generation of younger writers were now enjoying the boom he had enjoyed thirty years earlier and taking the novel in new directions. Virginia Woolf's *To the Lighthouse* had been published in 1927, Aldous Huxley's *Point Counter Point* in 1928, Hemingway's *A Farewell to Arms* in 1929 and Lawrence's *The Virgin and the Gypsy* in 1930. Yet his own fiction was showing no sign of any diminution in his imaginative powers. *Mr Blettsworthy on Rampole Island* revealed a freshness and narrative skill unequalled since his early romances and an impressive ability to handle allegory in a stimulating and meaningful way. Both *The Dream* and *The World of William Clissold* had been finely crafted novels, rich in characterisation and insight, whilst *Christina Alberta's Father* (1925) and *Meanwhile* (1927), though not up to the standard of his best work, displayed evidence of originality and skill in the use of imagery.

In July 1930 he decided to sell Easton Glebe – 'for me now it is no more than a nest of memories'[36] – and move into a flat at 47 Chiltern Court, Clarence Gate, NW1. This apartment above the rumble of Baker Street station became his London base. With the diagnosis of his diabetic condition in the following year his health dramatically improved; with renewed vitality he was full of plans for new novels and fresh initiatives.

Towards the end of 1928 Rebecca met a young man named Henry Maxwell Andrews who was immediately captivated by her. They met at a party given by the writer and feminist Vera Brittain and her economist husband George Catlin. Also present at the party were the novelist Winifred Holtby and a select group of writers and academics. Rebecca, Vera and Winifred were each associated with the weekly journal *Time and Tide* and had much in common, but it was Henry Andrews who received most of her attention that evening. The attraction was mutual.

Henry was a tall, gentle, shy man who had been born in Burma in 1894 of Anglo-German parents and educated at Uppingham and New College, Oxford. Despite his cosmopolitan background – his father had been employed by the British East India Company and had later lived in Hamburg – he had many English characteristics including diffidence, kindness and formality. By profession he was a merchant banker, and his leisure interests embraced literature, history and culture. Quiet and headmasterly, he was in the completest contrast to the mercurial Wells and the dynamic Beaverbrook. Rebecca decided that she liked this polite and cultivated man who had such a deep admiration for her work. He particularly admired *The Return of the Soldier*, which he had enjoyed both as a novel and a play, and shared Rebecca's enthusiasm for reading and the theatre. They began to see more of one another.

There was much in Henry that she found attractive, and vice versa. Though considerate and urbane he was at heart a deeply insecure man and Rebecca sensed this. Because of his mixed origins he had been interned in Germany throughout the First World War and this experience had exacerbated his lack of self-confidence. In his innermost self he was a frustrated academic and secretly longed to be a scholar; he had never really found banking congenial and had to indulge in his love of books outside working hours. His shyness in company was made worse by a slight deafness and a gravity of bearing that made him appear slow and over precise. On the other hand he exuded kindness, courtesy and solicitation. There could be no question of the genuineness of his concern for her both as a woman and as a writer: his devotion to her was total. In Rebecca he recognised a creative artist of great promise who had had to lead a life without settled roots. He grasped her need for an ordered existence and for a partner who could share her life, taking a daily interest in her writings and ideas. Rebecca was now weary of her unsettled life and longing for security and domesticity. When at length Henry proposed marriage she accepted his offer with gratitude. He made it clear that he had no capital (in common with Rebecca's father he had lost considerable sums in Stock Exchange speculations) but her reply to this was that they should pool their resources. It was not a love match comparable to the deep love she had felt for Wells or the fascination she had felt for Beaverbrook but they had a warm affection for one another and a genuine desire to make their marriage work. She was enormously buoyed up by Henry's devotion to her at a time when she was miserable with loneliness and insecurity and convinced of his evident need for her. They were married by special licence at Abinger, Surrey, on 1 November 1930.

Rebecca was now feeling more settled than she had been for many years. She was married to an eligible man who could provide her with security and stability; she was determined to make her marriage a success; and from now onwards she would have the peace of mind essential to her fulfilment as a creative writer. For Wells also a watershed had been reached. His decision to sell Easton Glebe marked the end of an important phase in his life and the beginning of a new chapter in which he felt able to take a firmer grip on his destiny. With Moura now back in England, his relationship with Odette rapidly deteriorating, and the resurgence of his health and his powers as a novelist he was clearly poised for a fresh start. For both Rebecca and Wells a new phase was about to begin.

Part III:

The Parting of the Ways

Chapter 7

Novelist and Prophet

Whatever else I have desired, invariably the leading thing I have desired has been personal response. And the next thing to that has been something hard to name, a kind of brightness, an elation, a material entanglement with beauty.

H. G. Wells, *The World of William Clissold*

Man comes into life to seek and find his sufficient beauty, to serve it, to win and increase it, to fight for it, to face anything and dare anything for it, counting death as nothing so long as the dying eyes still turn to it.

H. G. Wells, *The History of Mr Polly*

I

During 1931 two deaths occured which affected Wells profoundly. The first, on 27 March, was that of his old friend Arnold Bennett. He and Bennett had maintained a genial friendship since they first corresponded in 1897; they had been frequent visitors to each other's homes and had often met at the Reform Club; for many years both had entertained a lively admiration and respect for the other's work. Despite occasional disagreements they had never quarrelled on fundamentals and throughout their correspondence had discussed each other's novels with complete candour and good humour. Among all Wells's literary friendships that with Arnold Bennett was probably unique in this respect. The explanation is a perfectly simple one: that, though they were friendly rivals, they had a genuine liking for each other and took real pleasure in the other's company. They had much in common: they were almost exact contemporaries, they were both self-made men, they had both set out determined to make their mark as writers, they had the deepest curiosity about life and behaviour. Their liking for one another had enabled them to be perfectly candid without causing offence. Writing to Bennett apropos of his novel *Sacred and Profane Love*, for example, Wells had written: 'I doubt if ever you weep. You have no passion for Justice, You prefer 'style' to beauty.' In response Bennett told Wells a few home truths:

> You are not really interested in individual humanity. And when you write a 'non-scientific' novel, you always recur to a variation of the same type of hero, and you always will, because your curiosity about individualities won't lead you further. You are concerned in big crowd-movements. Art, really, you hate. It means to you what 'arty' means to me. You live in a nice house, but you know perfectly well you wouldn't care what sort of a house you lived in . . . You won't have anything to do with 'surface values' at all. You don't merely put them in a minor place; you reject them.[1]

One cannot imagine Wells taking comments like this from James, Gissing or Conrad without being stung into an elaborately defensive justification of his own position. From Bennett he took it all in good part: 'All I've said was right but I like your spirit', he told him. And now he was no more. Bennett's death of typhoid at the age of 63 meant that Bernard Shaw was now almost the only survivor from that distinguished literary circle who had befriended him in the 1890s – Bennett, Gissing, James, Conrad, Shaw, Stephen Crane. It was a further reminder, if reminder was needed, of the remorseless advance of time and the unpredictability of life.

When he came to write about Bennett in his autobiography Wells observed:

> While I was becoming more and more set upon changing my world and making it something entirely different and while Conrad was equally set upon wringing an unprecedented intensity of phrasing out of his, Bennett was taking the thing that is, for what it was, with a naive and eager zest.[2]

In this comment Wells is attempting to define, somewhat ungraciously, a real difference which he felt divided him from Bennett but which he found not easy to express in words. The truth was that he felt uneasy when critics bracketed him and Bennett together as if they were writers of the same type. Virginia Woolf had done precisely this in her influential essays 'Modern fiction' (1919) and 'Mr Bennett and Mrs Brown' (1924), and Rebecca West had done the same again in the 'Uncle Bennett' review that had so irritated him. Wells felt in his bones that in reality he and Bennett were poles apart in their approach to literature: a view which is surely confirmed by a comparison of *Clayhanger* and *The Old Wives Tale* with (say) *Tono-Bungay* and *The New Machiavelli*. Bennett was in essence a realistic novelist in the tradition of Balzac and Zola: a classic example of a writer whose novels are windows on reality. Wells, by contrast, was a novelist whose work departs significantly from the conventions of the Victorian realist novel as exemplified by George Eliot or the early Dickens. His novels are frequently self-conscious, pessimistic and fragmented; they do not take the thing that is for what it is; they implicitly question the conventions of the omniscient narrator and the ordered chronological narrative; and they make extensive use of symbolism and imagery. Indeed it can be argued that Wells was not really a novelist in the realist tradition at all – that he was fundamentally a transitional figure between realism and modernism – and that both in his practical and theoretical attitudes towards the novel he was in the sharpest contrast to Bennett.

But when all is said and done the fact remains that they had enjoyed a warm friendship over a period of more than thirty years. Re-reading all his letters to Bennett (he had collected them together in 1930 for his biographer, Geoffrey West) he had told him: 'Touching it is to read over those letters. What a good friendship it has been! What a good friend you have been!'[3] A year to the day after this letter was written Bennett died at his London home, 97 Chiltern Court, after a long and exhausting illness. It meant the end of one of the most steadfast and good natured friendships Wells had ever enjoyed. He was still blessed with many friends of both sexes and drawn from many walks of life but he knew it was unlikely that ever again would his life be enriched by a friend as genuine and unaffected as the kindly and plain-speaking Staffordshireman.

The second death, in September, was that of his first wife Isabel. He and Isabel had been on friendly terms for many years; he had provided her with a regular income, advised her in her business ventures, and welcomed her for long periods at Easton Glebe when convalescing after an operation. Her sudden passing was for Wells an emotional and psychological trauma for her slight and pretty figure had haunted him since he had first set eyes on her in 1886 at 181 Euston Road. 'I tethered my sexual and romantic imagination to her', he wrote.[4] Indeed he did, but beyond this it is this gentle-mannered girl who lives and breathes in so many of his novels and animates the dreams of his narrators. Ethel in *Love and Mr Lewisham*, Nettie in *In the Days of the Comet*, Marion in *Tono-Bungay* and Margaret in *The New Machiavelli* each reflect aspects of her personality and testify to the powerful hold her character exercised on his imagination. When George Ponderevo in *Tono-Bungay* leaves the unresponsive Marion for the sensuous and devoted Effie he is stricken with remorse for the wife he has left behind him: 'Yet at the back of it all Marion remained, stupid and tearful and infinitely distressful, so that I was almost intolerably unhappy for her – for her and the dead body of my married love.'[5] The plain fact is that since the age of 20 Wells had been obsessed by Isabel – a truth which Rebecca had not been slow to grasp. His decision to part from her in January 1894 after two years of marriage had wounded him far more deeply than he had admitted to anyone except Jane. The scars from this parting were very slow to heal and came to the surface in novel after novel during the early years of the twentieth century. For him she was the embodiment of all those qualities of mystery and promise which haunt the romances of classical mythology:

> she was the unconscious custodian of something that had gripped my most intimate instinct, she embodied the hope of a possibility, was the careless proprietor of a physical quality that had turned my head like strong wine . . . I saw her in dreams released, as it were, from herself, beautiful, worshipful, glowing.[6]

Her death meant the severance of the bonds of affection that had bound them together for more than forty years and released a flood of memories. Thinking over all she had meant to him, allowing his imagination to dwell on her quiet, thoughtful personality, he began to shape out a novel in which he could pay tribute to the nobility of her spirit.

The story he now commenced, *The Bulpington of Blup*, was conceived in part as a satire on his old acquaintance Ford Madox Ford. Both Wells and Rebecca had known Ford on and off for years and whilst Rebecca had admired some of Ford's novels neither of them liked him as a man. Both felt he was pompous and pretentious, Rebecca remarking acidly that being embraced by Ford 'was like being the toast under a poached egg'.[7] In his novel *The New Humpty-Dumpty* (1912) Ford had lampooned the Edwardian literary scene and included a hard-hitting caricature of Wells (as Herbert Pett) that had rankled deeply. Now Wells felt the time had come to pay off an old score. *The Bulpington of Blup* would relate the tangled mental history of a poseur modelled on Ford in a story that would encapsulate Wells's dislike of the aesthetic approach to literature.

To combine these two objectives in one novel – to satirise the aesthetes and at the same time pay tribute to the memory of Isabel Mary Wells – sounds a tall order, but in fact the novel works remarkably well. *The Bulpington of Blup* is one of the freshest and most readable works he had written since *The Dream*. The characterisation is deftly handled, the narrative is shaped with fine assurance and the work as a whole is set against a convincing backcloth of English intellectual life during the years 1880–1920. The novel's central character, Theodore Bulpington, is an effete young man who grows through life in a series of poses, unable or unwilling to come to terms with his real self. He dabbles in religion and Fabian politics and, in his daydreams, becomes 'The Bulpington of Blup', the ruler of a mystical kingdom. As an adolescent he is torn between his desire for the vivacious and worldly Rachel Bernstein and the enigmatic and beautiful

Margaret Broxted. It is Margaret who is the 'Isabel' figure – virginal, impalpable, desirable – and in portraying her Wells likens her to Michelangelo's portrait of the Delphic Sybil with her unfathomable smile and haunting expression. When Theodore eventually rejects Margaret in favour of Rachel he is tormented by a sense of loss:

> Suddenly his mind was irradiated by pain, pain of the soul and a sense of irrecoverable loss. Something deep and beautiful he felt had shone upon his life, had belonged to his life, and he had lost it or been robbed of it or anyhow it had gone out of his life for evermore. He knew certainly it had gone for evermore. This desolation was so real, this anguish was so acute, he could not remain indoors.[8]

The title of this chapter is 'Inexplicable heart-ache', which is a precise description of Theodore's sense of longing. He is troubled by an awareness of loss of innocence, a feeling that he has in some way betrayed Margaret and in doing so has lost faith with his fundamental instincts. He begs Margaret to become his mistress and, when she refuses, returns to Rachel. The heading of this section, 'Sacred and profane love', underlines the contrast between the two women. Theodore well understands the choice he has made and that in renouncing Margaret he has turned his back on an essential part of his nature. With the outbreak of war in 1914 Theodore prevaricates between his innate cowardice and his desire for heroic action. After a year of evading a decision he eventually enlists as a private and plays an ignominious role in the trenches. Fleeing in terror from the final German offensive he feigns shell-shock and is pardoned by a kindly doctor who turns a blind eye to his evident panic. After a spell in a psychiatric hospital he returns to London after the armistice and attempts to pick up the threads of his old life. Margaret now rejects him completely and, finding England unendurable, he decides to settle in Paris. There he becomes the co-proprietor of a pretentious dilettante magazine, *The Feet of the Young Men*, which he edits for ten years. The novel ends with Theodore retiring to a Devonshire cottage left him by an aunt, completely absorbed in the world of his delusions. He has convinced himself that he was a great war hero who captured the Kaiser single-handed and played a decisive role in defeating the last German advance. As a symbol of his final abandonment of all that Margaret represents – integrity, purity, beauty – he destroys a print of the Delphic Sybil he finds in the cottage and retires to bed in a drunken stupor.

On the whole, *The Bulpington of Blup* was well received by the critics and the chorus of praise did much to dispel Wells's notion that since the war he had dropped below 'the habitual novel reader's horizon'.[9] In addition to bringing out the book in a handsome hardback edition (with the Delphic Sybil reproduced on the endpapers) at the then standard price of eight shillings and sixpence, Hutchinsons published a paper-back edition which sold widely. The novel is significant for several reasons. First, it demonstrated that, in his mid-sixties, Wells was still perfectly capable of writing well-crafted fiction animated by solid, believable characters. When he claimed in the dust jacket text that Theodore 'keeps more of our sympathy to the end than perhaps some of us will care to admit' Wells was telling no more than the truth: that many people maintain a pose in their daily lives and his hero was by no means exceptional in living behind a series of masks. As a study of a divided character, Theodore Bulpington is one of his most fully realised creations and more than justified his renewal of confidence in his powers. Second, the book provides interesting evidence of Wells's growing preoccupation with the inner lives of his characters as distinct from the external details of their behaviour. For the novel is not simply a study of Theodore but of his parents, Raymond and Clorinda, both of whom are divided against themselves. The story of his adolescence is the story of the interaction of his mind with theirs, with Margaret and Rachel, with Margaret's brother Teddy and their circle of friends. The series of novels beginning with *The Bulpington of Blup* have been described as 'anatomies of egotism',[10] for each is an acutely perceptive analysis of a mind: a case study in the development of a personality. In dissecting Theodore's psyche Wells demonstrates his ability to look into the innermost self of his creation and to raise disturbing questions concerning the mainsprings of human emotion. Theodore is a more complex character than Kipps because he is made up of several different selves, some noble and some ignoble, and the reader is shown many facets of his personality. Third, and most importantly, the novel's tender portrayal of Margaret Broxted as the gracious and gentle heroine is moving testimony to Wells's abiding fixation with Isabel's memory. The heartache experienced by Theodore whenever he thinks about her is a physical sensation. It was this overwhelming sense of pain, of being bereft, that Wells had experienced when his first marriage came to an end. He knew that a vital element essential to his happiness and peace of mind had departed from his life, 'something deep and beautiful' had shone upon him. All his subsequent love adventures – with Amy Catherine Robbins, with Amber Reeves, with Rebecca West – can be seen as partially successful attempts to eradicate that sense of loss, to regain that elusive vision of beauty and desire which haunted him. Her death of diabetes in 1931 by no means exorcised the ghost. But it compelled him to come to terms with the fact of her passing and allowed his mind to speculate about her with a freedom he had hitherto found impossible. Isabel continued to haunt him – and would do for the remainder of his life.

The Bulpington of Blup was followed by a lengthy fantasia of the future, *The Shape of Things to Come*. The book purports to be a reprint of a manuscript written by the now deceased Dr Philip Raven, relating the history of the world from the beginning of the twentieth century to the year 2105. It is essentially a much fuller treatment of a thesis he had first elaborated in *Anticipations* (1901) and again in *The World Set Free* (1914): that a terrible and destructive world war would be succeeded by a gradual process of reconstruction and renaissance. In *Anticipations* he had forecast an open freemasonry of dedicated men and women who would remake the world. This open conspiracy of

> capable operative and administrative men inspired by the belief in a
> common theory of social order, will come about – peacefully and
> gradually as a process of change, or violently as a revolution – but
> inevitably as the outcome either of the imminence or else of the disasters
> of war.[11]

This is the scenario which Wells now expanded into a full-scale history, prophesying a 'Last war cyclone' which breaks out in 1940 and continues until 1950, followed by a disintegration into famine, disease and anarchy. The collapse of civilisation into a new dark age is prevented by an elite of technical revolutionaries who unite to impose their will on the shattered fragments of Europe and succeed in rebuilding a system of world order.

The idea of writing a history of the future was one which Wells found irresistibly appealing. Many of his early scientific speculations had taken this form – *The Time Machine* and *When the Sleeper Wakes*, for example – and a number of his short stories, including 'A dream of Armageddon', had been fascinating glimpses into the world of tomorrow. In 'The queer story of Brownlow's newspaper', an entertaining short story published in the *Strand Magazine* in 1932, he had played with the idea of a man who receives a daily newspaper dated forty years hence. He had long been interested in the time theories of J. W. Dunne and in the relationship between dreams and the future; *The Discovery of the Future*, his Royal Institution lecture of 1902, had been based on the notion that the future was 'inductive' and that its broad outlines could be inferred from present trends. To attempt a forecast of the main outlines of world history in the twentieth century was, then, an entirely logical and attractive proposal to one of Wells's temperament and background.

There are immense technical problems inherent in such an undertaking. In writing *The Shape of Things to Come* he chose the device of a partly deciphered manuscript, with its inevitable gaps and inconsistencies. It is a brave conception, but in presenting the history of the future as if narrated by an impartial historian instead of in the form of graphic eye-witness accounts (as he had done in *The World Set Free*) the book becomes a treatise instead of a living and vivid chronicle. There is a dryness about it, a sense of detachment which many readers found off-putting. Where 'The queer story of Brownlow's newspaper' was intriguing and thought-provoking, *The Shape of Things to Come* seemed soulless and autocratic by comparison. Wells's purpose in writing the book was an honourable one: to demonstrate the futility of modern warfare and the disastrous consequences of trying to achieve enduring peace in a world composed of independent sovereign states. As a warning the book was salutary. Unfortunately it simply confirmed the idea already held by many readers that he was an apostle of the inevitability of progress and material advancement at the expense of the human spirit. The titles of many of the chapters – 'Keying up the planet', 'Geogonic planning', 'Changes in the control of behaviour', 'Organisation of plenty' – seemed to confirm this view.The human interest that animates such works as *A Modern Utopia* and *Men Like Gods* was absent from his new scenario. Instead the reader was offered a vision of a planet ruled by benevolent technocrats: a prospect which many (including, one suspects, Wells himself) would have found repellent.

II

By May 1933 he realised he could no longer work effectively at Lou Pidou. It was, he wrote, 'an amateurish, pretty house with a peculiar charm of its own but it insisted upon growing and complicating itself; it became less and less a refuge and more and more of an irksome entanglement with its own baffling bothers and exactions.'[12] He had given the usufruct of the house to Odette Keun for the duration of her lifetime and, accepting that a parting was inevitable, left her in possession. He said farewell to the house and the garden, of which he had been very fond, and travelled to Ragusa (Dubrovnik) where he presided at the Congress of the International PEN Club. From there he went by train to Salzburg for a holiday with Moura. He and Moura were extremely happy together in Austria and Wells asked her to marry him. Moura was not willing to contemplate marriage – she wanted her own independence – but she made it clear she wanted to be his companion and his lover; she was willing to settle in London and to be his helpmate.

A legend has grown up around her, because of her romantic and Russian background, as if she was some kind of Mata Hari figure, a spy or double agent. The truth, though certainly colourful, is more prosaic than the legend. She was born Moura Zakrevsky in 1893 and had been brought up in the Ukraine, a member of an aristocratic family possessing a large house and country estates. In 1911 she had married John von Benckendorff, a Russian nobleman and diplomat, and had remained in Russia throughout the terrifying events of the revolution and the civil war. As a member of the nobility the Bolshevik revolution of 1917 meant the end of a way of life she had known since childhood. Her husband was assassinated in 1919 while staying at his estate near Tallinn in Estonia and thereafter she had spent some years in Petrograd. She had a brief affair with the British diplomat Robert Bruce Lockhart (who wrote about her in his book *Memoirs of a British Agent*) and became Gorky's secretary and interpreter. It was in this capacity that she met Wells in 1920. In 1921 she had married again, this time to an Estonian nobleman Baron Nicolai Budberg. This was purely a marriage of convenience to enable her to acquire Estonian citizenship. After the revolution she had remained in Petrograd (St Petersburg) to look after her sick mother but by doing so had lost her right to apply for Estonian citizenship; this placed her in a difficult position since most of her relatives lived in that country. Gorky's health was failing and he was anxious to move out of Russia to a warmer climate. Gorky was *persona grata* with Lenin and so long as she lived under his 'protection' she was in no danger from the Bolshevik authorities, despite the fact that she was a daughter of the landed gentry. She had no wish to remain in Russia without Gorky; on the other hand she could not make her home in Estonia without a passport. She was in an invidious position since the Estonian authorities, who viewed the Soviet Union with profound suspicion, were sceptical of her motives for wanting to return. Not unnaturally they suspected her of Bolshevik sympathies. Hence her marriage to Baron Budberg; a year after the wedding the Baron went to live in South America and they were divorced in 1926. From 1922 onwards she continued to act as Gorky's secretary, first in Berlin and later at Sorrento, Italy. When Gorky decided in 1933 to leave Sorrento and settle permanently in Moscow with his family, Moura decided not to accompany him. She had long been fascinated by Wells and decided that her loyalties lay with him.

Moura shared many of Rebecca's characteristics: a tendency to 'dress up' the past by romanticising or embroidering incidents; great charm and self-confidence; warmth and humour; and a decided preference for the limelight. Throughout the remaining years of Wells's life she provided him with the companionship and solace for which he craved. In return he provided her with a steadfast friendship and an entrée into English literary and intellectual life. Moura, he wrote in the last decade of his life, 'satisifed my craving for material intimacy more completely than any other human being. I still "belong" so much to her that I cannot really get away from her. I love her still."[13] Moura's daughter, Tania Alexander, described her as a survivor, 'determined to hold on to what she had salvaged and achieved; forced by circumstances to become independent'.[14] She had survived the Russian revolution, the death of her husband and the destruction of her home. She had seen the overthrowing of the Russian nobility and had had to build for herself a completely new life in a strange land. These experiences had given her a fierce independence of spirit, a resolve to make the most of her life regardless of fortune. She repaid Wells's friendship with a loyalty, sympathy and understanding he came to appreciate more and more with the passing of time.

Geoffrey West's biography, *H. G. Wells: A sketch for a portrait*, had been published in 1930. The name 'Geoffrey West' was a pseudonym: the author's real name was Geoffrey H. Wells (no relation by either surname). He had written a life of Annie Besant and a number of critical articles before embarking on his biography of Wells. He had approached his task with great thoroughness, receiving Wells's whole-hearted co-operation in amassing hitherto unpublished correspondence, tapping reminiscences of old friends, and disentangling the complicated history of Wells's literary beginnings. The final result was a readable, competent and reliable biography which, though necessarily incomplete (it had, of course, to stop short at 1930) was a solid attempt to present a rounded portrait of a many-sided personality. Submitting to his biographer's endless questions about his early life and re-reading hundreds of his early letters stimulated Wells's interest in his own life as a source of creative material. The idea of writing an autobiography began to appeal to him more and more, especially as it seemed to him that West had largely skirted round his tangled emotional history, including his love–hate relationship with his mother. The decline of his relationship with Odette was also bothering him and he felt that to spend a year or so in a detailed examination of his own life would be excellent therapy. The project was begun in earnest in the spring of 1933 and the bulk of it was completed by the summer of 1934. He decided to call the book *Experiment in Autobiography: Discoveries and conclusions of a very ordinary brain.*

Experiment in Autobiography is a fascinating account of his life and times from 1866 up to and including the First World War. He did not bring the story of his life beyond this point because this would have involved references to many individuals who were still living. Instead he chose to write a separate *Postscript* detailing his emotional life and instructed his literary executors to publish this volume after his death at a time they judged appropriate. (The *Postscript*, edited by his son G. P. Wells, was finally published in 1984 under the title *H. G. Wells in Love*). The nine chapters of the autobiography offer a highly readable and candid survey of Wells's mental and personal development including his years at Bromley, his schooling, his experiences as a science student in London, his breakdown in health, his years as a teacher and his early literary career. The autobiographical chapters are interspersed with two sections of analysis: an introductory section examining the 'quality of the brain and body concerned', and a lengthy chapter entitled 'Dissection', in which he subjects his own emotional self to a detailed and dispassionate scrutiny. The result is a refreshingly honest book in which Wells does his utmost to unravel the complications of his personality and in the process to arrive at a closer understanding of himself. There is a genuine attempt to present a balanced account of his two marriages, his feelings towards his parents, and the defects in his own make-up that had led him again and again to uproot himself from unpalatable situations. The overriding impression is of a continuing struggle against claustrophobia, ill health and frustration to win for himself a place in the sun: a determination to triumph over every obstacle. In its candour, humour, honesty and ebullience it remains one of his most engaging and characteristic works. Within its pages he encompasses the whole range of his life, work and thought and disentangles as far as any man can do the strengths and weaknesses of his own temperament.

On its publication in 1934 *Experiment in Autobiography* was widely reviewed and brought him an extensive correspondence. Many old friends took the opportunity to write to him including two colleagues from South Kensington days, R. A. Gregory and William Burton. Odette Keun, reviewing the autobiography in *Time and Tide*, took the opportunity to lambast him in a series of articles entitled 'H. G. Wells: the player', accusing him of changing 'almost from one moon to another, his ground, his angle, and his solutions'.[15] She insisted that he had betrayed the thousands of readers who had been inspired by such books as *A Modern Utopia* and *First and Last Things* and was a wholly inconsistent thinker. He found her outburst irritating but his anger soon passed. He was content to bide his time and take his revenge later.

Franklin Roosevelt's New Deal had been launched in the United States early in 1933 and for some time Wells had wanted to meet the new President. At the same time he was fascinated by developments in the USSR and longed to meet the Soviet leader, Stalin. In the spring and summer of 1934 he achieved his ambition by travelling to Washington and Moscow to interview the two statesmen. He was greatly encouraged by his meeting with Roosevelt, believing him to be 'the most effective transmitting instrument possible for the coming of the new world order'.[16] He recognised in Roosevelt a freshness of approach and a willingness to innovate that he found heartening; the President, he felt, was an 'open conspirator', a member of that elite of dedicated leaders who would help to remake the world. The meeting with Stalin was, by contrast, profoundly discouraging. During their three-hour meeting Stalin listened courteously enough to what he had to say but replied to his arguments with repetitions of Marxist dogma. Wells tried to persuade him that the notion of class war was now outmoded and that the USSR and the USA must learn to live peacefully together. Stalin would have none of it. Conflict between communism and capitalism was inevitable, he asserted, and Wells was being naïve in believing otherwise. All Wells's attempts to reason with him were in vain. Stalin countered his arguments with a reassertion of Marxist and Leninist theology, concluding that Wells was an incurable bourgeoise. Wells came away from the meeting with a favourable impression of Stalin as a man – he liked his brusque candour – but deeply depressed by his dogmatism, in such total contrast to Roosevelt's openness. He was even more depressed when he met Gorky, who had now lapsed from his former intellectual integrity into an uncritical supporter of Stalin's regime. Gorky died two years later, a pathetic shadow of his old self. Wells recorded his impressions of his American and Russian visits in two books, *The New America: The new world* and *Stalin – Wells Talk*. He had learned much from the experience, not least an appreciation of the immense difficulties impeding any effective movement towards international co-operation. Back in London he threw himself into the effort to project his ideas more widely, to explore every means of furthering the concept of world order.

Though Wells and Rebecca had not met for several years they continued to take a keen interest in each other's work and when in 1935 Rebecca published a new volume of short stories, *The Harsh Voice* – her first work of fiction since *Harriet Hume* in 1929 – he wrote requesting a copy. He was deeply impressed by the craftmanship of the stories. It seemed to him that she had lost the prolixity of her early work in favour of a more restrained and polished style. He wrote to congratulate her:

> You have a richness. I am simplicity. That is why I came off artistically from the beginning and got slovenly later and why you had to begin with such a spate of undisciplined imagination in *The Judge* before you got to the MASTERY of these stories.[17]

From this point onwards until the end of his life Wells and Rebecca were on terms of increasing warmth. The easy cordiality of their old relationship returned to them and they were able to forget the rancour that had marred their friendship before her departure for America. There were several reasons for this growing affection. One was that Jane Wells, whom Rebecca had always mistrusted and resented, was now dead. While Jane was alive Rebecca had found it impossible to come to terms with the hold his wife exercised over his mind and emotions; Rebecca felt she was simply a 'mistress' and as such occupied an inferior position. Jane's death dramatically altered the situation. Now there was no longer a Mrs H. G. Wells no one was in a secondary position and she no longer felt she was merely a pawn in the triangle of wife-mistress-home. Wells's readjustment to the fact of Jane's passing had been a slow one – she had, after all, played a central role in his life from 1892 onwards and her death created a void no one else could fill. His friendships with Odette Keun and Moura Budberg met his emotional needs but these were in no way comparable to the intimate relationship he had enjoyed with Jane.

Another reason was that disagreements about Anthony now seemed to be a thing of the past. He had come through the traumas of his schooling and his brief flirtation with religion and was now old enough to reach his own decisions about life. Rebecca had sometimes felt that Wells's keen interest in Anthony's education was a disruptive influence but now that Anthony was 21 this was a bone of contention which no longer rankled. A third reason was the fact that both had a genuine respect for the other's writings and ideas and shared a common concern for the deteriorating situation in Europe. With the rise of Nazism and Fascism both Wells and Rebecca clearly foresaw the coming of war and deeply deplored the ambivalent attitude of Baldwin and Chamberlain towards the dictators. They shared a fundamental belief in freedom of thought and expression and both worked through International PEN to warn against the rising tide of intolerance.

But the basic reason for their growing cordiality was that they had a fundamental liking for one another. Their friendship had survived the quarrels of 1923 and regained the warmth they had enjoyed for so many years. 'Our relations have mellowed more and more' he wrote, adding that she could live with her husband 'without the perpetual friction of antagonistic mental disposition and conflicting literary ambitions.'[18]

In writing his autobiography and the *Postscript* Wells had summarised his attitude of mind and the forces that had shaped his outlook on the world. He still felt the need to clarify his beliefs on matters of conduct and morality and in a new book, *The Anatomy of Frustration*, he set to work to produce an imitation of Burton's *Anatomy of Melancholy*, discussing the frustrations which impede the achievement of happiness. Because of the provisional nature of his beliefs and the fact that on many issues he was divided in his own mind he invented a fictitious author to be the vehicle of his thoughts: a device Carlyle had employed in *Sartor Resartus* and which he himself had adopted in *Boon*. This imaginary writer, William Burroughs Steele, is an industrialist who settles down in his retirement to present a distillation of his world, in much the same manner as William Clissold had done ten years earlier. *The Anatomy of Frustration* is an attempt to answer the question: What prevents us from achieving contentment? In a lengthy chapter entitled 'Frustration through loneliness and the craving for a lover' Wells in the guise of his *alter ego* discusses the contradictions within his personality that have prevented him from attaining a fully harmonious emotional relationship:

> After all my reasoning I come to the fact that I am quite irrational here. What I want in my heart is a Personal, Intimate, Subservient, Devoted, Private Divinity, a genius like the genius of Socrates, a confidant who will not know what I want to conceal but will know whatever I want to have known. And somehow this has got to be embodied in an attractive, variable, interesting woman who will respond to my desire.[19]

He has to admit that this is an impossible dream, that the idea of a 'private divinity' who will be utterly devoted to himself is at heart a selfish concept and that the pursuit of it is in any case an illusion. In an interesting passage Wells comments on Steele's views and in doing so tries to come to terms with the ambivalence in his own make-up. He is fascinated by the contradiction between, on the one hand, the idea of a fixation on one cherished and loved person and, on the other, the notion of a deliberate promiscuity. At last he has to admit that he cannot reconcile the two:

> He argues to and fro because he is obviously troubled and uncertain in his own mind about it. Nowhere else is he so much the dissatisfied explorer. He has a bias against his own convictions. He is divided against himself. Manifestly Steele was disposed imaginatively for an 'exclusive love', life in duet form – which his critical intelligence refused to endorse.[20]

Here and elsewhere in *The Anatomy of Frustration* Wells is debating with himself and trying to face the fact of his irrationality. Again and again there is an implicit contrast between his imaginative intuitions and his rational intellect, between the romantic and classical drives which had divided him psychologically since childhood. In this book he is thinking aloud – in a manner that recalls the discussions between Boon and Wilkins in *Boon* – and, as it were, arguing between the two sides of his personality. The book is not only a guide to his state of mind in 1936 but a fascinating commentary on his attitudes to human relationships. Temperamentally he was deeply attracted by the idea of an exclusive fixation on one human being who would be the embodiment of all his dreams and desires. Intellectually he rejected this and instead developed relationships with different partners to meet his emotional and creative needs. But the two ideas were warring in his mind simultaneously and could not be reconciled. In trying to follow both paths at the same time he was attempting the impossible. For all these reasons *The Anatomy of Frustration* is one of Wells's most personal and revealing works and merits much wider critical attention than it has yet received. The fact that he tries to define his attitude to love and human relationships in several different ways and, with each definition, discusses the emotional issues involved is an indication of the importance he attached to personal relationships and the uncertainties within his own mind concerning the roots of behaviour.

In the mid-1930s his interest in the film as an art form revived powerfully. *The King who was a King*, the scenario he had written in 1929, had not materialised as a film though he had learned much from the experiment. Now, stimulated by new developments in cinema technique and by his growing friendship with Alexander Korda he set to work to transform some of his stories into film treatments. During 1935 he adapted four of his works into scenarios: *Things to Come, The Man Who Could Work Miracles, The New Faust* (an adaptation of his short story 'The story of the late Mr Elvesham') and *The Food of the Gods*. Of these only the first two saw the light of day as films, both produced by Korda and directed by Cameron Menzies and Lothar Mendes respectively. *Things to Come*, launched in a tremendous fanfare of publicity in February 1936, was a considerable success for Korda – and for the young stars Ralph Richardson, Raymond Massey and Ann Todd – but a huge disappointment for Wells. He had invested immense hopes in its realisation, taken a keen interest in the work of production and worked closely with all concerned, including the composer Arthur Bliss, to achieve a satisfactory rendering of his ideas. 'It was, I saw plainly', he wrote, 'pretentious, clumsy and scamped. I had fumbled with it.'[21] Wells placed much of the blame for this on Alexander Korda and Cameron Menzies but some of the responsibility surely lay with himself. The film's brilliant opening sequences depicting an air raid on a typical English community were a powerful argument against war and an astonishingly accurate forecast of the reality of aerial warfare, but the scenes that lingered in the mind were those portraying the reconstruction after the world war and the building of underground cities. It is these sequences, with their apparent emphasis on technological advancement and the creation of a soulless megalopolis, which have done more than any other single work by Wells to foster the notion of science as a panacea for all the world's ills. Thousands (probably millions if one counts the television screenings) have seen *Things to Come* and based their knowledge of Wells on this one film. The result is a persistent myth that Wells advocated scientific and technical 'progress' *per se* as the simple solution to the problems of mankind. *Things to Come* – by distorting, telescoping and oversimplifying his ideas – must bear a large proportion of blame for this misconception. Of those who flocked to see the film only a tiny minority would have read his novels and stories and grasped the truth that the film was a noisy exaggeration of his ideas. Dissatisfied with *Things to Come* and *The Man Who Could Work Miracles* – though he had to admit that the latter was 'a more coherent work of art altogether than its predecessor'[22] – he cast about for a more effective medium for creative expression.

III

Once Moura had settled permanently in London – she established herself in a small apartment near the British Museum – he decided to give up the flat at Chiltern Court and move into 13 Hanover Terrace, Regents Park. This was an elegant and spacious Nash house and had been the home of the poet Alfred Noyes. He moved into Hanover Terrace in the spring of 1935 and this remained his home for the remainder of his life. Here he spent much of his time, writing, entertaining friends, going for walks around Regents Park or the Botanical Gardens, and often lunching at the Savile Club. At the bottom of the back garden was a mews flat which he christened 'Mr Mumford's', containing odds and ends of furniture he had originally acquired at Easton Glebe. Here Anthony lived when he stayed with his father. The two were now seeing each other frequently and during these years Wells and Anthony became good friends. 'I came to like him, and to respect him', Anthony wrote later. 'All that I have learned of him since his death has increased my respect for him.'[23] Moura came to see Wells at 13 Hanover Terrace almost daily and continued to do so until the end. Surrounded by his books, stimulated by his friends, he entered the closing phase of his life determined to do all he could to warn mankind of approaching catastrophe.

A glance at the bibliography of his published writings from 1936 to the outbreak of the Second World War in 1939 reveals an astonishingly prolific output including novellas, lectures, film scenarios and a wide variety of journalism. In addition to four novellas – *The Croquet Player*, *Star Begotten*, *The Camford Visitation* and *The Brothers* – he found time to write three collections of non-fiction pieces, *World Brain*, *Travels of a*

17. H. G. Wells, Maxim Gorky and Moura Benckendorff in 1920.

18. H. G. Wells, *circa* 1920. His reputation as a novelist was now fading and being replaced by renown as a journalist, prophet and popular educationist.

19. Anthony West, 1970. He was then aged 56 and had returned to Britain after a twenty-year spell as book reviewer for the *New Yorker*.

20. Anthony West, *circa* 1984. The year saw the publication of his biography, *H. G. Wells: Aspects of a life* and the publication of the first British edition of his novel, *Heritage*. He died in December 1987, aged 73.

21. H. G. Wells, 1930. With the death of his wife Jane he had reached a turning point in his life and was about to embark on writing his autobiography.

22. Rebecca West, *circa* 1932. She was now a critic of international renown, contributing regular book reviews to leading journals in Britain and the United States.

23. 13 Hanover
Terrace, Regent's
Park, Wells's
home during the
final decade of
his life. He
remained here
throughout the
war years,
Rebecca sending
him food parcels
from her
country home.

24. H. G. Wells,
circa 1940. He
remained a
prolific writer to
the end of his
life, publishing
his last novel,
*You Can't Be Too
Careful* at the age
of 75. He died
on 13 August
1946, aged 79.

Republican Radical and *The Fate of Homo Sapiens*, and three full-length novels, *Brynhild*, *Apropos of Dolores* and *The Holy Terror*. He was hammering away at his leading ideas and at the same time determined not to abandon fiction as a medium of expression.

From the beginning of the decade onwards he had been consciously experimenting with a variety of literary forms in his search for a congenial vehicle for his ideas. Looking back on his literary career in his autobiography he had written: 'I may write a story or so more – a dialogue, an adventure or an anecdote. But I shall never come as near to a deliberate attempt upon The Novel again as I did in *Tono-Bungay*.'[24] He had found the attempt to translate his ideas into scenario form both challenging and frustrating. Now in his seventieth year he realised that the genre with which he had launched himself as an imaginative writer forty years earlier, the allegory in the manner of Swift and Voltaire, could after all prove to be the ideal forum for a man of his talents. He set to work to write a novella, *The Croquet Player*, which would embody his growing sense of foreboding at the contagion of cruelty and evil in human affairs and express this in the form of a powerful and haunting allegory. The result was one of his most unforgettable stories, a beautifully written fable in which he returned to the manner of his early romances.

In form it belongs to the genre known as 'the tale within a tale', a device he had employed with great success in *The Time Machine* and such short stories as 'The door in the wall' and 'Aepyornis Island'. George Frobisher, an effeminate young man who delights in playing croquet and bridge, is sitting on a terrace at Les Noupets sipping a vermouth when he is accosted by a stranger, Dr Finchatton, who engages him in conversation. Finchatton describes a district in the Fens called Cains-marsh which is haunted by a brooding sense of fear and evil. He is convinced that the district was populated by Neanderthal man for vast periods of time and that the cruelty and savagery of the ape-man are infecting human behaviour.

> The animal fears again and the animal rages again and the old faiths no longer restrain it. The cave-man, the ancestral ape, the ancestral brute have returned . . . You have felt them in the marsh, but I tell you these resurrected savageries are breathing now and thrusting everywhere.

Finchatton is obsessed by 'the deep fountains of cruelty in the human make-up', by the irrational violence and fear that is spreading like a contagion through this peaceful area of England. He is shown a Neanderthal skull in a museum and has terrifying nightmares of blood and evil. Finchatton tells his story with such conviction that the croquet player is completely taken in by his yarn. At this point a psychiatrist

appears, Dr Norbert, who explains that Finchatton is a patient of his
and that the story he has told is a fable, a myth designed to simplify a
deeply disturbing truth: that the spirit of the ancestral ape is now at
large throughout the world.

> Man is still what he was. Invincibly bestial, envious, malicious, greedy.
> Man, sir, unmasked and disillusioned is the same fearing, snarling,
> fighting beast he was a hundred thousand years ago . . . The brute has
> been marking time and dreaming of a progress it has failed to make.

Frobisher takes an immediate dislike to the psychiatrist and at last
succeeds in ridding himself of his company by insisting that he has to
play croquet with his aunt. But he is haunted by the story Finchatton
has told him and has to admit to the reader that 'I have been talking to
two very queer individuals and they have produced a peculiar disturbance of my mind.' The croquet player, who has hitherto led an
easy-going, sheltered life untroubled by disturbing thoughts, is deeply
disoriented by the story of Cainsmarsh and realises he has been told a
metaphor to explain the resurgence of barbarism in Europe.

The Croquet Player is economically told – it runs to some 18,000 words –
and is written in prose of disarming simplicity and power. The
narrative possesses a haunting quality that lingers in the mind long
after it has been laid aside, so much so that certain images are etched
permanently on the reader's consciousness:

> One would hear the sheep upon the lavender-coloured hills, four or five
> miles away, or the scream of some distant water-fowl, like a long, harsh
> scratch of neon light across the silent blue, or the sound of the wind and
> the sea, a dozen miles away at Beacon Ness, like the world breathing in its
> sleep.

In writing it Wells sensed he had hit upon a medium through which he
could convey his growing unease concerning the human condition, and
could do so with greater effectiveness than in a full-scale novel on the
pattern of *Joan and Peter*. He was greatly sustained in this belief by the
unanimous praise of the critics. *The Daily Mail* described *The Croquet
Player* as a 'masterpiece of exact and dovetailed narrative'; *The Observer*
praised it as having 'all those maturities of style, wisdom and vision
which reveal the master'; *The Manchester Guardian* described Wells as 'a
master of human reactions to the uncanny'; while *The Sunday Times*
expressed gratitude to him 'for a fable so brilliantly provocative'.

The novella was published at a time of growing tension in European
affairs when torture, violence, persecution and intolerance were on the
ascendant. In September 1935 Jews had been outlawed in Nazi

Germany, in March 1936 German troops occupied the Rhineland and in July the Spanish Civil War began. There were ominous signs of a rise of intolerance and an abandonment of the norms of civilised behaviour. Faced with the rapid deterioration of standards of conduct and an erosion of the rule of law Wells was swift to grasp the urgency of the situation. Anthony West was seeing much more of his father at this time and had many opportunities of conversing with him about the world situation. Anthony wrote:

> In the end I believe, on the strength of conversations which I had with him on the particular subject of what he had meant by Dr Moreau, and on some related topics, that he came to feel that a realisation of the truth of the human situation, in all its ultimate hopelessness, was much more likely to stir men to present effort to make life more tolerable than any pretence . . . At the close of his life, from *The Croquet Player* onwards, he was trying to recapture the spirit in which he had written *The Island of Doctor Moreau*, and what haunted him, and made him exceedingly unhappy, was a tragic sense that he had returned to the real source of what could have been his strength too late.[25]

The Croquet Player merits a place alongside *Candide* and *Animal Farm* as one of those enduring myths which illuminate the human situation. It demonstrates that Wells's gifts as a storyteller were as formidable as ever and that the spirit of Swift walked with him as it had done since his days at Uppark.

With the approach of his seventieth birthday in 1936 the PEN Club organised a dinner in his honour at the Savoy Hotel. After tributes had been paid to him by J. B. Priestley and other distinguished guests, Wells rose to make a poignant speech in which he said that he felt like 'a little boy at a lovely party, who has been given quite a lot of jolly toys and who has spread his play about on the floor. Then comes his nurse. 'Now Master Bertie', she says, 'it's getting late. Time you began to put away your toys.' He spoke of his plans for more books and of his hopes for the PEN Club at a time of rising international tension, concluding with an affirmation of the need 'for freedom of expression, the utmost freedom of expression and criticism, and a frank and friendly brotherhood and mutual patience among all honest writers, thinkers and creators'.[26] It was a wistful speech expressing regret at the passing of the years and his feeling that there was still so much he wanted to do. As yet he felt little decline in his physical or mental powers; he was still vigorous and looked ten years younger than his actual age.

Among the many letters of congratulation he received from friends scattered throughout the world two must have given him especial pleasure. The first was from his old friend William Burton, who had kept in touch since student days:

My dear Wells,
Mrs Burton and I send you our heartiest congratulations on your
seventieth birthday. What courage it bespeaks in you to have done so
much of permanent value to humanity. It is splendid and no one can
rejoice more in your accomplishments than ourselves, who must surely,
now, rank among your oldest friends.

Your friend, ever,
William Burton

The second was dated 21 September 1936, the date of his birthday, and
ran as follows:

Dear Jaguar,
I was so happy to learn from today's newspapers that our old old habit of
forgetting each other's birthdays had not been broken. Congratulations,
dear Jaguar. Lots more of everything.

With best love,
Panther[27]

Brynhild, published in 1937, shows no diminution in his powers as a
storyteller and an impressive ability to look at situations from the point
of view of his female protagonist. Brynhild is the wife of a successful
popular novelist, Rowland Palace. He is obsessed with the search for
publicity in order to enhance his public reputation and engages an agent
to boost his image. His wife, who is described as 'a fair-haired young
woman, with a broad serene face and kind brown eyes' sees through his
poses and pretensions but nurses him through all his crises of confidence. Gentle, wise and understanding, she is utterly devoted to her
husband and knows how to handle his moods of tetchiness and doubt.
Her calm, sympathetic character is clearly based on that of Moura
Budberg. Re-reading the novel today it is Brynhild's character that
remains in the mind – dependable, shrewd and kindly – in the sharpest
contrast to the shallow and erratic Rowland Palace. What is so
remarkable about *Brynhild* is the way in which Wells succeeds in
reaching inside her mind and conveying to the reader her innermost
reflections. Throughout the novel but particularly in the chapters
'Nocturne' and 'Mrs Palace meditates on the lot of women' one is aware
of a conscious attempt to present the narrative from her perspective
rather than from the male standpoint one normally associates with
Wells's novels. Not since *Ann Veronica* had he succeeded so ably in
presenting a feminine perspective.

Brynhild is a sympathetic listener and when a rising young novelist,
Alfred Bunter, wishes to unburden his soul he turns naturally to her.
Bunter's wife Freda (a recognisable portrait of Odette Keun) is excit-
able, possessive and egotistical. The contrast between the wise and

gentle Brynhild and the loud and assertive Freda is sharply drawn; Wells is throwing into relief two contrasting personalities – one placid and understanding, the other flamboyant and malicious – both clearly drawn from life. Though Brynhild has no illusions concerning her husband's weaknesses there is a genuine bond of affection between them and at one point she reflects on how much she loves him:

> What a wonderful abundant realisation of life this love in marriage was, this intensive exploration of a personality into which one flowed and which flowed into one. It was like going through a vast gift mansion of treasures and discovering unsuspected rooms and corridors of quaint and amusing things.[28]

In the following year Wells drew another sketch of Moura as Catherine Farness in his novella *The Brothers*. She is depicted as the serene and gracious lover of Bolaris, the leader of one of the factions in a civil war. Bolaris 'had an intense affection for her, an admiration, a belief in a sort of textural wisdom of body and impulse in her, far surpassing his own mental processes'. In the characters of Brynhild and Catherine we glimpse something of Moura's spirit and an inkling of what her companionship and understanding must have meant to Wells. In Moura he had found a kindred spirit, a 'textural wisdom of body and impulse' that sustained him during the final decade of his life.

His next novel *Apropos of Dolores* is a deliciously funny book in which he drew freely on his recollections of Odette Keun to present a good-humoured portrait of an exasperating woman. It purports to be the memoirs of Stephen Wilbeck, a publisher who is writing about his now deceased wife, Dolores, and describing their life together in France. A genial opening chapter, 'Happy interlude', is followed by a series of chapters portraying their meeting, their subsequent marriage and their hilarious adventures in various resorts in Brittany and the Riviera. In writing the novel Wells found he could look back on Odette without malice and describe her with a detachment made possible by the passage of time. The long section entitled 'Dolores at Torquestol' is a bitingly humorous account of her ability to disrupt the most well ordered hotel (it would make an amusing television play) and this is followed by an equally droll account of Dolores's funeral. Despite the vociferous nature of Dolores the book is notable for its air of detached calm. Wilbeck notes that he has a 'Boswell self, beyond doubt the happiest of all my selves'. In these Boswell moods the narrator regards his world with genial benevolence, determined that nothing shall mar his disposition towards kindliness. The mood returns to him at the end of the novel when he reviews his life with calm detachment:

> Stoical agnosticism is the only possible religion for sane adults. Accept

and endure what happens to you, from within just as much as from without. Do what is right in your own eyes, for there is no other guide. Go on. Go on to your end. Go on without either absolutes of believing or disbelieving, without extremities either of hope or despair.[29]

Apropos of Dolores provides convincing evidence that at the age of 72 he had lost none of his ability to tell a good tale or to entertain. In its humour, wisdom and pathos it recalls the novels of his early maturity. But in addition to these qualities it possesses a dimension much less in evidence in the Edwardian novels: the ability to reach inside the mind of his characters and probe the driving forces of human behaviour. Stephen and Dolores Wilbeck are both deeply divided individuals; each is a tangle of warring motives and desires. The exploration of their personalities forms the substance of the novel, for in describing Dolores and in seeking to understand her character Wilbeck reveals much about himself. 'In the case of Stephen Wilbeck versus Dolores', he concludes, 'I condemn both parties, with a recommendation to mercy. Each had a wicked heart and if she was an uncontrollable scream, he was a deadly self-protective companion for her.'

IV

Meanwhile the steady drift towards war continued. In July 1937 fighting broke out between Japanese and Chinese troops; in November an Air Raid Precautions Bill was introduced in the House of Commons; in February 1938 the British Foreign Secretary, Anthony Eden, resigned in protest at Chamberlain's policy of appeasement. Three weeks later German troops invaded Austria which was immediately declared to be part of the German Reich. Japan was sweeping ahead with military victories in China and Franco was victorious in Spain. In September 1938 Chamberlain visited Hitler at Munich and agreed to the dismemberment of Czechoslovakia; in October Japan withdrew from the League of Nations. Wells watched the accelerating decline of international order with mounting alarm and a growing feeling of impotence. As long ago as 1908 in *The War in the Air* he had foreseen the aerial bombardment of cities and in the concluding chapters, 'The great collapse' and 'Epilogue' had described a civilisation shattered by war and pestilence. He had repeated the warning in *The World Set Free* and again in *The Shape of Things to Come*. His thesis was that developments in communication and technology meant that the earth was now one community and that in an age of mass destruction the government of the world by a patchwork quilt of independent sovereign states was a dangerous anachronism. In a spate of books, pamphlets and lectures he hammered away at his central idea that mankind was drifting inexorably towards disaster and that *Homo sapiens* must adapt or perish.

World Brain brings together a series of lectures and articles advocating a 'world encyclopaedia'. By this he meant the linking together of libraries and information services throughout the world into one integrated system covering all fields of knowledge. The idea was fifty years ahead of its time, but in a world without computer and microchip technology and increasingly obsessed by the rise of Hitler and Mussolini his pleas fell on deaf ears. In *The Camford Visitation*, a carefully written novella set in an imaginary university town, he attempted a fictional presentation of the same thesis. An inhuman voice disturbs the cloistered academic peace of Holy Innocents College, Camford, raising pointed questions concerning the meaning and purpose of education. The impact of the visitation on the sheltered community is vividly described: the initial intrusion of the voice, the shocked disbelief of the dons assembled in the dining room, their attempts to find a conventional explanation for the unseen presence. The technique is similar to that of *The Invisible Man* – the arrival of a strange visitant in a small community and its impact on a cross-section of the local population, like a stone dropped into a still pool. 'There is no salvation for races that will not save themselves', the voice concludes. 'Half the stars in the sky are the burning rubbish of worlds that might have been.'

Travels of a Republican Radical in Search of Hot Water contains a number of polemical articles on the world situation including an eloquent paper on 'The honour and dignity of the free mind', an address he had planned to deliver at the PEN Congress at Stockholm on the eve of the outbreak of war. The Congress did not take place but his address stands as a powerful summary of the liberal humanist attitude. *Travels of a Republican Radical* was published as a Penguin Special, the first of a series he wrote for Penguin Books and which were widely read and discussed. *The Fate of Homo Sapiens*, published by the new firm of Secker & Warburg in August 1939, has the subtitle: 'An unemotional statement of the things that are happening to him now, and of the immediate possibilities confronting him'. It is a survey of the world situation as he perceived it at that time and a recapitulation of his plea for world order and world education. 'There is no reason whatever to believe that the order of nature has any greater bias in favour of man than it had in favour of the icthyosaur or the pterodactyl', he concluded. 'Adapt or perish, that is and always has been the implacable law of life for all its children.'[30] In essence he was repeating the argument he had first advanced in his scientific essays of the 1890s: that man was subject to the same evolutionary laws as any other biological species. In 'The extinction of man' (*Pall Mall Gazette*, 25 September 1894) he had written:

'In the case of every other predominant animal the world has ever seen
. . . the hour of its complete ascendancy has been the eve of its entire
overthrow.' The stoical cosmic vision he had imbibed from Huxley had
never left him. As Europe capsized into war Wells's mood remained
that of the seer: the man who had studied evolution at South
Kensington, who saw all life as one process and now watched in horror
as civilisation collapsed about him.

When war was declared in September 1939 Wells took the view that
it was the duty of the citizen to support the war effort without
argument. He had no patience with Chamberlain and the appeasers but
equally did not agree with conscientious objectors. This attitude led to
some violent arguments with Anthony who held strong pacifist views,
but despite the arguments he and Anthony remained good friends. At
the age of 73 there was little he could do in practical terms to 'do his bit'
but he plunged with characteristic energy into the campaign to define
the war aims of the Allies. In a series of letters to *The Times* strongly
reminiscent of his 'Memorandum on propaganda policy' during the
First World War he pleaded for a clear definition of war aims including a
restatement of the fundamental rights of man.

Ritchie Calder, then science correspondent of the *Daily Herald*, took
up the debate. Soon Wells found himself invited to be chairman of a
drafting committee including his old friend Sir Richard Gregory, Lord
Horder, Margaret Bondfield, Sir Norman Angell and Lord Sankey,
entrusted with the task of defining a basic code of human rights.
Though Wells was temperamentally ill-suited to working as a member
of a committee (he soon bowed out of the chairmanship in favour of
Sankey) his enthusiasm and feverish energy carried the others along.
After many meetings and much hard work the group arrived at the
draft of the Sankey Declaration of the Rights of Man. It was an
eloquent and far-seeing document couched in unmistakably Wellsian
terms. 'Within the space of little more than a hundred years there has
been a complete revolution in the material conditions of human life', it
began: 'It becomes imperative to adjust man's life and institutions to the
increasing dangers and opportunities of these new circumstances.'[31]
The Declaration did not have the immediate impact Wells had hoped,
though he sent a personal copy to President Roosevelt and its ringing
phrases may have had some influence on the Atlantic Charter. He did
not live to see the essence of the Declaration incorporated in the
Universal Declaration of Human Rights (1948) but for the remainder of
his life the promulgation and discussion of fundamental human freedoms was an abiding concern.

In *The Holy Terror*, a novel published as war clouds gathered, his
imaginary hero, Rud Whitlow, is a disagreeable egomaniac whose
ambition is to become dictator of the world. *The Holy Terror* is an inferior

production which many readers found inexplicable, but it was followed by a much more promising experiment, *Babes in the Darkling Wood*. This is a courageous attempt to describe the impact of the war on a group of ordinary English people, in the same manner as *Mr Britling Sees it Through* had portrayed the impact of 1914. It focuses on two young lovers, Stella Kentlake and Gemini Twain, and describes their life and experiences between June 1939 and May 1940. In doing so it seeks to capture the mood in England during the months leading up to the outbreak of war and its immediate aftermath, tracing the change in attitudes through the adventures, thoughts and reflections of the young couple. Despite a tendency to *talk at* the reader (particularly evident in a lengthy final chapter, 'Hope and plan for living', in which he falls into a steady treatise on the world situation) the novel succeeds remarkably well in its intention. It is vivid, convincing, and has a strong narrative line that holds the reader's attention.

The novel is prefaced by an introduction headed 'The novel of ideas' in which he makes a vigorous defence of the dialogue novel, 'the tradition of discussing fundamental human problems in dialogue form'. After a review of his own contribution to the genre in such novels as *The Undying Fire* and *Joan and Peter*, he turns to a discussion of *Babes in the Darkling Wood*, describing it as 'the most comprehensive and ambitious dialogue novel I have ever attempted':

> So far as my observation and artistry as a novelist has enabled me to achieve it, there is not a single individual in this book that you might not meet and recognise in the street. If you have had any experience in writing fiction, I think you will find that you can take any of my characters out of this book and invent a meeting between them and the real people you know.[32]

The two principal characters Stella and Gemini, their landlady Mrs Greedle, Gemini's father, a forbidding magistrate, and Stella's mother Lucy Kentlake are all solid and believable people whose interaction forms a varied and accomplished story. One of the most interesting sections of the novel is the part entitled 'Nightmare of reality', describing Gemini's disappearance during a visit to Poland on the eve of the German invasion. His inexplicable silence compels Stella to re-examine her feelings towards him and to come to terms with the realisation that he may be dead. In discovering that he is alive, though mentally ill, Stella realises the depth of her love for him and the bonds of affection which unite them. The spirit and determination of the lovers in the face of a world that appears to be disintegrating all around them forms the most heartening element in the story.

In his Introduction Wells refers to 'the very great burthen of fresh philosophical matter that this novel has to carry'. At times the reader is almost overwhelmed by the torrent of ideas poured upon him or her – on philosophy, psychology, religion, the war. In this sense the novel is marred by the same faults that had weakened *Marriage* and *Joan and Peter*. Yet always one is aware of the novelist's guiding hand in the background, shaping and controlling. When Gemini's father, the irate William Twain, descends on the cottage where Gemini and Stella are 'living in sin' the subsequent confrontation is convincingly and amusingly realised, forming one of the main 'set pieces' of the novel. One can only admire Wells's tremendous energy in continuing to produce novels, journalism, lectures and essays as Europe capsized into war. For the second time in his lifetime the world was in conflict and civilised values and human freedoms were visibly in retreat. As he watched the growing conflagration and reflected on the fact that all his warnings of disaster had apparently been in vain he decided that his epitaph would have to be: 'I told you so. You *damned* fools.'[33]

On 16 July 1940 Hitler ordered the German armed forces to prepare for an invasion of England: 'As England, in spite of her hopeless military situation, still shows no sign of willingness to come to terms, I have decided to prepare, and if necessary to carry out, a landing operation against her.' In the same month, on the orders of Heinrich Himmler, Reichsführer of the SS and Chief of the State Police, a list was drawn up of prominent persons who were to be arrested immediately in the event of invasion. The list included 2,700 names who were to be rounded up by the Gestapo, including Cabinet ministers, writers, artists and Members of Parliament. Prominent on the list were H. G. Wells and Rebecca West. In the summer of 1940 a German invasion of Britain seemed a very real possibility. Fearing that a German landing was imminent and that Rebecca might be compromised if their correspondence fell into enemy hands Wells apparently decided to destroy all her letters. Virtually every letter she had sent him during their ten-year partnership was burnt.

Despite the threat of invasion and the constant bombing raids on London he remained at 13 Hanover Terrace throughout the war years, only varying his routine by occasional jaunts to Moura's daughter's home in the Oxfordshire countryside. Even then he did not depart from his routine of spending every morning writing. Early in the war Lance Sieveking was commissioned by RKO to write a film scenario based on *The History of Mr Polly* and Wells and Sieveking worked closely together on the project. Wells told him that *Mr Polly* was 'the most autobiographical of all his novels, and the one for which in old age he had most concern that it should be done justice to on the screen'.[34] In the event the film adaptation was never made (though John Mills was to make a fine version in 1949) but Wells's close attention to the script and his willingness to spend many hours working on the proposal is an indication of how deeply his heart lay in the writing of fiction and of his concern for his own early work. Sieveking recorded that Wells 'came back to it with the authentic freshness of fun and invention with which he had first told the story nearly forty years earlier'.

From the autumn of 1940 to the beginning of January 1941 he undertook a lecture tour of the United States, speaking on 'Two hemispheres or one world' and 'The immediate future of mankind'. The main argument of his lectures was a plea for the United States and the Soviet Union to work together to achieve a lasting peace and a stable post-war world: a thesis which requires no advocacy today but was considered faintly Utopian in 1940. On his return to London he threw himself into writing about the world crisis and the prospect of post-war reconstruction, producing in rapid succession *Guide to the New World*, *The Outlook for Homo Sapiens*, *Science and the World Mind* and *Phoenix: A summary of the inescapable conditions of world reorganisation*. In each of these books he was hammering away at the fundamental proposition he had argued in season and out of season since 1918: that the world was now one community and there was no hope of enduring peace without planetary institutions.

Much of 1941 was devoted to the writing of *You Can't Be Too Careful*, which he intended to be his 'best and most comprehensive novel'.[35] The death of James Joyce and Virginia Woolf early in that year may have led him to speculate afresh about the meaning and purpose of the novel as an art form and how his own conception of the role of the novelist differed fundamentally from theirs. In *You Can't Be Too Careful* he set out to produce a work which would embody his theory of fiction and at the same time be an entertaining and thought provoking parable highlighting the human dilemma. In form it is a *Bildungsroman*, telling the story of the life and loves of Edward Albert Tewler, a Pollyesque individual born in Camden Town in 1901. In its formal division into 'books' with titles reminiscent of Victorian fiction, its detailed descriptions of the physical characteristics of rooms and people and its tidying up of loose ends in the final chapter it follows many of the conventions of the nineteenth-century novel. It differs strikingly from them however in the unusual relationship between author and reader, as if the author is talking directly to the reader, sharing in the experience of absorbing the novel. The process is analogous to that of reading *Tristram Shandy*: an awareness that the narrator is sharing his thoughts with you as you read, commenting on the story and even passing opinions on the characters he has created:

Hitherto this record of the acts and sayings of Edward Albert has been a simple unemotional record of the facts of the case, and if at times a certain realisation of the immanent absurdity of his life has betrayed itself, it has, I hope, been kept for the most part below the level of derision. But what has to be told now of this young couple is something so pitiful that I find myself taking sides with them against the circumstances that brought them to this pass.

My case is that Edward Albert is not so much detestable as pitiful, and that for the rest I like nearly all my characters as they are – except Mr Chamble Pewter, whom manifestly I loathe.[36]

Throughout the novel one is aware of a dual focus, a continual shift in perspective from individual lives to humanity as a whole. On the one hand is the narrative which forms the substance of the book – the boyhood, adolescence and manhood of Edward Albert Tewler, his emotional life, and his experiences during the Second World War. The story is told with complete candour and with a wry humour that recalls the satires of Swift or the early novels of Orwell. It is as if a sample of human life is being scrutinised under a microscope and dissected for the edification of the reader. Particularly memorable are the chapters comprising 'The marrying, divorce and early middle age of Edward Albert Tewler' which are related with a veracity Wells rarely surpassed. The story of Edward's upbringing against a background of sexual ignorance, his love for Evangeline Birkenhead and his courtship, marriage and subsequent disillusionment is told with total conviction and the fluency of a born novelist. Wells's characters are believable because they echo situations and emotions that are typical of countless ordinary lives in the years between the wars.

Interwoven with this concentration on humdrum lives is a wider perspective, a constant reminder that the hero is a representative sample of the species which Wells terms 'Homo Tewler', a creature undergoing a crisis of adaptation. The interplay between the specific and the general, the individual and the species, is one of the most interesting aspects of the novel (the interplay is underlined by an Appendix on 'The evolution of the placental mammals' and 'The ancestry of man') and makes the reading of it a continually rewarding experience. Wells expresses this dualism in these terms:

This is the story of the Deeds and Sayings of Edward Albert Tewler. From *his* point of view. But like those amusing pictures you find in books on Optics that will turn inside out as you look at them, it is equally the story of this whole universe of Edward Albert Tewler, and he is just the empty shape of a human being at the centre of it – its resultant, its creature.[37]

In common with so many of his novels *You Can't Be Too Careful* ends on a note of uncertainty. A final chapter 'And after sapiens?' summarises the prospects for human advancement and concludes: 'Yet a vista of innumerable happy generations, an abundance of life at present inconceivable, and at the end, not extinction necessarily, not immortality, but complete uncertainty, is surely sufficient prospect for the present.' In its Shandean irreverence, its intimate relationship between creator and reader, its evolutionary perspective and final ambivalence it is a characteristic Wells text and a vindication of his didactic approach to the art of fiction. Though the novel was widely reviewed and reprinted in the same month as publication it has never received the critical attention it deserves and is today almost forgotten. It was to be his last novel, the final jest of the man who had given the world *Kipps* and *Mr Polly*.

V

Early in 1943, sensing that his life was drawing slowly but surely towards its end, he tried the experiment of writing his own obituary. 'My auto-obituary' is a brief but fascinating essay in which he reviews his life and work from the standpoint of a sympathetic but detached observer:

> Wells was a copious and repetitive essayist upon public affairs and a still more copious writer of fiction . . . He was much more the scientific man than the artist, though he dealt in literary forms. Scarcely anything remains of him now, and yet, without him and his like, the reef of common ideas on which our civilisation stands today could never have arisen.[38]

The 'auto-obituary' presents a picture of a frail and forgotten figure, with 'few associations for the younger generation', who dies at the age of 97, a neglected writer who was heard to mutter 'Some day I shall write a book, a *real* book.' His conception of himself as 'much more the scientific man than the artist' is interesting and a further reminder of the ambivalence in his nature between rational and imaginative drives. Though the literary historian sees him primarily as a novelist he regarded himself first and foremost as a thinker and scientist. In 1942 he had submitted a thesis to the University of London for the Doctorate of Science with the forbidding title 'A thesis on the quality of illusion in the continuity of the individual life in the higher Metazoa, with particular reference to the species *homo sapiens*'. Its central argument was that the concept of a single integrated personality was an illusion, that each individual is an amalgam of many different personalities, not necessarily acting in harmony with one another. This erudite paper, together with his continual revisions of *The Outline of History* and *The Science of Life*, his work on the idea of a world encyclopaedia, his description of the space-time continuum in *The Conquest of Time* and his wish to be accepted as a Fellow of the Royal Society, all witness to his desire to be remembered as a man of science. To the end the writing of fiction went hand in glove with his attempts to elucidate the world situation and to understand – and help his readers to understand – the challenges facing mankind in mid-century.

A final collection of essays, *'42 to '44: A contemporary memoir*, appeared in March 1944. Only 2,000 copies were printed at the prohibitive price of two guineas – a deliberate decision on Wells's part who wanted to make sure that 'that strange indiscriminate creature, the rare book collector, will get his money's worth'.[39] Much of *'42 to '44* is ephemeral in nature. It consists in the main of polemical articles commenting on the contemporary international political scene and on the conduct of the war. The material was hurriedly assembled in book form as he felt the sands of time were fast running out and he might not live to complete the task; a mistaken diagnosis had led him to believe that his death was imminent. He described the book as a 'memoir of my ideas and impressions of the contemporary world crisis'. Apart from the material of strictly topical interest the volume contains two pieces of more permanent value: his thesis 'On the quality of illusion' – an intriguing commentary on the dualism of the human temperament – and a carefully written essay on 'The passing of Beatrice Webb'. Beatrice, with whom he had had an uneasy friendship for many years, died on 30 April 1943. 'She counted for so much in the scenery of my life', he wrote, 'that it is almost as if a major planet had vanished from my sky.' With warm affection he looked back on Sidney and Beatrice Webb and on all that their association had meant to him, making amends in the process for some of his own intolerance of former years. He tried to imagine what her death must mean to Sidney in a beautiful metaphor:

> You might think then that for Sidney the sun must have gone out. But that is not what happens with those with whom we have lived very closely and for many years. I know. They live on in us and with us. For Sidney she is not dead. It will be as if she had just gone into another room for a time.[40]

In this obvious reference to Jane Wells he showed that her memory was still very much with him in his old age. She had 'just gone into another room for a time', living in him and with him, an abiding presence.

Wells spent the final years of his life in slowly failing health, suffering from cancer of the liver. Attended by a nurse and a house-keeper he pottered about the house and garden, often comatose for long periods. On fine days he would sit outside, carefully wrapped up and wearing a panama hat, alternately meditating and resting. He told J. L. Hodson, who called to see him three months before he died, 'You'll find me here, one foot in the grave, one foot waving about.' He painted a mural on a wall at the back of his house summarising the evolution of man from the first mammals to the emergence of *Homo sapiens*. Beneath the last panel he wrote 'Time to depart?'.

In February 1945 he drew up his will, a lucid and moving document in which he made generous dispositions for his family and his closest friends. At the end he wrote in his tiny spidery handwriting:

> And finally I want to put on record my loving recognition of the good and sane behaviour of all my offspring towards me and each other and the abundant interest and happiness with which they have enriched my life and I leave them my benediction.

During 1945 he published three short works, each completed during the previous year: *The Happy Turning, The Betterave Papers* and *Mind at the End of its Tether*, which appeared in February, July and November respectively. These are utterly different in nature and scope, and each presents an interesting indication of his state of mind as his life drew slowly to its close. *The Happy Turning: A dream of life* is a collection of genial essays describing his dreams and reveries at 13 Hanover Terrace. His dreams begin with a vision of a turning he has not noticed before on his daily walks:

> At first the Turning itself was the essence of the dream. Now, directly my dream unfolds I know where I am; it has become a mere key to this delightful land of my lifelong suppressions, in which my desires and unsatisfied fancies, hopes, memories and imaginations have accumulated inexhaustible treasure.[41]

After describing the dreams of his childhood he proceeds to an exhilarating account of his dreamland imaginations in which all he sees is wonderful and benign. In this world of fantasy he encounters Jesus of Nazareth and has a series of engaging conversations with him. Jesus discusses the discrepancies between the Gospel account of the miracles and the parables and what actually occurred, and goes on to converse with disarming frankness about the disciples and their habit of mis-understanding his teachings. '*Never* have disciples', says Jesus, 'It was my greatest mistake.' Ever since childhood Wells had been fascinated by theology. In such short stories as 'A vision of judgment', 'The last trump' and 'Answer to prayer' he had allowed his imagination to play with heavenly speculations, and in the 'Prologue in heaven' chapter of *The Undying Fire* and 'The elemental powers' sequence in *Man Who Could Work Miracles* he had displayed his gift for conveying eternal truths in the form of a metaphor. In *The Happy Turning* he claims that 'theology has always seemed to me an arena for clean fun that should do no harm to any properly constituted person.' Jesus is the 'most congenial' companion he encounters in the Beyond, but not by any means the only one. There is a Holy Carnival of divinities, a gathering of bishops, and a conference of architects and engineers who discuss their plans for the new world after the war: 'And though endless lovely new things are achieved, nothing a human heart has loved will ever be lost.' He describes his love of rural scenery, of wandering as a child through country lanes picking wild flowers, his delight in the sounds and sights of pastoral England.

The dream of the Happy Turning leads on to a vision of the Elysian Fields. Here Wells imagines he is talking to a gathering of poets, artists and writers about beauty and the creation of beautiful things. 'A point we found we were all agreed upon was that Beauty is eternal and final, a joy for ever.' The discussion turns to a meditation on poetry, Shakespeare and literature, culminating in the reflection that 'every new realisation, every fresh discovery, has for those who make it a quality of beauty, transitory indeed but otherwise as clear and pure as that enduring Beauty we cherish for ever . . . .'[42]

The Happy Turning is a very brief work (it runs to just fifty pages) but its pervading mood of happiness ensures it a permanent place in the canon of his writings. The benevolent attitude to life which breathes through its pages is in the sharpest contrast to the doom-laden prophecies of the early war years and strongly recalls the atmosphere of *The History of Mr Polly*. Clearly when he wrote it Wells was in a 'Boswell' mood: a mood in which he became 'a happy explorer telling of a delightful world he has come upon, beyond expectation'.

The Betterave Papers was published in *The Cornhill Magazine*, then edited by Peter Quennell, and appeared cheek by jowl with contributions by Harold Nicolson, Kenneth Clark and Denton Welch. It was printed under the name 'Wilfred B. Betterave' with the explanatory note 'written at the suggestion of H. G. Wells himself, who has given the Author (i.e. W. B. B.) *carte blanche* to relieve his mind in the matter without either interference or comment from (one has to admit it) his creator'. The longest section is a delightfully funny essay headed 'All's well that ends well: a complete exposé of this notorious literary humbug', in which the imaginary Betterave – who clearly strongly disapproves of Wells and all his works – surveys Wells's career as a prophet and novelist with devastating candour. The invention of

Betterave serves a similar purpose to the device of Reginald Bliss in *Boon*: it permits him to comment on his own life and writings with total dispassion and to look on himself *from the outside*. The result is an essay of sparkling wit which ranges over the whole of his intellectual career with hilarious results. In the process he gently deflates his literary pretensions and permits the reader to see him without illusions:

> After that [*The World of William Clissold*] Mr Wells might write what he liked and do his utmost. It was no longer the thing to read him. Reviewers might praise him and a dwindling band of dupes might get his books. They vanished from the shop windows and from the tables of cultured people . . . People whom once he had duped would perhaps mention him as a figure of some significance in English literature, but the established reply of the people who no longer read him and had nothing to say about him, was simply the grimace of those who scent decay. 'Oh, *Wells*' they would say, and leave it at that. So that Wells decays alive and will be buried a man already forgotten . . . .[43]

His eldest son, G. P. Wells, described *The Betterave Papers* as 'a bitter opusculum',[44] which perhaps suggests that the work is of comparatively minor importance. Because it appeared as a magazine essay, whereas his other two last books were published as separate works, the piece has received surprisingly little critical attention. *The Betterave Papers* should be treated on equal terms with these since it is essential to an understanding of Wells's attitude of mind in the closing months of his life and forms an interesting codicil to his autobiography. The invention of a hostile 'second self' who pours scorn on his life and achievements enables him to laugh at himself in a thoroughly endearing way. It also creates an unusual relationship between author, reader and text since the reader is aware that Wells is the author yet is seeing Wells's biography from Betterave's point of view. His ability to distance himself in this way, to place himself in the position of an unsympathetic observer, was one of Wells's most striking characteristics. The Jekyll–Hyde relationship between the real and ostensible author is maintained to the end. 'You have no existence apart from mine', says Wells finally, 'and so I shall make an end to you now.'

His last published work, *Mind at the End of its Tether*, has achieved some notoriety as a final recantation of faith, a bitter rejection of all he had stood for in his previous writings. A careful reading of it, however, shows that it is by no means consistent in its pessimism; nor does it represent the fundamental breach with his life's work which many critics have supposed it to be.

Its inconsistency is explained by the fact that *Mind at the End of its Tether* in its published form is an amalgamation of two drafts written at different times. One draft (the first three chapters of the present text) is unrelievedly pessimistic in outlook: 'The end of everything we call life is close at hand and cannot be evaded.' These chapters, barely coherent in tone, describe a universe intellectually and morally bankrupt, a world in which 'the attempt to trace a pattern of any sort is absolutely futile'. These pages are clearly the work of a writer who is tired and ill, a man who can see no glimmer of hope on the horizon. The second draft (chapters four to eight) was originally written as the concluding section of a revised edition of *A Short History of the World* on which he was working simultaneously. These chapters, which comprise the greater part of the book, contain a summary of organic evolution and a recapitulation of the biological attitude to life he had held since student days. After asserting that a new species must evolve to replace *Homo sapiens* he continued:

> That new animal may be an entirely alien strain, or it may arise as a new modification of the *hominidae*, and even as a direct continuation of the human phylum, but it will certainly not be human. There is no way out for Man but steeply up or steeply down. Adapt or perish, now as ever, is Nature's inexorable imperative.[45]

This seems to me to be no different in essence from the views he had postulated throughout his life. Fifty years earlier he had written:

> But since the Cephalapsis and the Coccosteus many a fine animal has increased and multiplied upon the earth, lorded it over land or sea without a rival, and passed at last into the night. Surely it is not unreasonable to ask why man should be an exception to the rule . . . *in no case does the record of the fossils show a really dominant species succeeded by its own descendants.*[46] [Wells's italics]

His first full-length work of fiction, *The Time Machine*, had concluded with the narrator's gloomy comment that the Time Traveller 'thought but cheerlessly of the Advancement of Mankind, and saw in the growing pile of civilisation only a foolish heaping that must inevitably fall back upon and destroy its makers in the end'. *The Time Machine* was published by Heinemann in July 1895. *Mind at the End of its Tether* was published by Heinemann almost exactly half a century later, in November 1945. His writings had come full circle. From first to last he regarded man as an imperfect animal species, a creature which had struggled from the primordial slime through countless adaptations and must now adapt to its rapidly changing environment or subside into extinction. Through all his fluctuating moods he never departed fundamentally from this basic attitude of mind: an attitude which is neither optimistic nor pessimistic but realistic – a stoical acceptance of the human condition. Man was no different from any other species and must adapt to his circumstances or go the way of the dinosaurs.

VI

In the last months of his life he had little energy for writing but began work on a film scenario, *The Way the World is Going*, an updated version of *Things to Come*. He toyed with the idea of writing a study of *The Decline and Fall of Monarchy and Competitive Imperialisms*, a summary of his conception of history. In the closing phases of his illness he was too weak for sustained periods of creative work but he left a number of abandoned manuscripts including *Exasperations*, a collection of polemical essays, and an earlier draft of *Mind at the End of its Tether* running to some 30,000 words. This includes a fascinating appendix, 'Aesop's quinine for Delphi', a series of gentle, whimsical additions to Aesop's Fables. The most touching of these, 'The world in slippers', is a plea for 'the total banishment of the jackboot and indeed of any sort of hard footwear from the world. You cannot trample on your fellow creatures in slippers.'[47]

In anticipation of his eightieth birthday on 21 September 1946 Penguin Books published a commemorative edition of ten of his works: *Tono-Bungay, The New Machiavelli, The War of the Worlds, A Short History of the World, The Time Machine, The Island of Doctor Moreau, The History of Mr Polly, Love and Mr Lewisham, The Invisible Man* and *Kipps*. One hundred thousand copies of each volume were printed. It was a tribute that meant much to him, for he cared far more for his posthumous reputation than he publicly acknowledged. But he did not live to see his birthday. Five weeks before, on 13 August 1946, he died peacefully in his sleep.

Three days later he was cremated at Golders Green. The funeral service was attended by a distinguished gathering of friends and relatives including both Rebecca and Anthony. J. B. Priestley delivered the address:

> His literary genius was rich and rare – the best of his novels and short stories are among the finest creations of our time – but he belongs not only to English Literature, but also to world history, as a great educator and as the chief prophet of this age of transition, long foreshadowing, with pity and passion, the shape of things to come.[48]

Rebecca had just returned from Nuremberg where she had been reporting the Nazi war trials. Had he lived, she had planned that very day to call on him at 13 Hanover Terrace to show him some photographs of the Nazi leaders. She wrote to his secretary, Marjorie Wells:

> I loved him all my life and always will, and I bitterly reproach myself for not having stayed with him, because I think I was fairly good for him. But you know the reverse of the medal, the tyranny that was the incorrigible part of him. I could not have submitted to it all my life – nor do I think that he could have loved me or that I could have loved him if I had been the kind of person that could. And indeed he got on pretty well without me.[49]

Chapter 8

The Thinking Reed

But then the problem, which occupied me more and more, was to know what kind of person she was, what she was, beyond being my mother. She was so many different people that it seemed impossible that she could be any one of them, much less all of them.

Anthony West, *Heritage*

I had never met anything quite like her before, and I doubt if there ever was anything like her before. Or ever will be again.

H. G. Wells, *H. G. Wells in Love*

I

Shortly after her marriage to Henry Andrews, Rebecca and her new husband moved into 15 Orchard Court, a pleasant apartment near Hyde Park. Here she settled into a life of domesticity and respectability, determined that her marriage should be a success.

Henry's work as a merchant banker necessitated a considerable amount of travelling throughout Europe. They frequently journeyed together on these visits, widening their knowledge of the European scene and making many contacts in the worlds of business and finance. Rebecca decided that she liked Henry more and more and that domestic life suited her. Meanwhile the 16-year-old Anthony had to come to terms with a new stepfather, which cannot have been an easy adjustment to make. Henry, with his formality, slowness, staidness and mannered charm was the opposite of the mercurial and dynamic Wells; Anthony was not impressed. Henry was kind and understanding and did his best to hit it off with the boy but the chemistry between them never really jelled. Something of Anthony's reaction to him may be deduced from the portrayal of 'the Colonel' in the semi-autobiographical novel *Heritage* where Henry is depicted as a bumbling but well-meaning member of the landed gentry. Anthony was quick to sense that inwardly his mother seethed at Henry's slowness and that deep inside the 'Cicely' role Henry imposed on her the real Rebecca was struggling to assert herself.

Anthony's academic career was not helped by this readjustment. He was unhappy at Stowe and, to make matters worse, failed Latin in his school certificate examination: an essential entry requirement for Oxford or Cambridge. Despite private tuition he again failed the examination at a second attempt and Rebecca had no alternative but to abandon her dream of Anthony going to university. His unsettlement at this time is hardly surprising in view of his divided upbringing, the normal traumas of adolescence, his unhappiness at school (though his parentage was no longer a shameful secret he was still bullied) and the change in his mother's emotional life. He knew in his heart that, despite her ambitions for him, he was simply not cut out for university: he wanted to be a painter. He left Stowe and, after undergoing extensive psychoanalysis, settled down happily to be an art student. With his worries about university now over he worked industriously and harmoniously for some years, painting and studying art. As soon as he reached the age of 21 he surprised his mother and his friends by announcing his intention to marry. His bride was the artist Katherine Church; she remained a loyal and loving wife to him for fourteen years.

Rebecca was contributing regular book reviews to journals in Britain and America and also writing features and short stories which were widely syndicated. Her frequent reviews in the London *Daily Telegraph* ranged widely over fiction, biography, history and current affairs and included novels by such popular writers as H. E. Bates, Vicki Baum and Leo Walmsley and scholarly works on politics, philosophy and psychology. Her literary articles revealed the catholicity of her reading and her loyalty to the enthusiasms she had formed in her youth. During these years she wrote essays on Dickens, Shaw, Bennett, Proust, James, Tolstoy and many others whilst simultaneously keeping herself up to date with contemporary developments in the English and European novel. At the same time she was contributing features on such diverse topics as the royal family, motherhood, servants, marriage, housing and travel in addition to weighty essays on politics and world affairs. Nor was she neglecting the writing of fiction. In 1935 four of her longer short stories were published in book form by Jonathan Cape in London and Doubleday in New York. This collection, *The Harsh Voice*, contains some of her finest writing and reveals a growing mastery in the handling of characterisation and dialogue. The stories anticipate the milieu of *The Thinking Reed*, for each explores the lives and relationships of wealthy people and the barriers of emotion and falsity that divide them. Their common theme is failure of communication and the way in which marriage and friendship can be destroyed by misunderstandings and hatreds. The stories are peopled with characters who have no shared interests, whose lives are made up of misconceptions and prejudice, whose overriding concern is self-assertion. Rebecca confided to Edward Sackville West that *The Harsh Voice* was written 'in the depths of gloomy contemplation of the destinies of the inarticulate damned'.[1] She herself was happily married but well knew from the experience of her parents that much bitterness could arise where there was not complete trust between husband and wife. *The Harsh Voice* is an expression of the darker, pessimistic side of her nature. Implicit in its pages is a questioning of human happiness, as if she is posing the question: Can there be a fully harmonious partnership? Or is communication an illusion? She returned to this theme in much greater depth in her next novel.

The Thinking Reed, published in 1936, was Rebecca's first full-length novel since *Harriet Hume* seven years earlier. Markedly different in style and theme from her previous novels, *The Thinking Reed* presents a picture of the life and reflections of a contemporary woman, Isabelle Sallafranque, whose social, mental and emotional world forms the substance of the book. Isabelle is a wealthy socialite who moves in the monied and leisured circles of the American and European rich, outwardly conforming to their lifestyle but inwardly loathing the shallowness and falsity of their existence. Her witty comments on the emptiness of their lives enrich the novel with a crossweave of irony and humour which makes it one of her funniest works of fiction.

The title is a quotation from Pascal's *Pensées*: 'Man is but a reed, the most feeble thing in nature; but he is a thinking reed.' It is Isabelle, the central character of the novel, who is the *thinker*, reflecting on the world around her and forming shrewd assessments of all whom she meets. She is married to a millionaire and is therefore accustomed to a way of life based upon wealth but is privately repelled by her friends' obsession with material values. She is struck by the fact that the propertied circles in which she and her husband mingle are 'noticeably more driven and irritable than the people in the world outside. They had refused all succour offered to them by the mind, and there is simply not enough for the body to do unassisted during the whole twenty-four hours.' A recurring theme in the novel is Isabelle's sharp perception of the vapidity of a life with no mental or creative stimulus, a routine founded on an endless preoccupation with clothes, money, gossip and possessions. In this sense *The Thinking Reed* is in the sharpest possible contrast to such anodyne best sellers of the 1930s as the works of Elinor Glyn and Ethel M. Dell. It is a much more *cerebral* novel, filled with aphorisms on life, love, friendship and marriage as the heroine thinks aloud about the values of her world. Isabelle's observations on the contemporary scene are written with an astringent wit characteristic of Rebecca at her most memorable. Her house in Paris was 'among over-handsome mansions like heavy-bosomed dowagers', a friend talks to her 'in a voice sad as the falling of leaves', an acquaintance she cannot stand pulls a face 'like an unmade bed'.

Beneath the mockery of empty lives a much more serious purpose is evident: a prolonged meditation on marriage. In a sense *The Thinking Reed* returns to the theme Wells had explored in *Marriage*, that of the intelligent woman with time on her hands who is resolved to make a success of her married life. Her husband, Marc, is strong, passionate and kind; she marries him initially without any firm emotional bond but comes to love him in the course of the novel. Other men come and go as the story proceeds: Laurence Vernon, reserved, cold and intellectual; Alan Fielding, quiet and artistic; André de Verviers, fascinating and frivolous; but it is Marc with his gentleness and warmth with whom she finds lasting happiness. In telling the story of an independent-minded woman who, after many vicissitudes, finds emotional security, Rebecca was expressing in fictional form themes that had dominated her life since childhood. 'Heiress as I am to ethical squalor', she tells one of her friends, 'and exposed throughout my childhood to every disadvantageous influence, I am driven through life by an insatiable craving for goodness . . . How I detest myself! But I must struggle on under the burden of what I am.' In this and many similar outbursts can be discerned the daughter of Charles Fairfield and Isabella Mackenzie trying to come to terms with the forces which had moulded her as a woman and as an artist. Marc possesses many of the qualities Rebecca's father had embodied: a passionate nature, dynamism, strength and forcefulness. At the same time he possesses a tenderness and understanding Charles Fairfield had lacked. He is an idealisation of all that Rebecca most admired in manhood.

The Thinking Reed has been described as a novel depicting 'a truly feminine life'.[2] By this is meant that Isabelle's thoughts and feelings are seen from *her* point of view, not from a male novelist's conception of that point of view as in Wells's *Ann Veronica* and *The Passionate Friends*. One senses that Isabelle would be quite capable of attaining happiness on her own, that she abides by the conventions of marriage and motherhood because this is what society expects of her. As a single woman living alone she would be frowned on by polite society. In a significant passage towards the end of the novel Isabelle gives free expression to her pent-up frustration:

> She had never been able to live according to her own soul, to describe her own course through life as her intellect would have been able to plan it. She had progressed erratically, dizzily, often losing sight of her goal, by repercussion after repercussion with men travelling at violent rates of speed on paths chosen for no other motive than the opportunities they gave for violence . . . In terror she thought, 'All men are my enemies, what am I doing with any of them?'[3]

Few readers in 1936 can have known that this was written with deep conviction borne of personal experience. Rebecca, like Isabelle, had 'never been able to live according to her own soul'. Her life had been deflected by Wells, by Anthony, by Beaverbrook, by the conflicting drives of conformity and independence. On one level *The Thinking Reed* is a reflection of her married happiness with Henry Andrews, to whom the book is dedicated; the heroine, after much soul searching, rejects one suitor after another in favour of Marc. Her final reconciliation with him represents the triumph of emotion over intellect, of enduring values over trivial pleasures. On a deeper level it is a myth embodying drives and tensions which had fractured her life since she had first begun to think for herself – on the one hand the desire to be a free spirit, answerable to no one; on the other, the need for emotional security and fulfilment. Behind the novel lies the question 'Can the two be reconciled?'

The Thinking Reed was widely and favourably reviewed, bringing Rebecca's name to the attention of a huge popular readership eager for fiction concerned with real issues. The *New Yorker* described it as a 'brilliant study of the heart and mind of a woman', while *Time* hailed it as 'among the best novels in the short memory of modern man'. Despite this enthusiastic reception she turned her back on the writing of fiction for many years; there was to be no new novel from her pen until *The Fountain Overflows* twenty years later. With the deteriorating international situation and the rise of Fascism and Nazism she turned her attention more and more to the writing of non-fiction: to the issues of history, politics, nationhood and belief which came increasingly to dominate her life.

II

Meanwhile Henry had been relieved of his post as head of the European division of Schroders – he had become more and more disillusioned with the growing influence of Nazis within the organisation – and was working as a freelance merchant banker. His contacts in many parts of Europe enabled both Rebecca and himself to understand the significance of Nazi ideas at an early stage and to grasp the fact that sooner or later war was inevitable.

From 1936 onwards she was consumed by a growing fascination with the Balkans, and Yugoslavia in particular. She made several journeys to Yugoslavia, sometimes with Henry and sometimes alone, intrigued by the atmosphere of the country and making notes for her monumental *Black Lamb and Grey Falcon*, which eventually appeared in 1941. Conceived originally as a travel book it grew and grew until it threatened to take over her life. By the time it was finished she had written half a million words embracing politics, mythology, religion and the spirit of landscape. Above all *Black Lamb and Grey Falcon* became the workshop in which she sought to define her fundamental attitudes to life and belief.

The book is at once a meditation on history, a study of the relations between East and West and a survey of the origins of the First World War. Vivid descriptions of towns and scenery are combined with trenchant analyses of history and politics and reflections on human nature. Her theme throughout is the contrast between freedom and totalitarianism, between the quest for beauty as exemplified in art and architecture and the impulse towards evil manifest in the rise of Fascism and Nazism. Implicit in her argument is the reflection that man at his finest has produced the work of Michelangelo and Mozart and at his worst is responsible for torture, persecution and barbarism. War, she suggests, has its roots in man's divided nature, in the urge to destroy and vilify. The assassination at Sarajevo in 1914 was the spark that set the world afire but the war had its roots in the past, in decades of mistrust, rivalry and intolerance. Similarly the Second World War, which she could see so clearly on the horizon, had its origins in the legacy of history. In its fusion of travelogue and political commentary, its ability to range widely over religion, art and morality and its idiosyncratic asides on the details of everyday living *Black Lamb and Grey Falcon* is entirely characteristic of her work and a monument to her industry.

By good fortune Henry's dismissal from Schroders was followed by a transformation in his horizons. In 1936 his wealthy uncle died, leaving him a considerable sum of money. This inheritance enabled him and Rebecca to purchase a house in the country, to which they moved at the end of 1939. Ibstone House, an imposing eighteenth-century building standing in its own grounds and surrounded by seventy acres of farmland, remained their home until Henry's death in 1968.

Despite wartime restrictions and food shortages Rebecca took to country life as if to the manner born. She assumed the role of countrywoman with enthusiasm, involving herself in the Women's Institute, keeping hens, reading books on husbandry and taking delight in farmhouse cooking. When Anthony came to satirise Ibstone as 'Marshwood' in his novel *Heritage* he was quick to notice the change of role:

> I decided not to ask why the Colonel had taken to calling her by the name she had dropped when she first went on the stage. I saw at a glance that she had assumed a new personality for which Emily [Cecily] was the best possible name. She was wearing a tweed coat and skirt, a pale pearl-grey blouse, and flat-heeled brogues.[4]

Anthony was not alone in finding this chameleon-like ability to adopt a new role rather confusing, but there can be no question of her enthusiasm in adapting to the country. She took an interest in village life, took over the running of the greenhouses and flower gardens, and enjoyed going for walks with her pet labrador. She enjoyed *organising* things: savings weeks, first aid classes, village concerts. Life at Ibstone during the war years brought real happiness to both Henry and Rebecca.

From the inception of the war Henry began working for the Ministry of Economic Warfare, drawing up plans for the economic reconstruction of the Balkans. His involvement with this work necessitated close contacts with liberal intellectuals and others opposed to the rise of totalitarianism in Europe. Rebecca shared his deep interest in and concern for the Slav peoples and devoted much of her time to speaking and writing on behalf of Yugoslav relief organisations. Together they did their utmost to assist refugees and to find homes for the stateless dispossessed. Much of her contentment during these years can be attributed to the fact that for the first time in her life she felt she was doing something *practical*. She had a sense of achievement which writing by itself could not bring her.

As soon as war had broken out Anthony decided to buy a farm and to make a serious attempt to be a cattle breeder and dairy farmer. He held deep pacifist convictions which prevented him from taking an active part in the war effort, and for some years made a success of running a sixty-eight acre farm. Later in the war he found employment with the British Broadcasting Corporation, working as a sub-editor at the Far Eastern Desk.

During the summer of 1946 Rebecca attended the closing sessions of the Nuremberg trials in which the surviving Nazi leaders were prosecuted by an international tribunal. She was intensely interested in the proceedings and observed the trials not simply as a journalist who had been commissioned to write a series of articles but as a writer who was passionately concerned with issues of justice and morality. The concern found its expression in *The Meaning of Treason* (1947) and *A Train of Powder* (1955), works remarkable for their perception and determination to arrive at the truth. She was fascinated by treachery, by the motivations that lead an individual to put the interests of an enemy nation above those of his own country. With insight and understanding she ranges over the actions of William Joyce, John Amery, Nunn May, Klaus Fuchs and others, discussing with frankness and honesty the psychology of the traitor. What makes a traitor?, she asks. Why are some men utterly loyal to their own country and others betray it at every opportunity? In disentangling the background to these stories of betrayal and duplicity she reveals a deep understanding of human psychology and her lifelong fascination with the mainsprings of conduct. Her concluding reflection is at once stimulating and humane:

> As a divorce sharply recalls what a happy marriage should be, so the treachery of these men recalled what a nation should be: a shelter where all talents are generously recognised, all forgivable oddities forgiven, all viciousness quietly frustrated, and those who lack talent honoured for equivalent contributions.[5]

She could never forget that Hitler rose to power on a tidal wave of genuine discontents, that both world wars had their origins in enmity and frustration. Treachery, she felt, has its roots in intolerance and misunderstanding, in the human weakness for mythologies that pander to envy and hatred. Her thesis is that treason can never be eradicated until statesmen understand that man is not a rational creature but a complex of warring motives driven by 'love or hate, good or evil, life or death, according to the inhabiting demon, whose reasons are never given'.

In 1949 Houghton Mifflin in the United States and Eyre and Spottiswoode in London published *On a Dark Night*, Anthony's first novel. It is a strange, haunting book which takes place in the hereafter, in a hell remarkably like Orwell's *Nineteen Eighty-Four*, published in the same year. The theme of the novel is individual responsibility, that each human being creates his own heaven or hell by his actions and by his concern for others; only by acknowledging the evil he has committed in his own life can a man achieve freedom. The novel begins with the suicide of the central character, a prosecutor at the Nuremberg trials, and proceeds to the love–hate relationship which binds him to the German general he has condemned to death. *On a Dark Night* was at once recognised as the work of an original and unusual talent. Walter Allen, writing in *The Year's Work in Literature*, described it as 'the first novel of a distinguished critic and probably the most ambitious novel of the year . . . Genuine imaginative power is matched by real brilliance of writing.'[6] The book won the Houghton Mifflin–Eyre and Spottiswoode Award for an English novel and earned wide critical acclaim for Anthony who had previously been known only as a writer of non-fiction.

The publication of *On a Dark Night* had important repercussions for the relationship between Anthony and his mother. His American publishers had announced the book as being written by Anthony West, 'the son of Rebecca West and H. G. Wells', and had also announced that Anthony was working on a biography of his father. Rebecca was greatly displeased by both these statements. While genuinely admiring the novel (she told her sister Winnie that it was 'magnificently written') she did not wish the facts of his parenthood to be widely known and shrank from any publicity linking her and Anthony's name with Wells's. From her point of view it seemed that Anthony and his publishers were intent on exploiting an old scandal. At Rebecca's behest Henry came down to Anthony's home in Dorset to remonstrate with him, insisting that there should be no reference to the name of his mother and father. Anthony wrote later: 'I was taken aback by his proposition, and could only tell him that I couldn't possibly do or say anything that might seem to suggest that I had any reason to be ashamed of being the child of either one of my parents.'[7] Henry demanded from Anthony a solemn undertaking never to exploit in any way the fact that he was the son of Wells and Rebecca. Not surprisingly Anthony felt unable to give any such guarantee. He was proud of the fact that he was the son of two such distinguished writers and had already started work on a biography of Wells. Henry, hurt and angry, gave him time to reconsider but eventually removed all reference to Anthony from his will. Anthony's position had been transformed from being the principal beneficiary to having no expectations at all.

This disagreement was typical of the quarrels and misunderstandings which disfigured the relationship between Rebecca and Anthony for the remainder of their lives. To her it appeared that her son was bent on causing her embarrassment by re-opening old wounds. Any reference to his parentage was, from her vantage point, an intolerable intrusion into her private life. To him it seemed that she was ashamed of her association with Wells and that to insist on silence would place him in a strait-jacket. The tragedy of this and all their quarrels was that *from their own point of view* each of their attitudes was entirely reasonable and understandable. Given that Rebecca guarded her private life so jealously and abhorred any newspaper publicity about her personal affairs, her reluctance to advertise the details of Anthony's parentage is perfectly justifiable. Given Anthony's feelings towards his father, his wish to write a book about Wells and to acknowledge the facts of his own parentage is eminently understandable. That their intentions and desires could not be reconciled and that to each of them it seemed that the other was bent on wrecking their happiness was characteristic of their relations from this point onwards. By their own lights each was behaving rationally and neither could understand the hostility and suspicion of the other. On the title page of his novel *Heritage*, which appeared some years later, Anthony placed an epitaph: 'These are long vendettas, a peculiar people, neither forgivers nor forgetters. . .'.

They were indeed long vendettas. Relations between mother and son were poisoned by disagreements and suspicions that found their expression in lengthy and angry correspondence between them. To Anthony it seemed that his mother was being wilfully obstructive, determined to misinterpret his motives and actions and bent on spoiling his happiness. Wells in his autobiography had written 'Rebecca could produce voluminous imaginative interpretations of action and situation that dwarfed my own fairly considerable imaginative fluctuations altogether.'[8] How fully Anthony would have concurred as he saw his mother in letter after letter reinterpreting his life, dramatising his behaviour or imputing motives for his actions. From her point of view, of course, the situation looked entirely different. As he grew older Anthony reminded Rebecca more and more of Wells, not only in his physical appearance but in his wilfulness and tendency to impulsive decisions. She feared he was repeating the pattern of the past and saw in his waywardness the hand of Joseph Wells and of her own father Charles Fairfield. There seems little doubt that for both Rebecca and Anthony the profound animus between them satisfied some deep psychological imperative. Both needed a scapegoat. Rebecca tended to blame him for interrupting her literary career at a crucial stage in its development and for being the cause of many of her disagreements with Wells. Anthony tended to hold her responsible for much that had gone wrong in his own life, for his emotional insecurity and ignorance of many aspects of his father. With such deep disagreements between them it is not surprising that misunderstanding and grievances multiplied. What Rebecca intended as motherly concern Anthony construed as meddling interference. What he regarded as an honourable regard for Wells's literary reputation she saw as a spiteful attempt to rake up the past. The gap between them became more and more unbridgeable with the passage of time.

With relations with his mother and stepfather at a low ebb and his own marriage passing through a difficult phase it seemed to Anthony there was little reason to remain in England. He sensed moreover that critical and scholarly interest in Wells was virtually extinct – following Wells's death in 1946 there had been an inevitable reaction against his work – and that now was not an opportune time to bring out a biography. He decided to make a completely fresh start and, leaving his wife and children in England, emigrated to the United States in 1950. There he attained a new reputation as a book reviewer for the *New Yorker*, a role he fulfilled with distinction for the next twenty years. He divorced Katherine in 1952 and in the following year married Lily Emmet, a college student. He was still determined to write his biography in his own good time.

His second novel *Heritage*, published by Random House, New York, in 1955 is a *roman-à-clef* in which he drew freely on his memories of boyhood to create a moving and fascinating account of a young man torn by divided loyalties. It purports to be written by Richard Savage, the illegitimate son of a popular writer and a famous actress, who recounts the story of his life beginning with his earliest memories of elegant living in South Kensington. Though fictitious names are used for the characters the identity of the narrator's parents is easily apparent and it is clear that the reviewers were not fooled. When a widely selling paperback edition was published by Pocket Books, New York, in 1957 a quotation from the *Time* review appeared on the cover: 'As the son of famed British writers Rebecca West and H. G. Wells, novelist Anthony West has a pretty fair idea of his subject . . . An intelligent, witty, tolerant book.'

Rebecca was horrified both by the novel and the publicity associated with it. It is not difficult to understand why she found *Heritage* so distasteful. In addition to recognisable portraits of herself (Naomi Savage) and Wells (Max Town) there are easily identified caricatures of Henry Andrews, Odette Keun and Moura Budberg. The story is a skilful mixture of fact and fiction but in describing Richard Savage's childhood and adolescence Anthony does not depart fundamentally from his recollections of his own early life. With sensitivity and insight born of personal experience he vividly conveys the anguish and uncertainty of a thoughtful young man confused about his parenthood and ambivalent about his direction in life. The relationship between the narrator and his gifted parents is described with deep conviction; the reader has a powerful sense of his love–hate feelings towards his vivacious and strong-willed mother and his growing affection for his charismatic father. Not the least interesting aspect of the book is its insight into Anthony's own personality. In describing his hero's journey from boyhood to adolescence and his slow emergence from gaucheness to maturity he depicts the traumas of a sensitive youth coming to terms with his own emotional needs:

> For the first time I really became aware of a need greater than my own, of the identity of another person. I had, it abruptly dawned on me, no experience of life at all beyond my own desire for it, and no conception of how to enter into a human relationship.[9]

Heritage has the fascination common to autobiographical novels told in the first person, the fascination of such books as *Great Expectations* and *The New Machiavelli*: that of unravelling the complex relationship between fiction and reality. It is written with deep feeling, so much so that many scenes remain etched in the mind long after the book has been set aside. The narrator's childhood and schooling, his first encounters with the unforgettable Max Town, his visit to his father in the South of France, his sexual awakening, are all described with vividness and a novelist's gift of language. *Heritage* is significant not only as a passionate account of a tormented childhood but as a masterly novel in its own right in which Anthony reveals his growing self-confidence as a writer. He was indeed the son of Rebecca West and H. G. Wells and had inherited from each of them the creative artist's power of illuminating a scene with the striking detail that gives it life.

It cannot have pleased Rebecca that the novel received almost unanimous praise from the critics. The *Chicago Tribune* hailed the book as 'A penetrating, amusing, often satirical, often affectionate picture of highly individualistic human beings, and a fascinating and penetrating study of the effect of an uncommon heritage', while the *New York Herald Tribune* praised it as 'Clever, undeniably fascinating and enormously readable'. She was incensed at the book's success and determined to do her utmost to prevent its publication in England. Since *Heritage* also contains recognisable caricatures of Gip and Frank Wells and their wives, Rebecca consulted them and together they agreed on a concerted plan of action. By threatening legal action they were able to prevent publication in London and also to remove the possibility of serialisation in British newspapers. *Heritage* did not appear in Britain until 1984, by which time Rebecca was dead.

III

One day in the early 1950s Rebecca had a sudden urge to write a story about a musical family. Her original intention was to write a short story about two musical sisters but the project became more and more ambitious until it eventually became a full-length novel, *The Fountain Overflows*, and she began planning a number of sequels. *The Fountain Overflows* presents a child's view of the world, an evocation of the life Rebecca had known and loved during her years as a girl in London. The situation described in the novel closely parallels her own background in the final years of Victoria's reign and the beginning of the twentieth century. The narrator, Rose Aubrey (a surrogate for Rebecca) is the daughter of a gifted and devoted mother and a charismatic and wayward father who surround their close-knit family with enduring bonds of love and affection. With child-like innocence Rose describes the powerful influence of her mother in holding the family together, the pains of growing up, the resilience of her sisters in coping with the traumas and crises of childhood. The reader has a powerful sense of immediacy, an awareness that what is being described is happening *now*. One senses, as in *The Judge*, the voice of a writer with an eye for detail and a striking gift of metaphor. A field of heather is described as 'rich like a bass chord sustained by the pedal'; wet earth is 'dark as plum cake'; a lit gas mantle glimmers 'like a little man risen from the dead whose cerements partook in the light of his immortality'. With total recall the narrator presents a picture of her childhood world and the cultured, bookish household which is the centre of her life. It is a home where music, ideas and politics are daily currency and where the children are encouraged to think for themselves and express their own views. Rose's sister Cordelia (a fictionalised version of Rebecca's sister Letitia Fairfield, to whom the book is dedicated) is determined to become a concert violinist though she possesses little talent and much of the novel is the story of the family's attempts to dissuade Cordelia from this laudable but misguided ambition. Her brother, Richard Quin, is an idealised version of Anthony as a boy: the angelic, delightful child who can do no wrong. In describing Richard and his endearing sayings and ways Rebecca is subconsciously looking back to the happiness she had known at Quinbury and Leigh-on-Sea when Anthony was the light of her life and she was captivated by his precocity and lovable disposition.

Rose's mother, Clare Aubrey, is a sensitive and loving woman who is utterly devoted to her enigmatic husband and, though aware of his shortcomings, regards him with mingled admiration and respect. Rose remarks of her: 'She often did seem to look to her daughters for protection, which was not unnatural in a very feminine woman who had not only no masculine protection but was threatened by its negative.' Talented, loyal, tenacious, Clare Aubrey is the anchor whose dependability welds the family together and provides her children with the security and discipline they crave. Like Isabella Fairfield, she is herself an accomplished musician but foregoes any thought of a professional career in devoting herself to her husband and family. Since her husband is frequently absent from home and when he is at home shuts himself away in his study, it is Clare who is the children's principal companion and it is her standards they seek to emulate. She is the moral yardstick of their lives.

Rose's father, Piers Aubrey, is a journalist who deeply loves his wife and children but is preoccupied with his own concerns to the extent that he lives in a world of his own. Beset by financial worries and increasingly at odds with his employers he at last deserts his family, leaving a vacuum in their lives which cannot be filled. The impact of their father's desertion on such a close-knit family is catastrophic: Rose and her sisters 'suffered wounds which were never to heal'. Writing fifty years after her own father had walked out it is clear that the enormity of the event was still vivid in Rebecca's mind. The scene in which Mrs Aubrey breaks the news to the children that 'Your Papa has gone away and is not coming back' is one of the turning points in the novel: a traumatic moment frozen in time. Yet both the mother and the children look back on him with regret, recalling his generosity and manliness, savouring the many happinesses they had shared. Without him they are bereft; they continue to love him despite his abandonment of the family home.

The abiding impression left in the mind of the reader is of an acutely perceptive authorial voice, a narrator who is at once a child looking at the grown-up world with wonder and innocence and an adult observing with sympathetic understanding the fledgling she once was. It is this dual perspective – the adult Rose looking back with mingled nostalgia and puzzlement on her own girlhood – which gives the novel such a powerful aura of truth. One is aware of a narrator who can reach inside the mind of her characters to present a picture of a thoroughly believable world, a microcosm of a society in the process of dissolution. Rose looks back with affection on Christmasses and summer holidays, on visits to relatives and friends, seeing through the pretension and hypocrisy of adults and the constant effort to keep up appearances. She is a child who longs for stability and order, who is proud of her unusual parents while conscious at the same time that other homes are not like hers. She is quick to perceive that her friends' parents are not beset by financial worries, that they live in an atmosphere of security and calm uncluttered with books, music and political discussion.

The Fountain Overflows is an autobiographical novel in the same sense that *David Copperfield* and *Tono-Bungay* can be described as autobiographical novels: it is a re-creation of the world of her childhood in which she looks back with evident nostalgia on life in an unconventional home in Edwardian London. The title is taken from a quotation by Blake: 'The cistern contains: the fountain overflows', and refers to the emotional and creative bonds which hold the narrator's family together through all the vicissitudes that afflict them. At the end of the story the narrator declares:

> I could not face the task of being a human being, because I did not fully exist. It was my father and mother who existed. I could see them as two springs, bursting from a stony cliff, and rushing down a mountainside in torrent, and joining to flow through the world as a great river.[10]

In Jungian psychology a fountain is a symbol of the soul as the source of inner life and spiritual energy. The energy and creativity of Clare and Piers Aubrey overflows to their children, imbuing them with the imaginative power with which to overcome life's obstacles. (The fountain is a symbol used by Wells in many novels and stories, most notably in *Men Like Gods* and *Mr Blettsworthy on Rampole Island*. Both Wells and Rebecca employ the symbol as an image of life and renewal[11]).

Rebecca also seems to have intended it as a symbol of unity – the bonds of affection, like a rushing stream, merge the separate individuals into a oneness, linking them in a mystical affinity. As with all works of fiction which draw on memory, the relationship between the author's own past and the imaginative version depicted in the novel is a complex one. The world created in a novel has been described as 'another world, related to the real world by analogy'.[12] The events depicted in *The Fountain Overflows* and its sequels are in no sense a photographic reproduction of actual occurrences but they convey the *atmosphere* of Rebecca's childhood and adolescence with remarkable veracity. The trilogy is dominated by themes and motifs which preoccupied her throughout her life – her love for her dedicated mother and feckless father; her pervading sense that life is a struggle between good and evil, light and darkness; her ambivalent attitude towards the male sex; her fear of poverty and insecurity; her growing awareness of her own divided nature. In writing it she was giving fictional expression to some of her deepest intuitions.

The Fountain Overflows was conceived as the first part of a trilogy relating the story of the Aubrey family, though this ambitious scheme was not completed during Rebecca's lifetime. She continued to work on the sequels for some years and these were published posthumously under the titles *This Real Night* and *Cousin Rosamund*. These novels are remarkable for their verisimilitude and their wonderfully detailed evocation of life during the years 1900–30. One is reminded of the technique employed by Proust in *Remembrance of Things Past* or Dorothy Richardson in *Pilgrimage*: a leisurely distillation of the fabric of daily living. *This Real Night* continues the saga of the family from the beginning of the century onwards and culminates in the First World War with the death of Richard Quin and of Clare Aubrey. One notes, as in the first volume, the frequent references to the absentee father and the dread of insecurity: 'The homes of our school-fellows often startled and pleased us by their air of stability . . . It was beyond the capacity of my father to give his wife and children a home not constantly threatened by ruin.' The narrator's longing for security, for the reassurance of continuity and acceptance, is a recurring motif. Rose takes delight in the pleasures of daily life, in the conversation, games and rituals beloved of children. She is also prone to reverie and imaginative longings. She yearns for a place in the world, for respect and self-confidence. She senses that her father, unreliable though he was, embodied qualities and values that are important: a passion for clear statement, a determination to root out hypocrisy, the ability to inspire and influence others. For all these reasons her father commanded respect. All that Rose tells us concerning her father corresponds with what we know of Charles Fairfield and confirms the significance of the trilogy as a personal document. *This Real Night* is also valuable for its insight into Rebecca's own nature and for its growing awareness of evil. In a crucial passage the narrator acknowledges that she is torn between a love of discipline and a love of freedom:

> I was like a sea pulled by two moons. This must mean a boiling of the waters, tides that rushed up and carried away structures meant for living in, and then receded till earth that should be covered lay naked. I wanted to play the piano, and I did not want to be stretched on the rack of that calling. This was my secret, which I did not dare to speak, for fear of undermining life as I knew it.[13]

This confession to the reader underlines the dichotomy within Rebecca's personality and is strongly reminiscent of similar passages in Wells's autobiographical novels in which the narrator draws attention to his own divided nature. Part of her wanted public recognition and the kudos associated with this, even though this meant discipline, hard work and dedication. Part of her 'did not want to be stretched on the rack of that calling' and longed to be a free spirit. This contradiction within her temperament becomes slowly more apparent as Rose matures and is forced to acknowledge her emotional self. Most remarkable of all is Rose's burgeoning awareness of evil, of the darkness that lies at the heart of so much human activity: 'The real world was indeed that strange world where a dark wood could feel poor and rivers had business, and nameless forces could set trees alight for a message that had no meaning. For there death could be. . . .' Her recognition of 'nameless forces' underlying and influencing behaviour pervades the novel. Time and again she is reminded of the powers of darkness: first her beloved father disappears, then her saintly brother Richard Quin is killed on the battlefield, then her mother dies an agonising death. These events wound Rose by reminding her that goodness does not always triumph over evil, that life is a constant struggle between integrity and duplicity, altruism and selfishness.

The theme is resumed in *Cousin Rosamund* which continues the story of the family from the nightmare of war – 'we saw a fungoid bloom of ruin slowly creep across the familiar objects among which we had been reared' – to the Wall Street crash of 1929 and its aftermath. Again and again the novel demonstrates how individuals are affected by the values held by their parents and friends, and how these influences continue to affect us long after the people concerned are dead. The repercussions continue through time, shaping our lives in ways of which we are not always aware. Rebecca's characters are individuals in their own right with their own idiosyncracies and weaknesses but are also symbolic of forces she felt to be of immense importance – integrity (Clare Aubrey), goodness (Rosamund, Richard Quin), creativity (Rose,

Cordelia), duplicity (Piers Aubrey). Through the interplay of these forces the personalities of her characters are shaped and refined. Cousin Rosamund with her religiosity and selflessness is an embodiment of pure goodness; she represents the human spirit at its finest. Rose and Cordelia are both obsessed by art but do not see that there is more to life than the pursuit of artistic perfection. With great subtlety Rebecca helps the reader to see Rose's limitations as a narrator and as a human being: Rose never really understands Rosamund because she cannot comprehend spirituality, a quality possessed by Rosamund but not by herself.

The literary historian can but regret that this great project, to which Rebecca gave the overall title *A Saga of the Century*, was never completed. Her notes make it clear that she intended to bring the story up to the Second World War and the Nuremberg trials and perhaps even to extend the trilogy to a quatrain. But even in the unfinished form that we have the novels, the project remains an outstanding memorial to her skills as a writer and an abiding testament to her belief that each individual is shaped by forces rooted in the past. The writing of it helped her to see her own past in perspective and to clarify her attitudes to her parents and sisters. At about the same age Wells had settled down in Provence to write *The World of William Clissold*, a long novel which helped him to clarify his ideas and view his life and work in due proportion. *The Fountain Overflows* and its sequels fulfilled for her a similar purpose: it enabled her to come to terms with her childhood, to sort out in her own mind her feelings towards her parents and the scars of her upbringing. Had she written nothing else, she would still merit an honoured place in the history of the English novel.

IV

Her critical book *The Court and the Castle*, published in 1957, is an expanded version of three lectures she delivered at Yale University and marks a return to the preoccupations she had first aired in *The Strange Necessity*: What is the nature of art and what is – or should be – the relationship between art and life? *The Court and the Castle*, despite its forbidding subtitle, 'A study of the interactions of political and religious ideas in imaginative literature', is a series of sparkling critical essays in which she ranged over the whole field of English and European literature. Beginning with a discussion of Shakespeare's plays she continues with a lively resumé of the work of Fielding, Thackeray, Dickens and Trollope before turning to an examination of the modernists, including Proust, Lawrence, Woolf and Kafka. Her overriding theme is the interplay between 'the court' (the secular world of politics and statecraft) and 'the castle' (the world of religion and morality), showing how the two strands are interwoven in drama and the novel. Her juxtaposition of secular and sacred, public and private, is characteristic of her dual approach to life and literature and the dichotomy in her make-up between action and belief. Particularly illuminating is her discussion of Kafka's *The Trial* and *The Castle* as religious allegories; although she was not breaking new ground here her analysis is always refreshing and thought provoking. *The Court and the Castle* is literary criticism at its best. It contains evidence of wide reading without being in any way condescending and it succeeds in whetting the student's appetite to re-read the books under discussion. Many works of literary analysis only have the effect of driving the reader away from the novel or poem being discussed. But *The Court and the Castle* has the opposite effect: it enables the student to look at a range of novels and plays with greater insight and enjoyment and in doing so to appreciate afresh the balance between life and faith.

In 1959 Rebecca became Dame Rebecca West, an honour she was proud to receive and which probably meant more to her than all her other honours and awards. She felt very strongly that women writers were a disadvantaged class and in accepting this title was conscious that she was helping to raise their prestige. She never lost sight of the fact that she herself had sprung from humble origins and was proud to think that her name was known throughout the English-speaking world. Dame Rebecca West became increasingly a name to conjure with: a fearless writer who delighted in aiming cockshies at sacred cows, in exposing hypocrisy and double-think, in demolishing inflated reputations and searching out the truth however unpalatable it might be.

Meanwhile developments were taking place in the fields of biography and scholarship which exercised Rebecca considerably. In 1954 the University of Illinois purchased from the Wells Estate the substantial archive of letters, papers and manuscripts which had been in Wells's possession at the time of his death. Some of his friends expressed surprise that a literary treasure-house of this kind should find a permanent home in America rather than the country of his birth, but his sons felt strongly that Illinois was a logical home for the archive. The University already possessed a fine collection of literary manuscripts and its Professor, Gordon N. Ray, was planning to write a major biography of Wells and edit Wells's correspondence. It dawned on her that sooner or later biographers would have to present an account of his life and that within such an account a resumé of her relationship with him would inevitably find a place.

Wells's correspondence with Henry James was published in 1958, with Arnold Bennett in 1960 and with George Gissing in 1961. The H. G. Wells Society was founded in 1960 and Rebecca was invited to become a Vice-President. She replied that she would be 'honoured' to do so. When ambitious plans were drawn up to celebrate the centenary of his birth in 1966 she declined to take part. 'It is not that I wish to dissociate myself from H. G.', she wrote, 'I am extremely proud of my association with him, and my regard for his work has grown greater every year. But I do not wish to seem to exploit that association.' [14]

The publication in 1961 of Bernard Bergonzi's critical study *The Early H. G. Wells* stimulated considerable scholarly interest in Wells – an interest that had laid dormant since 1946 – and a growing number of academic books and papers on aspects of his life and work began to appear. In 1970 Gordon Ray suggested to Rebecca that, in addition to the biography on which he had been working for many years, he should write a study of the love affair between her and Wells. She consented to this suggestion on condition that she would have the right to vet the book before publication, and that Anthony would not be consulted in any way. The resulting book, published in 1974, was based on an examination of Wells's letters supplemented by Rebecca's recollections of their ten-year partnership. The weakness of this approach lay in the fact that Ray was relying on her memories of events that had occurred fifty or even sixty years earlier. Apart from the inevitable fallibility of memory, her recollections were coloured by a natural anxiety to present her own version of events. 'I want to do everything I can to get the situation as I want it before I die', she told a friend. [15] On its publication Anthony reviewed the book savagely in *Books and Bookmen*, accusing Ray of having impugned his standing as a scholar. To him it seemed inexplicable that an academic should write a study of his parents and their relationship without at least talking to him. For Anthony this was one more instance of his mother's perverseness, her determination that hers should be the only version of the truth which prevailed. When Norman and Jeanne Mackenzie's biography, *The Time Traveller*, was published in 1973 Rebecca reviewed the book at length under the title 'The real H. G. Wells'. Their biography, she wrote

> makes it seem as if, in a society exclusively composed of dull dogs, he was the dullest dog of all. It also makes him seem hateful, which is really astonishing in view of the number of friends who to the end loved nothing better than to be with him to an even inconvenient degree. [16]

Ranging widely over Wells's life, work and personal relationships she stressed the substance that lay behind the charm and illustrated his gift of transforming situations through the power of his personality. In doing so she drew attention to a limitation inherent in the nature of biography. The reader of a biography, she asserted, should ask him- or herself the question: 'When I die how much will those who come after me be able to discover about my most intimate relationships?' Even when the facts are known the facts often admit of several different interpretations and it is this *interpretation* which is the biographer's most difficult task. Rebecca was now 80. She well knew that in the nature of things her life was drawing to its close and that future biographers would want to arrive at a balanced judgement concerning both her own life and achievement and her association with Wells. She resolved that in the years remaining to her she would compose a volume of memoirs which would record all that she know of her parents and grandparents and all she could remember of family history and anecdotage. She continued to work on this project for the remainder of her life, neither completing nor abandoning it but never finally satisfied with the various drafts and outlines. The book was published posthumously in 1987 under the title *Family Memories*, edited and introduced by Faith Evans.

   The fact that she was working on the book on and off for so many years and that in the process it underwent countless changes of style, order and content reflects her own deep ambivalence regarding her ancestry and also her inability in some instances to distinguish between reminiscence and legend. Her memories became so intermingled with her own interpretation of events and her subconscious impressions of the past that Faith Evans described *Family Memories* as 'more like a sequence of interrelated novellas than a verifiable history', adding pointedly 'It has been decided not to include an index, to avoid conflict with the partly imaginary style of the narration.' [17] Despite its semi-fictional status the book remains a memorable portrait of her ancestors, providing fascinating insights into Rebecca's conception of herself and her background. In tracing the history of her mother's family, the Mackenzies, and contrasting this with the characteristics and environment of her father's family, the Fairfields, she throws into opposition attitudes and traits which powerfully influenced her early life. The qualities that stand out when discussing the Mackenzies are resilience, determination, pride and self-sufficiency. Time and again her Mackenzie forebears triumph over adversity, bringing up large families against heavy odds, surviving domestic crises, combatting hardship with thrift. Their quintessential attributes are respectability, strength of spirit and a dogged resolve to hold their heads up high. Stability and survival are their hallmarks. The Fairfields, by contrast, are adventurous, unpredictable and picaresque. Their background is filled with tales of foreign travel, colourful exploits and itinerant occupations. The Fairfields are romantic, gifted and emotional; Bohemianism rather than conventionality is their watchword. It is the implicit contrast between continuity and insecurity, conformity and rebellion, which provides the book with its dominating theme.

A secondary theme underlying *Family Memories* is that of betrayal. Treachery in both private and public life was a concept that exercised her imagination for many years. A recurring pattern in her memoirs is that of betrayal by the male sex: the unreliability of the male in comparison with the strength and dependability of the female. It is clear from her account that her father possessed many fine qualities – affection, subtlety, sensitivity, generosity. But equally clear is her inability to come to terms with the fatal flaw in his character, his failure to be a reliable breadwinner, husband and father. This weakness in his make-up – as she expressed it, 'the detachment of my father from the consequences of his actions' – was to her incomprehensible and inexcusable. She simply could not understand his blatant sexuality, his unfaithfulness, his gambling, his lack of compunction in deserting them. To her this was the ultimate treachery: to walk out on a wife and family who trusted and respected him. His extra-marital relationships in her opinion 'made him indifferent as to whether my mother and my sisters starved or not'. This seems an extravagant claim. But there can be no question that Rebecca firmly believed it, just as she believed that the inconstancy of her father was a hereditary trait. To her we are all the victims of our environment, the product of an unending struggle between good and evil, happiness and sorrow, light and darkness.

Her last novel *The Birds Fall Down* – a gripping story of intrigue and adventure in pre-revolutionary Russia – was published in 1966. In it she returned to her favourite themes of treachery and integrity, showing how the seeds of the 1917 revolution were sown in Russia's past and how deception in statecraft is inextricably linked with duplicity in private life. For some of the details of life in Tsarist Russia she consulted Moura Budberg. It would be too much to claim that Laura, the young heroine of the novel, is based on Moura as a young woman but one may reasonably assume that the character was inspired at least in part by Moura's colourful exploits: certainly the novel owes much to her 'feel' for period atmosphere and her understanding of the snares of intrigue in pre-1914 Europe. *The Birds Fall Down* became a book club choice and sold well despite its inordinate length. It brought her name before a new public brought up on the works of Eric Ambler and Hammond Innes who had somehow not associated the author of *The Fountain Overflows* and *The Thinking Reed* with stories of international betrayal.

During the autumn of 1968 Henry's health began to deteriorate. He was 74 and had been suffering for some time from an ulcer. He died of cancer on 3 November 1968. Rebecca was distraught. She and Henry had been partners since 1930; she had come to depend on him for so much. Her immediate reaction was to sell Ibstone, as the house was now far too large for her needs. She acquired a comfortable flat in Kensington Gardens which remained her home for the rest of her days. She sold Ibstone for much the same reason that Wells disposed of Easton Glebe after the death of his wife: though the house was dearly loved it held too many memories. She enjoyed living in London again after an absence of so many years and kept herself busy with journalism, book reviewing, going to theatres and shows.

Anthony returned to London in 1970 and devoted himself to writing the biography of his father which he had had on his mind for many years. During his twenty years in the United States he had consolidated his reputation as a critic and published *Principles and Persuasions*, a collection of his literary essays, and a number of novels and critical works. Back in England he concentrated all his energies on the biography, though he agreed to become a Vice-President of the H. G. Wells Society and to address a meeting of the Society in which he talked about some of the biographical problems he had encountered. He had originally undertaken to deliver the completed manuscript to the publishers by the end of 1977 but as the project grew and he found himself becoming increasingly fascinated by Wells's life and work the deadline was more and more unrealistic. It was not until the end of 1983 that he delivered the final text to Hutchinson; it was published in 1984 under the title *H. G. Wells: Aspects of a life*.

The biography is a full-scale work which surveys the entire span of Wells's life and writings and places his work in its literary and intellectual context. Anthony decided to adopt the unusual device of commencing the biography in 1914, the year of his own birth, then – after describing Wells's life from 1914 onwards – going on to describe his early life and that of his partents and so bringing the story full circle. It is a fascinating and highly readable account of Wells's life and work which deserves to take its place alongside Norman and Jeanne Mackenzie's *The Time Traveller* as one of the outstanding literary biographies of our time. There can be no doubt that in writing it Anthony felt he was paying his debt to his father for the inspiration of his life and achievement and, with the best of intentions, seeking to explain and re-interpret Wells's behaviour. It is unfortunate that in his anxiety to present Wells in the most favourable light Anthony does less than justice to some of his contemporaries including in particular Shaw, James and Gissing, all of whom come in for a drubbing. Not surprisingly Anthony reserves most of his ire for his own mother. The opening chapters are devoted to a splenetic account of the relationship between Wells and Rebecca in which he seeks to pay off a number of old scores by portraying Rebecca as naïve, unbalanced and high-handed. The fact that Anthony is so emotionally involved with the events and personalities being described discounts him as a dispassionate witness and tends to weaken the credibility of the biography as a scholarly work. This is regrettable, for the book is in many ways an honourable attempt to place Wells's life and work in perspective and to understand the mainsprings of his behaviour and attitudes. It is especially perceptive in its account of Joseph and Sarah Wells and their impact on their mercurial and gifted son. As the son of two brilliant and headstrong individuals Anthony possessed a deep insight into the influence of parents on their children and well understood the complex of desires and emotions that moulded the young Herbert George Wells. In writing of Wells as a young man he detected the influence of his ancestry at many crucial stages in his life and the competing motivations which drove him onwards. The biography is particularly skilful in unravelling the tangled skein of hereditary and psychological influences which shaped Wells as a man and as a novelist, and in probing deeper into incidents in *Experiment in Autobiography* where he feels that Wells is disingenuous. For all its faults *H. G. Wells: Aspects of a life* remains indispensable reading for all who seek a deeper understanding of Wells. Anthony knew his father very well indeed and came nearer than most to appreciate the conflicting drives that tormented and inspired him.

V

The final years of Rebecca's life were crowded with activity. She took a close interest in the television adaptation of *The Birds Fall Down* and travelled to Paris on location to advise on details of production. She also gave her approval to the making of a new film version of *The Return of the Soldier*, starring Alan Bates and Jule Christie. In 1977 The Viking Press in the United States and Macmillan in Britain published *Rebecca West: A celebration*, an anthology of her best work. The volume included *The Return of the Soldier* in its entirety together with selections from *The Harsh Voice, The Thinking Reed, The Strange Necessity* and *Black Lamb and Grey Falcon* and a number of uncollected essays. Rebecca worked closely with the publishers over the choice of contents and took great satisfaction in assisting in the editorial process. In his Introduction, 'In communion with reality', Samuel Hynes wrote: 'That fine, strong androgynous mind that we meet in her books is her achievement; knowing it, we could not wish that her work were anything except what it is.' The anthology was subsequently reprinted in paperback and remains an impressive tribute to the breadth of her work and the vitality of her writing.

In 1980 Virago, the feminist publishers, reissued *The Judge* and *Harriet Hume* as the first stage of a major programme of reprinting her novels and critical works. These were followed by *The Young Rebecca*, a collection of her early polemical essays and book reviews. It gave her immense pleasure to see the republication of her books, some of which had been out of print for many years, and to know that her work would reach a new generation of readers for whom the radical causes of the early twentieth century were an unknown world. Her regular book reviews for the *Daily Telegraph* and *Sunday Telegraph* continued until a few months before her death – always coruscating, lively and unpredictable. To the end she took the keenest interest in her journalism and current affairs, despite being in increasing pain from arthritis. She entertained widely and liked to keep in touch with all that was going on in the worlds of literature and art.

Her last book, *1900* – an impressionistic essay on life at the dawn of the century – appeared in 1981. Writing was now becoming more and more difficult as she was in so much pain. Reluctant to concede defeat she struggled to write a short story and completed an Introduction to a new edition of R. S. Surtees' *Ask Mamma*. Latterly she became completely housebound – an imperious but always dignified old lady with an ailing body and a mind of incredible sharpness. At last, as her mental powers began to wane, she took to her bed. In her less coherent moments she held imaginary conversations with Anthony, with Wells, even with her own mother. Then lucidity would return and it would upset her that slowly but irrevocably her faculties were declining. She died on 15 March 1983, aged 90.

By her own choice she was buried at Brookwood Cemetery near Woking in Surrey. There, among the rhododendrons, azaleas and bluebells, and surrounded by stately pines and oak trees, she found her peace. The cemetery is only a mile or two from Horsell Common where Wells had placed the first Martian landing in *The War of the Worlds* and close to the modest villa in Woking where he and Jane had lived in the early years of their marriage. Four miles away is Sutton Place, the 'Lady Grove' of *Tono-Bungay* and the scene of George Ponderevo's aeronautical experiments. A short journey to the South is Guildford, the 'altogether charming old town' to which Mr Hoopdriver cycled in search of romance and adventure in *The Wheels of Chance*. In death she was still linked to the man who had so powerfully affected her life and with whose imagination and emotions she was inseparably fused.

Chapter 9

The Summing Up

I stumble and flounder, but I know that over all these merry immediate things, there are other things that are great and serene, very high, beautiful things – the reality. I haven't got it, but it's there nevertheless. I'm a spiritual guttersnipe in love with unimaginable goddesses.

H. G. Wells, *Tono-Bungay*

That is the great handicap of sexual love, that lovers can share everything except what explains the past, of which their enjoyment is a part.

Rebecca West, *Cousin Rosamund*

I

The partnership between H. G. Wells and Rebecca West affected them both profoundly. It was a friendship between two writers who were torn by powerful emotional and creative drives, each of whom saw in the other the fulfilment of a deeply felt need. It was a friendship which had significant consequences for them both as literary figures and which exercised them long after their love affair had come to an end. To reflect on their partnership and its consequences raises a number of questions that are pertinent not only to the two principals as individuals but to literary history. What impact did each have upon the other's creative life? What were their fundamental attitudes to literature and how did these differ? Why did the partnership come to an end? And what are the enduring elements in their literary achievement? To these questions we will now turn.

Rebecca came into Wells's life at a crucial stage in his emotional and creative development. In his personal life he was dissatisfied with his relationship with Elizabeth von Arnim and desperately in need of reassurance. The scars of the love affair with Amber Reeves that had almost torn his life apart were still fresh in his mind, leaving him prey to moods of depression in which all his world seemed dark and hopeless. This malaise is evident in the closing pages of *Boon* with the deepening pessimism which almost overwhelms the writer and in the striking passage in *The Passionate Friends* when the narrator admits that at times 'a sense of life as of an abyssmal flood, full of cruelty, densely futile, blackly aimless, penetrates my defences'.[1] To Wells, profoundly discontented with his emotional life and at odds with the world, Rebecca, young, vibrant and eager, crossed his horizon at precisely the point when he was most in need of the qualities she embodied.

Likewise in his creative life he had reached a turning point. After a brilliant beginning as a creator of haunting apocalyptic and mythopoeic fables he had turned with growing mastery to the writing of novels and in the early years of the new century had produced a series of memorable works of art including *Love and Mr Lewisham, Kipps, Tono-Bungay, Ann Veronica* and *The History of Mr Polly*. These had wrung from Henry James the assertion that 'You must at moments make dear old Dickens turn – for envy of the eye and the ear and the nose and the mouth of you – in his grave.'[2] They had won for him a reputation throughout the English-speaking world and beyond as a novelist of the foremost rank and an imaginative writer of distinction. But by 1912 it was clear he had reached a watershed in his practical and theoretical approach to literature. *The New Machiavelli* and *Marriage* had both displayed an increasing preoccupation with ideas, a fascination with politics and sociology at the expense of human character. To many readers he seemed to be moving away from the qualities that had so animated his earlier fiction – vivid interest in personalities, a concern with communities, a love of rural life – towards a dry and humourless obsession with putting the world to rights. This growing concern for ideology was accompanied by a marked distancing of himself from James and his circle. In his 1911 lecture to the Times Book Club, 'The contemporary novel', he had deliberately scorned what he termed 'the Weary Giant' theory of literature – the notion that the function of the novel was to entertain and that it must not on any account stimulate thought or introduce controversial matter – and proclaimed his intention to discuss a wide range of contemporary social problems through the medium of fiction. *Marriage*, the novel which brought Rebecca into his world, is a praiseworthy attempt to achieve this end but it is clearly the work of a writer who is still feeling his way towards the fusion of discussion and narrative and cannot resist the temptation to lecture the reader. It is moreover the work of a novelist who, recoiling after the frankness of *Ann Veronica* and *Tono-Bungay*, was still remarkably coy and laboured in his descriptions of dialogue between lovers. Rebecca was quick to detect these weaknesses and in labelling him 'the old maid among novelists' was drawing attention not simply to his coyness but to the unreality of so many of his female characters. Beatrice Normandy in *Tono-Bungay*, Margaret Seddon in *The New Machiavelli*, Marjorie Pope in *Marriage* and Lady Mary Christian in *The Passionate*

Friends are all gracious, beautiful women who seem utterly remote from the everyday world of work and domesticity. Rebecca found their idleness and spiritlessness infuriating and made her opinions known in no uncertain terms. From this point onwards his heroines are not only far more believable as characters but their relationships carry far more conviction. In part this is attributable to the change in moral climate between the Edwardian years and the 1920s – *The Dream*, published in 1924, is in many ways a more outspoken novel than *Ann Veronica*, published fifteen years earlier, but it did not cause any furore – but it is also plain that he had taken Rebecca's criticisms to heart and that her youth and vitality was having a material effect on his fiction.

To what extent did Wells make use of Rebecca as a character in his novels? If we examine this question we are faced at once with an impressive list of heroines who animate his fiction:

Amanda Morris	:	*The Research Magnificent*
Cecily Corner	:	*Mr Britling Sees It Through*
Joan Debenham	:	*Joan and Peter*
Martin Leeds	:	*The Secret Places of the Heart*
Fanny Smith	:	*The Dream*
Helen	:	*The World of William Clissold*

Each of these characters is vivacious, animated and *alive*; each is a world removed from the gentle, passive heroines of his Edwardian novels. It is not simply that the characters themselves are vigorous and lifelike but that each transforms the novel through her impact on her protagonist. Fanny Smith in *The Dream* and Helen in *The World of William Clissold*, for example, are described in terms which render them unforgettable. They remain in the reader's mind long after the book has been closed and haunt the imagination by their loveliness. When Clissold tells the reader that Helen 'not only evoked and satisfied my sense of beauty in herself, but she had the faculty of creating a kind of victorious beauty in the scene about her' [3] one finds oneself assenting. This is the kind of detail which brings a character to life and compels belief.

Rebecca's influence on Wells as a creative artist does not end here. During their ten-year partnership he produced some of his finest work – *Mr Britling Sees It Through*, *Joan and Peter* and *The Dream* – novels which pulsate with the questioning and vitality of a new generation. In these novels he was gaining growing mastery in the handling of dialogue and incident, a mastery which would come to fruition in *The Bulpington of Blup*. He also produced two novels which mark a turning point in his intellectual development: *Boon* and *Men Like Gods*. *Boon* has its place in literary history as the novel in which he said farewell to the world of James and his circle, the intensely art-conscious group of writers who had lived within cycling distance of his home at Sandgate. It is a symbolic renunciation of all that they stood for. *Men Like Gods* is of equal significance as the work in which he caricatured his own Utopian writings and in doing so recognised the futility of his idealistic dreams. It marks the end of innocence. These two novels, written at the beginning and the end of his partnership with Rebecca West, neatly encapsulate its impact upon him. The decade 1913–23 was for him a period of enormous creative importance. It saw the end of his flirtation with James and the aesthetes and a decisive shift away from the traditions of the Victorian novel towards the novel of discussion and social comment. It saw the tremendous concussion of the First World War, sweeping away the world of his youth and forcing him to abandon the facile optimism of *A Modern Utopia* and *In the Days of the Comet*. Above all it saw his passionate friendship with a young, vital writer who embodied the spirit of youth and brought him in touch with the aspirations of a radical generation. It is perhaps in this respect – the fact that Rebecca symbolised in her own person an intense eagerness for life and experience, and in doing so enabled him to recreate the vigour and drive of his own youth – that she made her most decisive impact.

Wells entered Rebecca's life at an equally significant stage. When she first met him at the age of 19 she was a young writer of great promise who had earned a reputation as a fearless critic and iconoclast. Her reputation was confined to feminist and socialist journals but she was already determined to make her mark as a novelist and writer on social questions. After her brilliant debut as a novelist in *The Return of the Soldier* (1918) no full-length work of fiction appeared from her pen until *The Judge* four years later. The long gap is partly explained by the upheaval in her life of trying to combine a literary career with motherhood but it is also explained by the fact that in writing *The Judge* she was working out the essential battle of her approach to life and art. Not the least of the reasons why it remains essential reading for all who seek to understand Rebecca West is that in the turmoil of its creation she was coming to terms with herself as an artist. It is a powerfully written story with a haunting theme and an engaging and lifelike central character but is flawed by its uneven quality and excessive prolixity. Wells once defined their differing approaches to literature by saying 'You have a richness. I am simplicity.' In the same letter he described *The Judge* as 'a spate of undisciplined imagination'.[4] Just as he had taken her strictures over *Marriage* to heart, the evidence of her novels strongly suggests that, while professing to disagree with him, she had learned the lesson. The works she wrote after *The Judge* – *Sunflower*, *Harriet Hume*, *The Harsh Voice*, *The Thinking Reed* and *The Fountain Overflows* – are far more disciplined, far more carefully wrought than her earlier work and bear all the marks of meticulous planning and revision. Of these it is *Sunflower* and *Harriet Hume*, written in the aftermath of their parting, which offer the deepest insight into his impact on her life.

Rebecca poured into *Sunflower* all her anguish at parting from Wells. Essington is a man with a mind 'as large as life', 'full of sweetness', a man possessed by ideas that dominate his life who cannot do without the reassurance Sunflower means to him. Sunflower is attracted towards the manly and powerful Francis Pitt but it is Essington, for all his moodiness, whom she finds lovable and kind. She cannot bring herself to leave him because that would be 'to abandon the whole of life that was good'. *Sunflower* is memorable not simply for its portrayal of Wells as Essington but for the power of its writing. What remains in the mind is its maturity, the conviction with which the novel portrays the divided feelings of a perceptive and sensitive woman. It possesses in abundance the ring of truth: *this*, one says to oneself, really happened. But *Sunflower* is also notable because interwoven in the narrative is a skilful deployment of symbols drawn from the language of dreams and the unconscious. When the heroine is trying to choose between Eassington and Pitt the car in which she is travelling passes along an avenue of trees. The trees are described as confused between the seasons, being 'bright with white candles celebrating spring, but casting beneath them a shadow damp with the rich, rotting airs of autumn, in which the downward thrusting spears of sunshine seem to be forged of the strong light of midsummer'.[5] This is a vivid metaphor for Sunflow-er's ambivalent state of mind, torn between the spring-like quality of her first love for Essington and the autumn of its decline. But its language is extremely interesting – 'white candles', 'rich, rotting airs of autumn', 'downward thrusting spears', 'strong light of midsummer' – and strongly reminiscent of Wells's short stories such as 'Mr Skelmersdale in fairyland' and 'The beautiful suit' and the complex imagery of *The Time Machine*. In this and subsequent novels Rebecca seems to be much more conscious of Jungian imagery and to make extensive use of symbolism.

During their years together she and Wells allowed their imaginations free rein in a world of fantasy, finding happiness in reveries of country inns, eccentric animals and imaginary people. The love of fantasy which they shared found its expression in *Harriet Hume*, a novel he described as 'her all too little appreciated book'.[6] This story of the attraction between two mystical lovers and the pursuit of Harriet against a background of a garden like 'a green sanctuary' is at once Rebecca at her most fanciful and an etherealised version of her love for Wells. In its widespread use of dream imagery derived from 'The door in the wall' it is, of all her novels, the one most obviously influenced by his work. The frequent use of the phrase 'the door in the wall' as a symbol for passing from the conscious to the unconcious mind makes it plain she is aware of the derivation and is employing the symbol as a deliberate motif. Harriet is a typical anima figure – beautiful, elusive, captivating – and the novel is characteristic of its genre in its emphasis on the theme of the eternal quest. *Harriet Hume* embodies, in fact, many of the themes and tensions implicit in Rebecca's relationship with Wells: the happiness of the two lovers, their delight in one another, their recognition of their differences, their puzzled attempt to come to terms with their strengths and weaknesses.

The garden motif which permeates so many of Wells's stories, most notably *The Time Machine*, 'The door in the wall', *The History of Mr Polly* and *Men Like Gods*, became an increasingly common element in her novels, particularly when recalling scenes she and Wells had shared. So many of their happiest times together had taken place against a background of English rural scenery – Monkey Island, Virginia Water, the Sussex Weald, Dorset – that the pastoral idyll became for them both a reminder of all that was best in their friendship. The third chapter of *The Return of the Soldier* with its lyrical description of Monkey Island is unforgettable in its beauty and haunting nostalgia. Most striking of all are her descriptions of the Thames Valley in *This Real Night* and *Cousin Rosamund* and the loving evocation of a riverside inn, 'the Dog and Duck', which becomes for Rose Aubrey a haven of happiness. The stretch of the river around Bray and Maidenhead – the location of Monkey Island and of Wells's boyhood paradise Surly Hall – is depicted with glowing affection:

'Look at those trees across the river', he said absently. 'That line of poplars at the back, then the beeches below, then those weeping willows, with their tumbled branches in front of them, and in the foreground the flat meadow, and the same hedge of loosestrife on the water's edge as we have, and then the water. It is a composition!' [7]

Compare Wells's description of the same scene in *The History of Mr Polly*:

It was about two o'clock in the afternoon, one hot day in May, when Mr Polly, unhurrying and serene, came upon that broad bend of the river to which the little lawn and garden of the Potwell Inn run down . . . A hedge separated the premises from a buttercup-yellow meadow, and beyond stood three poplars in a group against the sky, three exceptionally tall, graceful, and harmonious poplars. It is hard to say what there was about them that made them so beautiful to Mr Polly, but they seemed to him to touch a pleasant scene with a distinction almost divine. [8]

Clearly the Thames riverscape was for both of them a special place, rich in memories. It held for them the association of a romantic idyll, a retreat where they could be alone.

Wells's impression on her creative life is difficult to quantify but the aspects identified here – a more disciplined approach to the art of fiction and a wider use of psychological and pastoral imagery – are readily identifiable and traceable to his influence. Throughout ten stormy years together they merged their imaginative selves in a continual flow of fantasy, reverie and make-believe. At the end of it each emerged a different person, changed mentally and emotionally by contact with the other.

II

As their creative lives progressed their differing approaches to literature became more evident. Wells's mentors were and remained Dickens, Sterne and Fielding; Rebecca's mentors were and remained Lawrence, James and Proust. In part the difference reflects the gap in their ages. Where Wells placed emphasis on the novel as a medium for the discussion of social and moral questions and the exploration of human character, Rebecca saw the novel as an instrument for the fulfilment of aesthetic values. The difference was one of both theory and practice. A comparison of his essay 'The contemporary novel' with *The Strange Necessity* reveals a fundamental dichotomy in their critical approach. Wells insists that the novel should be 'a powerful instrument of moral suggestion' through the discussion of human conduct and that the difference between the Victorian and modern novels lies in the fact 'that formerly there was a feeling of certitude about moral values and standards of conduct that is altogether absent today'. The whole tenor of his argument is that there can be no absolute standards in morality, art or literature and that art is incidental to the writing of fiction: what matters is not the creation of beautifully crafted works of art but the illumination of human behaviour. Rebecca's position is the opposite of this. *The Strange Necessity* insists that art *matters*, that it is fundamental to human happiness and fulfilment and that the role of the artist is to give asethetic pleasure by producing works of art. The artist's function is 'to light up the world with the beauty of his work'. Her position is essentially that adopted by Henry James in his 1915 quarrel with Wells: art is the only enduring reality and the role of the creative artist is to serve it to his utmost.

The difference becomes clear when one compares their work in practice. To compare *Tono-Bungay* with, say, *The Fountain Overflows* or

Britling Sees It Through with *The Return of the Soldier* is an illuminating exercise revealing much about both writers. All four novels are accomplished and rich in literary qualities but are plainly the outcome of very different attitudes to life. What interests Wells are human emotions, the way in which individuals react on one another and respond to changes in their situation. Like Dickens he is fascinated by the role of chance in human affairs, the way in which circumstances can be transformed by sudden changes of fortune. His dominating themes are challenge and response, the catalyst impinging on its surroundings. His style is readable and fluent but he is more interested in narrative than in the creation of memorable effects. Rebecca's concerns are much more introspective. She too is interested in the individual's response to change but has far more patience than Wells in working out its implications through the nuances of daily life. Where *Tono-Bungay* moves at a breathtaking pace offering a panoramic vision of life, *The Fountain Overflows* is content to move with measured tread through the small events of everyday living, studying the minutia of behaviour over long periods of time. She is concerned with the mainsprings of behaviour rather than outward events, with causes rather than effects. The same divergence is evident in their war novels. *Mr Britling Sees It Through* describes the impact of war on a representative Englishman and the changes in his attitudes, beliefs and lifestyle as the conflict proceeds. It broadens out into a vision of the world transformed as a result of the lessons learned by the war. *The Return of the Soldier* also focuses on a small group of Englishmen and women but the visionary quality of Wells's novel is altogether absent. Rebecca is content to examine the effect of the war on one man's mind; she is concerned with individual psychology rather than the huge issues of war and peace. Both novels are perfect of their kind but one has the impression that whereas *Mr Britling* was written in a white heat of enthusiasm, *The Return of the Soldier* was fashioned with laborious care, every word chosen with Lawrencian intensity.

At the root of their differing attitudes to literature was a profound divergence in their vision of life and behaviour. To Wells each individual is responsible for his own destiny; to Rebecca each individual is shaped by hereditary forces. This fundamental difference in approach underlay many of their quarrels and deeply affected their conception of the role of the imaginative writer.

Wells's conviction that the individual is responsible for his own fate, that 'if the world does not please you, you can change it',[9] stemmed in large measure from his personal history. Again and again in his life he had been struck by the fact that determined action can alter the most unpromising situations. Either wholly or partly as a result of his own actions he had succeeded in escaping from the draper's shop, from the

Holt Academy, from the correspondence college, from his first marriage. Instead of blindly accepting his lot he had rebelled against it on each occasion when his circumstances seemed limiting or frustrating. The pattern of disentanglement and flight became ingrained in his nature, as it had done for his father before him. On each occasion when Joseph Wells had found his employment as a gardener uncongenial he had quarrelled with his superior or simply moved on to a different post. When he found shopkeeping in Bromley intolerable he took up cricket coaching, which involved frequent absences from home, or threatened to emigrate to America. The same pattern is repeated in Wells's novels. Kipps escapes from the world of retail trade which had seemed to be his irrevocable destiny and extricates himself from a marriage he senses will bring him nothing but misery; Polly flees from his lacklustre wife and home and finds happiness at a country inn; George Ponderevo disentangles himself from an unhappy marriage and finds a purpose in life by throwing all his energies into aeronautical experiments. The typical Wells hero, both in the novels and the short stories, is a man who frees himself from a constricting environment through his own actions.

Rebecca's conception of life was very different. To her one's destiny is shaped not by individual will but by drives and traits rooted deep in the past. In her view each human being is swayed by hereditary factors making for good or ill, factors beyond the control of the self. The epigraph she placed at the beginning of her novel *The Judge* – 'Every mother is a judge who sentences the children for the sins of the father' – is an expression of this habit of mind: a conviction that one's propensity to good or evil, light or darkness, has its origins in ancestral forces. She derived this Manichean view of life from her observation of her own parents (and especially of the actions of her father) and her study of family history. In her eyes the feckless behaviour of her father was simply a recurrence of a long history of erratic behaviour on the part of the Fairfields, whereas her mother had inherited from her ancestors, the Mackenzies, qualities of independence, thrift and dependability that could be traced far back in the mists of time. When she came to express her ideas in fiction this view of destiny inevitably coloured her approach to character. Ellen Melville in *The Judge* falls in love with the illegitimate son of a woman who has been betrayed by a man. When the lovers seek to overcome the legacy of the past they themselves re-enact what has elapsed before. The lovers in *The Thinking Reed* are moulded by forces and attitudes rooted in their ancestry; none can escape from the consquences of the past. The Aubrey family and their circle in *The Fountain Overflows* and its sequels each embody good or evil and their lives follow a pattern predetermined by their inborn nature. The sense of a working out of irrevocable destiny, of a fulfilment of the past, removes from her characters the ability to fashion their own lives and gives to her fiction a sombre quality reminiscent of Hardy.

III

Superficially Wells and Rebecca had much in common. They were both writers with a keen interest in literature and literary expression. Both possessed a radical attitude of mind, questioning received notions on politics and morality. Both had a love of fantasy. Both had formidable intellectual powers and delighted in the world of ideas. Both were powerful personalities, inspiring strong feelings in all who knew them. The differences between them are equally striking. They first met when he was 46, a famous novelist with a growing world-wide reputation; she was 19, a young girl on the brink of her career. By comparison with her inexperience of life he possessed immense advantages of experience and maturity. He had been writing for twenty years and had already produced an impressive body of work including novels, short stories, scientific romances and sociological essays; he had learned his craft through a long process of trial and error. She had still to write her first novel and had yet to grapple with the problems of sustained imaginative creation. He was a married man with a household and a country home; she was a single girl with few possessions and still living at home with her mother.

Ten years later their respective situations were still widely different. He was now a world figure with a huge new following as a popular educator, the best-selling author of *The Outline of History* and *A Short History of the World*. He retained his pleasant country home in Essex and was happy in his wife and sons. He commanded substantial fees for lectures and articles and was increasingly preoccupied with politics and world affairs. He was editing a collected edition of his works. Rebecca, by contrast, was still finding her feet as a literary artist. In the intervening decade she had published two novels of considerable promise but her career had been deflected by the pressures of motherhood and the necessity of leading a *sub rosa* existence during the moral climate of the war years. She was steadily building up a reputation as a journalist and public figure but as a single woman with a child her position remained ambiguous. In the end the tensions inherent in their relationship proved insurmountable and she took the initiative in severing it. But to find the underlying reasons for their divergence one needs to look deeply into their psychology and attitudes. In the last analysis the partnership between H. G. Wells and Rebecca West failed to become permanent because each wanted from it fundamentally different things. Rebecca wanted security, reassurance, stability: all that her father had so lamentably failed to provide. But Wells wanted a goddess.

Rebecca's need for security stemmed from her profoundly ambivalent attitude towards her father, Charles Fairfield, and her deeply ingrained conviction that the male sex could not be trusted to provide protection and dependability. It is clear from *Family Memories* and *The Fountain Overflows* and its sequels that she, her mother and her sisters dearly loved their father but found his desertion of them cruel and inexplicable. This belief that men were unreliable, that they were inherently incapable of providing security, coloured her attitude towards the opposite sex all her life and strongly affected her feelings towards Wells. At several points in *This Real Night*, for example, Rose Aubrey reflects on the duplicity of the male sex:

> and there was the darker, and bewildering, realisation that men find a special pleasure in rejecting women, and will contrive to do it even to women who have not been offered to them.
> There was, in fact, a full force of husbands and dancing-partners available, had they only come forward; and I could not account then, and cannot account now, for their reluctance except by supposing that men do not like women and find pleasure in preventing them from doing what they want to do.[10]

The notion that 'men find a special pleasure in rejecting women' and that basically men do not like women was one of her most fundamental convictions. In the light of her family background her mistrust of men was perfectly understandable. She had seen her mother made deeply unhappy by her father's unfaithfulness and fecklessness and had witnessed the devastation of her home through his desertion. This profound mistrust was an ineradicable part of her make-up long before she met Wells and was fuelled by his prevarication and inconstancy. When he was unfaithful to her with Moura this confirmed her worst fears regarding masculine behaviour and seemed merely a repetition of her father's infidelity. When, in response to her repeated requests, he declined to leave his wife and marry her this seemed to her a confirmation of male treachery. His refusal to be pinned down was from her point of view proof of his inconsistency.

From childhood onwards Wells had been fascinated by the 'tall and lovely feminine figures' he had seen in volumes of *Punch*: idealised representations of Britannia, Erin and Columbia. 'My first consciousness of women', he wrote, 'my first stirrings of desire were roused by these heroic divinities', adding that alongside the world of adventure and exploration he derived from his boyhood reading he was aware of 'a cavernous world of nameless goddess mistresses of which I never breathed a word to any human being'.[11] There is a revealing moment in

The Secret Places of the Heart when his *alter ego* Sir Richmond Hardy is talking to the psychoanalyst Dr Martineau apropos of his attitude to women:

> 'On the whole I came up to adolescence pretty straight and clean,' said Sir Richmond. 'What stands out in my memory now is this idea of a sort of woman goddess who was very lovely and kind and powerful and wonderful. That ruled by secret imaginations as a boy, but it was very much in my mind as I grew up.'
> 'The mother complex,' said Dr Martineau as a passing botanist might recognise and name a flower.
> Sir Richmond stared at him for a moment.
> 'It had not the slightest connexion with my mother or any mother or any particular woman at all. Far better to call it the goddess complex.'
> 'The connexion is not perhaps immediately visible,' said the doctor.
> 'There was no connexion,' said Sir Richmond. 'The women of my adolescent dreams were stripped and strong and lovely. They were great creatures. They came, it was clearly traceable, from pictures, sculpture – and from a definite response in myself to their beauty.' [12]

This fixation, which Wells termed 'the goddess complex', haunted him throughout his life. The idea of a 'woman goddess who was very lovely and kind and powerful and wonderful' became an obsession that coloured all his relations with women; it was an ideal against which the reality had to be measured. As George Ponderevo expressed it in *Tono-Bungay*: 'I was torn between the urgency of the body and a habit of romantic fantasy that wanted every phase of the adventure to be generous and beautiful.' [13] The obsession recurs again and again in his fiction. It can be seen in the tall, fair girl who leads Wallace by the hand in 'The door in the wall' and takes him to the enchanted garden, the mermaid in *The Sea Lady* who lures Chatteris to his death, Marion in *Tono-Bungay* whom George sees 'in dreams released, as it were, from herself, beautiful, worshipful, glowing', the romantic daydreams of Mr Polly who is haunted by a vision of a simple-mannered girl in a pink print dress 'faintly smiling and yet earnest, parting the branches of the hedgerows and reaching down, apple in hand'. It can be seen in the narrator's love for Hetty Marcus in *The Dream* and his pursuit of the elusive quality she seems to embody, the emotional life of William Clissold and his quest for 'a material entanglement with beauty', Stephen Wilbeck's encounter in *Apropos of Dolores* with a tall, blonde, sunburnt woman outside the inn at Questombec. It can be seen in the paradisal imagery with which so many of his fictional heroines are surrounded. Weena in *The Time Machine* is depicted against the setting of a beautiful garden resembling the Garden of Eden, Christabel in *The History of Mr Polly* is encountered amidst idyllic pastoral scenery 'sitting in dappled sunshine upon grey and crumbling walls', Amanda in *The Research Magnificent* inspires her suitor with an image of two armour-clad lovers 'striding and flourishing through the lit wilderness of his imagination'.

This lifelong search for a goddess figure haunted his imagination and led him into a long series of emotional entanglements. He defined the search in these terms:

> All my life has been at bottom, *seeking*, disbelieving always, dissatisfied always with the thing seen and the thing believed, seeking something in toil, in force, in danger, something whose name and nature I do not clearly understand, something beautiful, worshipful, enduring, mine profoundly and fundamentally, and the utter redemption of myself; I don't know, – all I can tell is that it is something I have ever failed to find.[14]

This sense of life as a quest, as a search for a beautiful and enduring experience, had preoccupied him ever since his boyhood days in Bromley when his imagination had been fired by visions of womanhood derived from his reading.

Linked to the goddess fixation was a deep reticence in his make-up, a congenital inability to give himself wholly to another human being. Among the many autobiographical statements scattered throughout his fiction few are more revealing than the candid admission in *Tono-Bungay* that he was an ineffectual partner: 'I shall have much to say of love in this story, but I may break it to the reader now that it is my role to be a rather ineffectual lover. Desire I know well enough – indeed, too well; but love I have been shy of.'[15]

There were many reasons for this 'shyness' of love, this reluctance to commit himself to a partner. Claustrophobia, fear of entanglement, a goddess fixation which caused him to place before himself an impossibly high ideal: all contributed to this failure. In a perceptive article written long after his death Rebecca drew attention to the fact that 'Wells never made a normally satisfactory marriage, in which husband and wife share life day in, day out, under the same roof.'[16] The nearest he came to this was during the early years of his second marriage – the period from 1895–1900 when he and Jane were seeking to achieve a *modus vivendi* – though one suspects that even then he was smitten by wanderlust. It is difficult to resist the conclusion that deep in his make-up was an urge towards rebellion which led him time and again to seek refuge from constricting situations in fantasy or flight. Rebecca touches the kernel of the problem in pointing out his failure to achieve a normally satisfactory marriage, his reluctance to give himself to another human being. He could be the most delightful companion and

the most congenial of suitors but sooner or later one came across a
barrier when he would want to return to his work or leave for another
destination. Amanda in *The Research Magnificent* realises to her dismay
that in the last analysis Benham regards his work as more important to
his happiness than herself. In Wells's case the reluctance to commit
himself to a lasting union stemmed in part from a deep rooted
antipathy towards 'settling down' and in part from a driving impatience
that led him to overwork. He had inherited from his father Joseph
Wells a dislike of authority and routine, coupled with a determination
to be his own master. He had also inherited his father's impatience and
lack of staying power. He himself defined the problem in these terms.
Writing apropos of his wife Jane he confessed:

> I am a far less stable creature than she was, with a driving quality that
> holds my instabilities together. I have more drive than strength, and little
> patience; I am hasty and incompetent about much of the detailed business
> of life because I put too large a proportion of my available will and energy
> into issues that dominate me.[17]

There was unquestionably a deeply routed claustrophobia in his make-
up, a trait which made him rebel against conformity and any suggestion
that he was trapped by circumstances.

But his quest for a goddess-figure was symptomatic of deeply
ambivalent attitudes towards the role of women. In a series of novels
and tracts he had consistently argued for the emancipation of women
and their economic independence of men. *Ann Veronica* had played an
immense role in polarising conflicting attitudes to female emancipation
and bringing into the limelight issues that had lain under the carpet of
polite society since the reign of Queen Victoria. *New Worlds for Old, A
Modern Utopia* and *Socialism and the Family* had fuelled the debate by
preaching the Endowment of Motherhood and insisting that women
should be as free as men. He had nailed his flag firmly to the mast of
full sexual equality. However, his attitudes as revealed in his fiction and
his personal life led Rebecca to doubt that he meant what he said. Many
of his novels are variations on the theme of a dominant male who
marries and then becomes disenchanted; but in almost every case it is
the woman who is content to adopt a secondary role. Whilst he created
a number of spirited heroines – Ann Veronica and Christina Alberta for
example – who defy convention and take their destiny in their own
hands, many of his female characters are remarkably passive in their
attitudes towards life. One thinks of Marion in *Tono-Bungay*, Miriam in
The History of Mr Polly, Margaret in *The New Machiavelli* and Rachel in *The
Passionate Friends*. It is difficult to resist the conclusion that whilst in
theory he wanted the fullest possible sexual equality between men and

woman, in practice he shrank from the implications of his own advocacy. It is this contradiction between his principled views about women and his treatment of them in practice that Rebecca found inexplicable.

Of all Wells's fictional portraits of his relationship with Rebecca it is perhaps *The Research Magnificent* with its depiction of the lovely and spirited Amanda and her attraction for the priggish and divided Benham that offers the most penetrating commentary on their situation. When Benham first meets Amanda he recognises in her the divinity of his dreams. 'He had no doubt that she herself had the spirit and quality of divinity . . . We love not persons but revelations. The woman one loves is like a goddess hidden in a shrine; for her sake we live on hope and suffer the kindred priestesses that make up herself.' In the early phases of their love affair he continually imagines her in romantic encounters, clad in armour, exploring wildernesses, defeating wild beasts. For a time they are fearless allies embarking on life's journey, striding side by side in a common endeavour. Disillusionment follows gradually. As Benham comes to know Amanda more closely it dawns on him that their conceptions of life differ profoundly. Where she wants a social life in London, possessions and outings, he wants to get to grips with the world of thought and research. Where she is 'just a nest of vigorous appetites' he is conscious of much more serious drives, the urge to understand society and tackle its problems.

Benham is troubled by a sense of divergence, 'as though he was being pulled in opposite directions by two irresistible forces'. He senses that there is a deep contradiction between the social world of her desires and his own preoccupation with the world of ideas. He is convinced that the intellectual life he craves is incompatible with domestic life, that those who would pursue the research magnificent – those who are concerned for the future of mankind and place that concern over their own individual lives – must be 'untrammelled by domestic servitudes and family relationships'. The novel concludes with Benham leaving Amanda behind in England while he embarks alone on his philanthropic quest. As he puts it: 'One cannot serve at once the intricacies of the wider issues of life and the intricacies of another human being.' *The Research Magnificent* was completed before the end of 1914 yet it anticipates many of the tensions that divided Wells and Rebecca and offers numerous insights into their personalities. It is at once a reflection of the deep happiness each found in the other's company and a summary of the incompatibilities that tore them apart.

The Research Magnificent is characteristic of Wells's fiction in its opposition of the self and the wider world, its contrast between domesticity and social service. Benham summarises this contrast in a passage which encapsulates much that divided Rebecca and Wells:

The normal woman centres upon herself; her mission is her own charm and her own beauty and her own setting; her place is her home. She demands the concentration of a man. Not to be able to command that is her failure. Not to give her that is to shame her.[18]

It is this tension between the home and the world outside, between the individual and society, that divides Lewisham and Ethel in *Love and Mr Lewisham*, Remington and Margaret in *The New Machiavelli* and Stratton and Marjorie in *Marriage*. When Wells came to write about his parting from Rebecca in *The World of William Clissold* he defined the cause of their separation in the same terms – as a dichotomy between the self and creative work. 'I had made my last attempt to reconcile them', writes Clissold, 'and it had failed. I had decided for creation and broken my servitude to this romantic love, but at a price.'[19] The opposition between creative passion and romantic love which Clissold admits is 'the perennial conflict in my nature' was undoubtedly a very real one in Wells's mind but one is bound to ask the question whether it is equally valid in reality. In insisting that the two are irreconcilable was he not simply rationalising a duality in his own temperament?

The truth of their situation was that he and Rebecca could have succeeded in reconciling the two needs, but only at the cost of ending his marriage: this was a price he was not prepared to pay. Rebecca never fully understood Jane, and Wells found her misconception of his marriage hurtful and irritating. Equally it has to be said that he never fully understood Rebecca's secondary position as an unmarried mother. The inherent falsity of her status as the mistress of a married man – and the fact that she found this deeply provoking – was something he consistently failed to grasp. He failed to make allowances for the fact that she was the subject of gossip, that she had to make do with truculent servants, that whereas he could live a full public life she had to spend years living a clandestine existence as a single parent. His tendency to compartmentalise his life, to insist on a complete separation between his emotional and intellectual needs, meant that – despite her wish to enter fully into his world – she was aware of areas she could not penetrate. More and more she had the feeling that she was one half of his life and not the whole. He seemed quite content with this situation but to Rebecca it was not enough. And it cannot have escaped her notice that in novel after novel he presented their situation as if it was *she* who was interfering with his work rather than vice versa. His tendency to present himself as the injured innocent, the pursued rather than the pursuer, became increasingly unreal with the passage of time. At last she came to feel that, though parting from him would be a wrench that would sever her life, she had no alternative but to take the decisive step.

Would they have remained together longer had it not been for Anthony? One can only speculate. Certainly Anthony's presence aggravated the tensions already inherent in their relationship. When he was a baby the necessity for a nurse and domestic help was a continual source of friction between them; as he grew older they differed more and more acrimoniously over his upbringing. But one suspects that with or without Anthony their partnership would have come to an end sooner or later simply because the contradictions dividing them were ultimately more powerful than the bonds holding them together. Despite genuine attempts by them both they failed to arrive at a workable and mutually harmonious *modus vivendi*. Anthony's significance in their story lies in the fact that, simply by his existence, he was a tangible reminder of their love for one another. As he grew into manhood the physical resemblances between himself and Wells became increasingly striking. Long after the partnership between Wells and Rebecca had come to an end it must have galled Rebecca that he and Wells became excellent friends and companions. He whom she had loved so much as a baby turned more and more to the man she had rejected; it became increasingly apparent that he thought the world of his father and less and less of his mother. When he began to publish autobiographical books and articles recapitulating the past this rubbed salt in the wounds by compelling her to relive her former life with Wells. Her notebooks are filled with page after page of recrimination about Anthony, going over the past again and again, giving her own interpretations of his actions, commenting *in extenso* on incidents in *Heritage* or the Mackenzies' biography. As she declined into senility her attitude towards her son came to be poisoned with animosity. She came to regard him as a scapegoat for all that had gone wrong in her life with Wells and to convince herself that his motives in wanting to write a biography of Wells were wholly dishonourable. In this sense Anthony's role in their story can only be described as tragic. Unwanted as a boy, misunderstood as a man, the bitter quarrels of his parents marked him for life and hampered his own creative development. Torn by his feelings for his unusually gifted parents he was caught up inevitably in their disputes and became for them both a symbol of the deep affection that had once united them and the exasperations which drove them apart.

IV

H. G. Wells and Rebecca West were both remarkable literary figures, commanding in their heyday a readership of millions. Through their books and newspaper articles they reached an immense audience and exercised a very considerable influence on the intellectual life of their times. What is of enduring worth in their literary achievement? And what is their significance for the modern world?

Wells was a man of many contradictions. Trained as a scientist, he possessed the creative powers and vision of an artist. Profoundly pessimistic concerning the human condition, his name has come to be associated with a belief in the inevitability of progress and the power of science to cure all human ills. A novelist and storyteller of formidable imaginative power, he wished to be remembered as an educationalist and writer on social questions. The central contradiction of his life seems to me that while he insisted he was the antithesis of James Joyce and that his writings were of contemporary value only, the evidence of his work belies his protestations. The fact is that the bulk of his fiction was written with meticulous care, that he was a compulsive reviser of his own work and that he cared deeply about his literary reputation, despite his public assertions to the contrary. We now know far more about his methods of work than was apparent in his lifetime. From his manuscripts (now preserved at the University of Illinois), his letters to literary friends and the reminiscences of those who knew him it is possible to build up a picture of a writer who worried away at the drafts of his novels, passing them through revision after revision until he was satisfied. He cared passionately about words and the meaning of words and at his best – in his autobiography and such novels as *The History of Mr Polly* and *Tono-Bungay* – was a stylist of rare accomplishment. Given that he attached so much importance to language, how are we to account for his uncertain literary reputation today and the fact that he is bypassed by so much academic literary criticism?

Today his novels, scientific romances and short stories are still widely read but he is paying the price for having written too much of too variable a standard. His tendency to unevenness and overproduction has meant that the bulk of his immense output is out of print and largely forgotten. Twenty-two of his novels are currently in print in a variety of paperback and hardback editions (about half his total output of fiction) but virtually all his non-fiction has been submerged by the passage of time. Only *Experiment in Autobiography* and *A Short History of the World* survive from the fifty or so volumes on social and political questions he wrote between 1900 and 1945. The late John Raymond expressed a widely held view when he wrote apropos of his literary reputation:

> His generous unwisdom in the cause of human progress was Wells's artistic undoing. But when all his plans and pamphlets have blown away, the best of the novels, the scientific romances and the short stories are still there – wonderful and indestructible. They are alive and kicking.[20]

To concur with this judgement is not in any way to denigrate Wells's ideas – his advocacy of federal world institutions and the teaching of planetary rather than national history seem to me to be eminently sensible – but simply to point out that he expressed these ideas far more effectively and influentially in his novels than in the flow of blueprints, outlines, pamphlets and manifestos which poured from his pen. Who reads *The Open Conspiracy* today? Who reads *The Salvaging of Civilisation* or *The New World Order*? For any one person who studies these, thousands will encounter his ideas through such works as *Tono-Bungay*, *The New Machiavelli* and *Mr Britling Sees It Through*. If his ideas are to live and influence new generations of readers in the twenty-first century, it is much more likely to be through his novels than his non-fiction.

So far as popular taste is concerned, then, he remains a widely read author. Thanks to the scientific romances, the short stories and such novels as *Kipps*, *Tono-Bungay* and *The New Machiavelli* he remains a figure to be reckoned with, a writer who made a significant contribution to English literature and brought whole cross-sections of life into the novel. His critical reputation is much more difficult to assess. In his book *The Novelist at the Crossroads* David Lodge observed that 'The centenary in 1966 of the birth of H. G. Wells found the literary and intellectual world still divided and perplexed as to how to assess his importance.' [21] Despite the fact that the years since 1966 have seen an impressive number of biographical and critical studies, and a steadily growing understanding of Wells's methods of work and approach to the art of fiction, his critical standing remains uncertain. The reputation of Joyce, James, Lawrence, Conrad and Woolf seems in no doubt: all their work has the seal of academic respectability and as such is studied and analysed at universities throughout the Western hemisphere. Wells by comparison occupies a somewhat peripheral place on the fringe of English studies, neither wholly respectable nor wholly rejected. The reason for this ambiguity is not hard to find.

Wells was a writer in many different genres. He was a novelist in the English discursive tradition of Fielding and Dickens. He was a scientific romancer in the manner of Poe and Verne. He was a prolific author of short stories. Beyond this he wrote volumes on sociology, history, politics, metaphysics and current affairs. He remains a difficult writer to assess dispassionately largely because it is by no means easy to classify him under any conventional rubric. The position is complicated by the fact that he occupies a transitional place midway between realism and modernism. Whilst for many years he was regarded as a novelist in the realist tradition of Trollope and Bennett, more and more critics now discern elements of symbolism in his work. Writing in 1957 Northrop Frye in *Anatomy of Criticism* dismissed Wells as 'a low mimetic writer not much given to introducing hieratic symbols'.[22] In the light of the work of scholars such as Bernard Bergonzi, Patrick Parrinder, Robert Bloom, John Huntington and William J. Scheick it would be far more difficult to make that judgement today. My own assessment of his life and work is that he remains an extraordinarily interesting writer who dissipated much of his formidable talent in the production of ephemeral works but who left behind him an imperishable legacy of masterpieces. When he told Henry James 'I had rather be called a journalist than an artist' [23] and insisted that his own writings would not stand the test of time he was doing less than justice to himself. It will soon be one hundred years since the first publication of *The Time Machine*. This little book is imbued with the qualities that will ensure for H. G. Wells a lasting place in literary history: a sense of wonder, poetic imagination, vivid narrative power and the gift of compelling belief. Above all it epitomises that ability to create a myth of enduring relevance to the human condition which may yet prove to be his finest contribution to life and thought.

Thanks to widely selling paperback editions of her principal works the bulk of Rebecca West's writings are as popular today as in her lifetime. She commands a steadily growing reputation as a novelist and critic of distinction, a fearless writer on feminist issues and a shrewd observer of world affairs. It is perhaps as a novelist that she made her most permanent contribution to English literature and would most prefer to be remembered, for it is through her fiction that she expressed most fully her conception of life.

What immediately strikes the reader on entering a Rebecca West novel is the sheer power of the writing: 'Birds sat on the telegraph wires that span the river there as the black notes sit on a stave of music.' 'Our dead were like the constellations; we could not touch them but we could not doubt their existence.' 'Wide bays of brightness scalloped the pathway, for there were but half the number of trees on the valley side that there were on the side of the rising ground, so that at her elbow were wide windows of landscape, a landscape of vague radiant woods that seemed to be adhering to hills sticky with moonlight in the manner of treacle-caught moths.' [24] Her stories are littered with vivid metaphors, striking turns of phrase and unusual ways of looking at familiar objects. She has the gift of enabling the reader to share her perspective, as if she is saying 'Look at this'. It was this gift that so delighted Wells and compelled his admiration. To read a West novel is to enter a world of exhilarating freshness in which the reader is seeing individuals and scenes with new insight. All her writing possesses this astringent quality, the gift of illuminating a scene with dazzling penetration. The technique is analogous to comparing a colour photograph with the same view taken in black and white. One thinks of the first sight of the soldier in *The Return of the Soldier*, the descriptions of Edinburgh in *The Judge*, the pursuit of the lovers across Hyde Park in *Harriet Hume* or the encounters with Francis Pitt in *Sunflower*. There is nothing unusual about any of these situations but each is portrayed with a vividness that lifts them out of the commonplace. The reader is aware that he is in the presence of a distinctive authorial voice shaping a fresh perspective on life and humanity.

This perspective owes much of its impact to its *honesty*. In common with George Orwell she will be remembered as a fearless writer who was determined to arrive at the truth as she saw it. Whether she is writing a major novel or a newspaper article her concern is always for the truth, regardless of embarrassment in high places or the demolition of sacred cows. This determination to reach the heart of a problem gives all her prose a cutting edge that makes it immediately recognisable as her own. It is much more a question of approach than of style: a willingness to ask unpalatable questions, to probe behind accepted ideas, to find fresh ways of describing everyday situations. She possessed the tenacity to pursue an argument wherever it leads, even to the extent of following a train of thought along unfamiliar byways. Thus, *Black Lamb and Grey Falcon* appears at first to be a conventional travel book but soon becomes a meditation on history and the rise and decline of Western values; *The Court and the Castle* begins as a work of literary criticism then, as her fascination with her subject deepens, becomes a profoundly stimulating essay on politics and religion; *The Meaning of Treason* is ostensibly a study of William Joyce and John Amery but soon widens into a discussion of human psychology and the nature of belief.

It seems inevitable that with the passage of time the relevance of her non-fiction work to the modern world will decline. My own view is that all the non-fiction, including her literary criticism and studies of treason, will slowly fade. It will suffer the same fate as Wells's works on politics and sociology: relevant and readable in its time but of diminishing significance as the twentieth century draws towards its end. What will survive to posterity will be six novels: *The Return of the Soldier, Harriet Hume, Sunflower, The Fountain Overflows, This Real Night* and *Cousin Rosamund*. These are her literary inheritance; it is through these that her name and spirit will be remembered.

Of these it is the novels most closely associated with Wells, *The Return of the Soldier, Sunflower* and *Harriet Hume*, which embody the essence of her vitality. They will be remembered long after her polemical and critical writings have been forgotten because they encapsulate fundamental human truths. They are concerned with life and love, happiness and anguish, and the dichotomy between the search for contentment and the eternal quest for romance. They record the journey of the self towards adulthood and coming to terms with one's own identity. And they enshrine, supremely and simply, the story of her partnership with a man who transformed her life and in doing so brought out the best in her creative self.

References

As the novels of H. G. Wells and Rebecca West are available in a wide variety of editions, quotations from their fiction are identified by chapter and section in each case, rather than page number.

Chapter 1   A Man of His Time

1. *The New Machiavelli* (London: John Lane, 1911), book 1, 2, 5.
2. *ibid.*, 2, 5.
3. *ibid.*, 2, 3.
4. *Tono-Bungay* (London: Macmillan, 1909), book 1, 1, 3.
5. Sarah Wells's diary, 7 September 1850.
6. From an unpublished manuscript by William Baxter in the H. G. Wells Collection, Bromley Public Library.
7. *The New Machiavelli*, book 1, 3, 1.
8. Sarah Wells's diary, 23 October and 8 November, 1855.
9. *Experiment in Autobiography* (London: Gollancz, 1934), 72.
10. *The New Machiavelli*, book 1, 1, 2.
11. *Experiment in Autobiography*, 64.
12. Introduction to *The Atlantic Edition of the Works of H. G. Wells* (London: Fisher Unwin, 1924; New York: Charles Scribner's), vol. 1.
13. *Experiment in Autobiography*, 109.
14. Wells to his mother, 4 July 1880. Quoted in *Experiment in Autobiography*, 120–1.
15. *Experiment in Autobiography*, 137.
16. Anthony West, 'My father's unpaid debts of love', *The Observer*, 11 January 1976.
17. *Tono-Bungay*, book 1, 1, 3; book 1, 2, 8.
18. Wells to W. W. Cowap, 29 September 1934.
19. *Experiment in Autobiography*, 146.
20. *ibid.*, 148, 151.
21. *Tono-Bungay*, book 1, 2, 3.
22. *Love and Mr Lewisham* (London: Harper, 1900), chapter 1.
23. 'My lucky moment', *View*, 29 April 1911.
24. *Experiment in Autobiography*, 181.
25. *Love and Mr Lewisham*, chapter 8.
26. *Experiment in Autobiography*, 193.

27. *The Fate of Homo Sapiens* (London: Secker & Warburg, 1939) 10.
28. *Text-Book of Biology* (London: University Correspondence College, 1893) vol. 1, 131.
29. *Experiment in Autobiography*, 287.
30. *Love and Mr Lewisham*, chapter 17.
31. Reproduced in Geoffrey West, *H. G. Wells: A sketch for a portrait* (London: Howe, 1930) 59.
32. *Tono-Bungay*, book 2, 4, 1.
33. Quoted in Geoffrey West, *H. G. Wells*, 287.
34. *Experiment in Autobiography*, 309.
35. *ibid.*, 291.
36. *Text-book of Biology*, vii.
37. 'Scepticism of the instrument', published as an appendix to *A Modern Utopia* (London: Chapman & Hall, 1905) 375–93.
38. Geoffrey West, *H. G. Wells*, 289.
39. *Experiment in Autobiography*, 422.
40. *Tono-Bungay*, book 2, 1, 5.
41. *Experiment in Autobiography*, 363.
42. *ibid.*
43. *ibid.*, 427.

Chapter 2   The Divided Self

1. *Experiment in Autobiography* (London: Gollancz, 1934), 425.
2. *ibid.*, 430.
3. Introduction to *The Atlantic Edition of the Works of H. G. Wells* (London: Fisher Unwin, 1924; New York: Charles Scribner's) vol. 1.
4. *Experiment in Autobiography*, 430.
5. Introduction to *The Country of the Blind and Other Stories* (London: Nelson, 1911).
6. *The War of the Worlds* (London: Heinemann, 1898), book 1, 7.
7. Wells to Gissing, 1 January 1898.
8. James to Wells, 17 June 1900.
9. *Mankind in the Making* (London: Chapman & Hall, 1903), 300–1.
10. *Boon* (London: Fisher Unwin, 1915), 226.
11. *Experiment in Autobiography*, 468.
12. *The World of William Clissold* (London: Ernest Benn, 1926), book 1, 5.
13. *Experiment in Autobiography*, 461.
14. *H. G. Wells in Love* (London: Faber & Faber, 1984), 61.
15. Kingsley Martin, *Editor: A volume of autobiography* (London: Hutchinson, 1968), 85.
16. *The World of William Clissold*, book 4, 11.
17. *Experiment in Autobiography*, 378.
18. *Tono-Bungay* (London: Macmillan, 1909), book 1, 2, 7.
19. Wells to Bennett, 15 June 1900.
20. A. C. Ward, *Twentieth Century Literature* (London: Methuen, 1956), 28.

21. *Experiment in Autobiography*, 639.
22. *Tono-Bungay*, book, 1, 1, 5.
23. Introduction to 1914 edition of *Anticipations* (London: Chapman & Hall).
24. *The New Machiavelli* (London: John Lane, 1911), book 4, 1, 4.
25. *Ann Veronica* (London: Fisher Unwin, 1909), chapter 14, 5.
26. Quoted in Janet Dunbar, *J. M. Barrie: The man behind the image* (London: Reader's Union, 1971), 178.
27. *Experiment in Autobiography*, 468.
28. *H. G. Wells in Love*, 81.
29. Geoffrey West, *H. G. Wells: A sketch for a portrait* (London: Howe, 1930), 271.
30. *The New Machiavelli*, book 1, 3, 1.
31. Wells to James, 25 March 1912; James to Wells, 25 March 1912.
32. 'The contemporary novel'. Reprinted as chapter 9 of *An Englishman Looks at the World* (London: Cassell, 1914).
33. *H. G. Wells in Love*, 94–5.

Chapter 3   A Free Woman

1. The Rebecca West Papers, University of Tulsa, Notebook 19.
2. *The Judge* (London: Hutchinson, 1922), book 1, 4, 5.
3. *Family Memories* (London: Virago, 1987), 'My father'.
4. *ibid.*
5. Quoted by Faith Evans, Introduction to *Family Memories*.
6. *The Fountain Overflows* (London: Macmillan, 1956), chapter 7.
7. *ibid.*, chapter 2.
8. *ibid.*
9. *Black Lamb and Grey Falcon* (London: Macmillan, 1942), vol. 2, 478.
10. *Family Memories*, 'Streatham Place'.
11. *The Fountain Overflows*, chapter 15.
12. *The Judge*, book 1, 1, 1.
13. *ibid.*
14. Quoted in Harold Orel, *The Literary Achievement of Rebecca West* (London: Macmillan, 1986), 4.
15. *Family Memories*, 'My relations with music'.
16. 'The position of women in Indian Life', *The Freewoman*, 30 November 1911.
17. A selection of her contributions to *The Freewoman* is reprinted in *The Young Rebecca: Writings of Rebecca West 1911–17* edited by Jane Marcus (London: Virago, 1982).
18. Quoted by Jane Marcus in *The Young Rebecca*, 89.
19. *ibid.*, ix.
20. 'The contemporary novel', *Fortnightly Review*, November 1911. Reprinted as chapter 9 of *An Englishman Looks at the World* (London: Cassell, 1914).
21. *H. G. Wells in Love* (London: Faber & Faber, 1984), 95.
22. Wells to Rebecca, early February 1913.

Chapter 4   The Woman of My Life

1. Wells to Rebecca, June 1913.
2. Wells to Rebecca, July 1913.
3. *The Passionate Friends* (London: Macmillan, 1913), 2, 1.
4. James to Wells, 21 September 1913.
5. James to Wells, *ibid*.
6. *Experiment in Autobiography* (London: Gollancz, 1934), 436.
7. *H. G. Wells in Love* (London: Faber & Faber, 1984), 94.
8. *The World of William Clissold* (London: Ernest Benn, 1926), book 1, 5.
9. *The Research Magnificent* (London: Macmillan, 1915), 3, 4.
10. 'Autumn', *Clarion*, 4 April 1913.
11. *H. G. Wells in Love*, 96.
12. Wells to Rebecca, January 1914.
13. *Experiment in Autobiography*, 498.
14. *The Research Magnificent*, 3, 2 and 4.
15. *ibid*., 4, 3.
16. *Experiment in Autobiography*, 498.
17. Wells to Rebecca, January 1914.
18. 'The human adventure' in *An Englishman Looks at the World* (London: Cassell, 1914).
19. Wells to Rebecca, September 1914.
20. 'Women of England', *Atlantic Monthly*, January 1916.
21. *Boon* (London: Unwin, 1915), 267.
22. *ibid*., 104.
23. 'Mr Hueffer's new novel', *Daily News*, 2 April 1915.
24. James to Wells, 6 July 1915. Wells to James, 8 July 1915. James to Wells, 10 July 1915. Wells to James, 13 July 1915. The correspondence is reprinted in *Henry James & H. G. Wells*, edited by Leon Edel and Gordon N. Ray (London: Rupert Hart-Davis, 1958).
25. Wells to Rebecca, April 1915.
26. Wells to Rebecca, 8 October 1915.
27. *Henry James* (London: Nisbet, 1916), 98–9.
28. Wells to Walpole, late 1917. Quoted in Norman and Jeanne Mackenzie, *The Time Traveller* (London: Weidenfeld & Nicolson, 1973), 292.
29. *The Return of the Soldier* (London: Nisbet, 1918), chapters 3 and 4.
30. *Mr Britling Sees It Through* (London: Cassell, 1916), book 3, 1, 3.
31. *ibid*., book 1, 4, 4.
32. *Experiment in Autobiography*, 106.
33. *The Return of the Soldier*, 1.
34. *H. G. Wells in Love*, 99.
35. *The Return of the Soldier*, 4.
36. Rebecca to Wells, September 1916.
37. Pimlico is described in detail in *The Dream* (London: Cape, 1924), chapter 4, 3 and 5.
38. *The Judge* (London: Hutchinson, 1922), 5.

39. Notes prepared for Gordon Ray. Rebecca West Collection, McFarlin Library, University of Tulsa, Oklahoma.
40. *The Judge*, 5.
41. *ibid.*
42. *The World of William Clissold* (London: Ernest Benn, 1926), book 1, 13.
43. *Joan and Peter* (London: Cassell, 1918), 14, 1.
44. Wells to Jane, 1914. Quoted in Norman and Jeanne Mackenzie, *The Time Traveller*, 304.
45. *H. G. Wells in Love*, 111.

Chapter 5   Discords

1. *Experiment in Autobiography* (London: Gollancz, 1934), 72.
2. *Memorandum on Propaganda Policy Against Germany*, reprinted in *Secrets of Crewe House* by Sir Campbell Stuart (London: Hodder & Stoughton, 1920), pp. 61–81, and in Wells, *The Commonsense of War and Peace* (Harmondsworth: Penguin, 1940), pp. 101–14).
3. 'What is success?', *T. P.'s Weekly*, 24 November 1923.
4. Introduction to *Joan and Peter*, Atlantic Edition London: Fisher Unwin, 1924; New York: Charles Scribner's).
5. *ibid.*
6. *ibid.*
7. *Joan and Peter* (London: Cassell, 1918), 11, 5.
8. *ibid.*, 12, 11.
9. *ibid.*, 9, 5.
10. Bennett to Wells, 30 September 1905.
11. *Joan and Peter*, 14, 9.
12. *The Judge* (London: Hutchinson, 1922), 1, 3.
13. *The Undying Fire* (London: Cassell, 1919), 2, 3.
14. Quoted in Geoffrey West, *H. G. Wells: A sketch for a portrait* (London: Howe, 1930), 229.
15. *Heritage* (New York: Random House, 1955), chapter 1.
16. *H. G. Wells in Love* (London: Faber & Faber, 1984), 103.
17. *ibid.*, 95.
18. Wells to Rebecca, October 1920.
19. Wells to Rebecca, November 1920.
20. 'Life with Aunty Panther and H. G. Wells', *The Observer*, 4 January 1976.
21. *H. G. Wells in Love*, 102.
22. *ibid.*
23. *ibid.*, 97.
24. *The Judge*, 3, 2.
25. *ibid.*, 2, 10.
26. Virginia Woolf to Ottoline Morrell, 18 August 1922.
27. *The Judge*, 2, 2.
28. *The Secret Places of the Heart* (London: Cassell, 1922), 4, 6.
29. *ibid.*, 8, 1.

30. *ibid.*, 5, 2.
31. *Things That Have Interested Me* (1921–6), 191.
32. 'The novel of ideas', Introduction to *Babes in the Darkling Wood* (London: Secker & Warburg, 1940).
33. *ibid.*
34. *Experiment in Autobiography*, 106.
35. *Men Like Gods* (London: Cassell, 1923), 8, 1. For a fuller discussion of *Men Like Gods* as an allegory see J. R. Hammond, *H. G. Wells and the Modern Novel* (London: Macmillan, 1988), 126–43.
36. *Experiment in Autobiography*, 501.
37. *Principles and Persuasions* (London: Eyre & Spottiswoode, 1958), 16–17.
38. *The Story of a Great Schoolmaster* (London: Chatto & Windus, 1924), 1, 150.
39. *The Undying Fire*, 6; *The Secret Places of the Heart*, 9, 5; *Men Like Gods*, book 2, 3, 6.
40. *Experiment in Autobiography*, 737–9.
41. *Principles and Persuasions*, 14.
42. Introduction to *The Food of the Gods*, Atlantic Edition (London: Fisher Unwin, 1924; New York: Charles Scribner's).
43. 'The real H. G. Wells', *Sunday Telegraph*, 17 June 1973.
44. *ibid.*
45. *The Dream* (London: Cape, 1924), 7, 8.
46. Wells to Bennett, July 1909.

Chapter 6   The Aftermath

1. *The World of William Clissold* (London: Ernst Benn, 1926), book 4, 13.
2. *The Dream* (London: Cape, 1924), 3, 3 and 5.
3. *ibid.*, 5, 12.
4. *ibid.*, 6, 8.
5. *The Observer*, 4 January 1976.
6. *ibid.*
7. General Introduction to Atlantic Edition.
8. Wells to Bennett, 19 August 1901; 8 February 1902.
9. *A Year of Prophesying* (London: Fisher Unwin, 1924), 269–70.
10. *The World of William Clissold*, book 4, 13.
11. *H. G. Wells in Love* (London: Faber & Faber, 1984), 136–7.
12. *Experiment in Autobiography* (London: Gollancz, 1934), 740.
13. *The World of William Clissold*, book 1, 2.
14. 'The Betterave Papers', *Cornhill Magazine*, July 1945.
15. *The World of William Clissold*, book 4, 11.
16. *ibid.*, book 4, 12.
17. *ibid.*
18. *ibid.*
19. *ibid.*, book 4, 11.
20. Wells to Jane, 10 May 1927.
21. *The Book of Catherine Wells* (London: Chatto & Windus, 1928), 27.
22. *Family Memories* (London: Virago, 1987), 'My father'.

23. *The Book of Catherine Wells*, 26.
24. *Experiment in Autobiography*, 378.
25. *ibid.*, 501.
26. *Mr Blettsworthy on Rampole Island* (London: Ernest Benn, 1928), 3, 9.
27. *The Strange Necessity* (London: Cape, 1928), 50.
28. *ibid.*, 200.
29. Wells to Rebecca, 26 July 1928.
30. Wells to Rebecca, 3 August 1928.
31. *Harriet Hume* (London: Hutchinson, 1929), 2.
32. *ibid.*, 4.
33. *ibid.*, 3.
34. *The Observer*, 11 January 1976.
35. *H. G. Wells in Love*, 161–2.
36. *The Book of Catherine Wells*, 21.

Chapter 7   Novelist and Prophet

1. Bennett to Wells, 30 September 1905.
2. *Experiment in Autobiography* (London: Gollancz, 1934), 627.
3. Wells to Bennett, 27 March 1930.
4. *Experiment in Autobiography*, 287.
5. *Tono-Bungay* (London: Macmillan, 1909), book 2, 4, 10.
6. *ibid.*, book 2, 1, 4.
7. Victoria Glendinning, *Rebecca West: A Life* (London: Weidenfeld & Nicolson, 1987), 38.
8. *The Bulpington of Blup* (London: Hutchinson, 1932), 4, 3.
9. *Experiment in Autobiography*, 718.
10. Robert Bloom, *Anatomies of Egotism* (Lincoln: University of Nebraska, 1977) *passim*.
11. *Anticipations* (London: Chapman & Hall, 1901), 165.
12. *Experiment in Autobiography*, 741.
13. *H. G. Wells in Love* (London: Faber & Faber, 1984), 162.
14. Introduction, *An Estonian Childhood* (London: Heinemann, 1989).
15. *Time and Tide*, 15 (1934), 1309.
16. Quoted in Norman and Jeanne Mackenzie, *The Time Traveller* (London: Weidenfeld & Nicolson, 1973), 379.
17. Wells to Rebecca, 5 March 1935.
18. *H. G. Wells in Love*, 114.
19. *The Anatomy of Frustration* (London: The Cresset Press, 1936), 227.
20. *ibid.*, 217.
21. *H. G. Wells in Love*, 211.
22. *ibid.*, 213.
23. *The Observer*, 11 January 1976.
24. *Experiment in Autobiography*, 503.
25. *Principles and Persuasions* (London: Eyre & Spottiswoode, 1958), 20.
26. Quoted in Mackenzie, *The Time Traveller*, 395.

27. Burton to Wells, 21 October 1936; Rebecca to Wells 21 September 1936. The originals of both these letters are at the University of Illinois.
28. *Brynhild* (London: Methuen, 1937), 4, 1.
29. *Apropos of Dolores* (London: Cape, 1938), 7, 6.
30. *The Fate of Homo Sapiens* (London: Secker & Warburg, 1939), 311.
31. The full text of the Declaration is contained in *Phoenix*, 186-92. See also Wells's Penguin Special *The Rights of Man* (1940).
32. Introduction, *Babes in the Darkling Wood* (London: Secker & Warburg, 1940).
33. Preface to 1941 edition, *The War in the Air* (Harmondsworth: Penguin).
34. Lance Sieveking, *The Eye of the Beholder* (London: Hutton Press 1957), 224-35.
35. *H. G. Wells in Love*, 225.
36. *You Can't Be Too Careful* (London: Secker & Warburg, 1941), book 3, 11; book 6, 3.
37. Introduction, *You Can't Be Too Careful.*
38. *Strand Magazine*, vol. 104a, January 1943, 45-7.
39. Preface, *Mind at the End of its Tether* (London: Heinemann, 1945).
40. *'42 to '44* (London: Secker & Warburg, 1944), 127.
41. *The Happy Turning* (London: Heinemann, 1945), 2.
42. *ibid.*, 49.
43. *Cornhill Magazine*, July 1945, 362-3.
44. Introduction, *The Last Books of H. G. Wells* (London: H. G. Wells Society, 1968).
45. *Mind at the End of its Tether*, 19.
46. 'The extinction of man', *Pall Mall Gazette*, 25 September 1894. Reprinted in *Certain Personal Matters* (London: Lawrence & Bullen), 172-9.
47. A selection from 'Aesop's quinine for Delphi' is included in Wagar (ed.), *H. G. Wells: Journalism and prophecy* (Boston: Houghton Mifflin, 1964), 439-42.
48. The full text of J. B. Priestley's address is included in Brian Ash, *Who's Who in H. G. Wells* (London: Elm Tree Books, 1979), 295-7.
49. Rebecca to Marjorie Wells, 21 August 1946.

Chapter 8   *The Thinking Reed*

1. Quoted in Introduction to *The Harsh Voice* (London: Virago, 1982), x.
2. Anne Morrow Lindbergh, *The Flower and the Nettle* (New York: Harcourt Brace Jovanovich, 1976), 126.
3. *The Thinking Reed* (London: Hutchinson, 1936), 13.
4. *Heritage* (New York: Random House, 1955), chapter 3.
5. *The Meaning of Treason* (London: Macmillan, 1949), 339.
6. *The Year's Work in Literature* (London: Longmans, Green, 1950), 32.
7. Introduction to 1984 edition of *Heritage* (Secker & Warburg), iii.
8. *H. G. Wells in Love* (London: Faber & Faber, 1984), 97.
9. *Heritage*, chapter 6.
10. *The Fountain Overflows* (London: Macmillan, 1956), 17.

11. cf. *Men Like Gods* (London: Cassell, 1923), book 2, 4, 4 and *Mr Blettsworthy on Rampole Island* (London: Ernest Benn, 1928), 3, 9.
12. Graham Hough, *An Essay on Criticism* (London: Duckworth, 1966), 44.
13. *This Real Night* (London: Macmillan, 1984), 5.
14. Letter to Society of Authors, 25 May 1966.
15. Rebecca to E. Hutchinson, 10 October 1973.
16. 'The real H. G. Wells', *Sunday Telegraph*, 17 June 1973.
17. *Family Memories* (London: Virago, 1987), 4, 255.

Chapter 9 The Summing Up

1. *The Passionate Friends* (London: Macmillan, 1913), 11, 1.
2. James to Wells, 14 October 1909.
3. *The World of William Clissold* (London: Ernest Benn, 1926), book 4, 12.
4. Wells to Rebecca, 5 March 1935.
5. *Sunflower* (London: Virago, 1986), 3.
6. *H. G. Wells in Love* (London: Faber & Faber, 1984), 99.
7. *Cousin Rosamund* (London: Macmillan, 1985), 7.
8. *The History of Mr Polly* (London: Nelson, 1910), 9, 3.
9. ibid., 9, 1.
10. *This Real Night* (London: Macmillan, 1984), 6.
11. *Experiment in Autobiography*, (London: Gollancz, 1934), 79, 82.
12. *The Secret Places of the Heart*, (London: Cassell, 1922), 4, 2.
13. *Tono-Bungay* (London: Macmillan, 1909), book 1, 3, 2.
14. ibid., book 2, 4, 10.
15. ibid., book 1, 3, 2.
16. 'The real H. G. Wells', *Sunday Telegraph*, 17 June 1973.
17. *The Book of Catherine Wells* (London: Chatto & Windus, 1928), 25–6.
18. *The Research Magnificent* (London: Macmillan, 1915), 5, 21.
19. *The World of William Clissold*, book 4, 13.
20. *New Statesman*, 10 January 1959.
21. *The Novelist at the Crossroads* (London: Routledge, 1971), 205.
22. *Anatomy of Criticism* (Princeton, NJ: Princeton University Press, 1957), 155.
23. Wells to James, 8 July 1915.
24. *The Return of the Soldier* (London: Nisbet, 1918), 3; *Cousin Rosamund*, 1; *Sunflower*, 3.

Bibliography

Primary sources

Dickson, Lovat, *H. G. Wells: His turbulent life and times*, 1969, London: Macmillan.

Edel, Leon and Gordon N. Ray (eds), *Henry James and H. G. Wells: A record of their friendship, their debate on the art of fiction and their quarrel*, 1958, London: Rupert Hart-Davis.

Glendinning, Victoria, *Rebecca West: A life*, 1987, London: Weidenfeld & Nicolson.

Hammond, J. R. *An H. G. Wells Companion*, 1979, London: Macmillan; New Jersey: Barnes & Noble.

Hammond, J. R., *H. G. Wells and the Modern Novel*, 1988, London: Macmillan; New York, St Martins Press.

Hammond, J. R., *H. G. Wells: An annotated bibliography of his works*, 1977. New York: Garland.

Mackenzie, Norman and Jeanne, *The Time Traveller: The life of H. G. Wells*, 1973, London: Weidenfeld & Nicolson. Reissued by Hogarth Press, 1987.

Ray, Gordon N., *H. G. Wells and Rebecca West*, 1974, London: Macmillan; New Haven: Yale University Press.

Smith, David C., *H. G. Wells, Desperately Mortal*, 1986, New Haven: Yale University Press.

Wells, H. G., *Ann Veronica*, 1909, London: Unwin; New York: Harper. Reissued by Virago, 1980.

Wells, H. G., *Boon*, 1915, London: Unwin; New York: Doran.

Wells, H. G., *Experiment in Autobiography*, 1934, London: Gollancz; New York: Macmillan. Reissued by Faber & Faber, 1984.

Wells, H. G., *H. G. Wells in Love: Postscript to experiment in autobiography*, 1984, London: Faber & Faber.

Wells, H. G., *Joan and Peter*, 1918, London: Cassell; New York: Macmillan.

Wells, H. G., *Marriage*, 1912, London: Macmillan; New York: Duffield. Reissued by Hogarth Press, 1986.

Wells, H. G., *Men Like Gods*, 1923, London: Cassell; New York: Macmillan. Reissued by Penguin Books, 1980.

Wells, H. G., *Mr Britling Sees It Through*, 1916, London: Cassell; New York: Macmillan. Reissued by Hogarth Press, 1985.

Wells, H. G., *The Dream*, 1924, London: Cape; New York: Macmillan. Reissued by Hogarth Press, 1987.

Wells, H. G., *The New Machiavelli*, 1911, London: John Lane; New York: Duffield. Reissued by Penguin Books, 1985.

Wells, H. G., *The Research Magnificent*, 1915, London: Macmillan; New York: Macmillan.

Wells, H. G., *The Sea Lady*, 1902, London: Methuen; New York: Appleton.

Wells, H. G., *The Secret Places of the Heart*, 1922, London: Cassell; New York: Macmillan.

Wells, H. G., *Tono-Bungay*, 1909, London: Macmillan; New York: Duffield. Reissued by Pan Books, 1972.

Wells, H. G., *The World of William Clissold*, 1926. London: Benn; New York: Doran.

West, Anthony, *David Rees Among Others*, 1970, London: Hamish Hamilton.

West, Anthony, *Heritage*, 1955, New York: Random House; London: Secker & Warburg, 1984.

West, Anthony, *H. G. Wells: Aspects of a life*, 1984, London: Hutchinson.

West, Anthony, 'Life with Aunty Panther and H. G. Wells', *The Observer*, 4 January 1976.

West, Anthony, 'My father's unpaid debts of love', *The Observer*, 11 January 1976.

West, Anthony, *Principles and Persuasions*, 1958, London: Eyre & Spottiswoode.

West, Geoffrey, *H. G. Wells: A sketch for a portrait*, 1930, London: Howe.

West, Rebecca, *The Birds Fall Down*, 1966, London: Macmillan; New York: Viking. Reissued by Virago, 1986.

West, Rebecca, *Cousin Rosamund*, 1985, London: Macmillan; New York: Viking. Reissued by Virago, 1988.

West, Rebecca, *Family Memories*, 1987, London: Virago.

West, Rebecca, *Harriet Hume*, 1929, London: Hutchinson; New York: Doubleday. Reissued by Virago, 1980.

West, Rebecca, *Sunflower*, 1986, London: Virago; New York: Viking.

West, Rebecca, *The Harsh Voice*, 1935, London: Cape; New York: Doubleday. Reissued by Virago, 1982.

West, Rebecca, *Henry James*, 1916, London: Nisbet; New York: Holt.

West, Rebecca, *The Fountain Overflows*, 1956, London: Macmillan; New York: Viking. Reissued by Virago, 1987.

West, Rebecca, *The Judge*, 1922, London: Hutchinson; New York: Doran. Reissued by Virago, 1980.

West, Rebecca, *The Return of the Soldier*, 1918, London: Nisbet; New York: Century. Reissued by Virago, 1982.

West, Rebecca, *The Strange Necessity*, 1928, London: Cape; New York: Doubleday. Reissued by Virago, 1987.

West, Rebecca, *The Thinking Reed*, 1936, London: Hutchinson; New York: Viking. Reissued by Virago, 1984.

West, Rebecca, *This Real Night*, 1984, London: Macmillan; New York: Viking. Reissued by Virago, 1987.

West, Rebecca, *The Young Rebecca, Writings of Rebecca West, 1911–17*, 1982, London: Virago. Reissued by Virago, 1983.

Wilson, Harris (ed.), *Arnold Bennett and H. G. Wells: A record of a personal and a literary friendship*, 1960, London: Rupert Hart-Davis.

Secondary sources

Alexander, Tania, *An Estonian Childhood*, 1989, London: Heinemann.

Beauman, Nicola, *A Very Great Profession: The woman's novel 1914–39*, 1983, London: Virago.

Bergonzi, Bernard (ed.), *H. G. Wells: A collection of critical essays*, 1976, New Jersey: Prentice-Hall.

Cirlot, J. E., *A Dictionary of Symbols*, 1962, London: Routledge & Kegan Paul.

Gregory, Horace, *Dorothy Richardson: An adventure in self-discovery*, 1967, New York: Holt.

Horsburgh, E. L. S., *Bromley, Kent, from the Earliest Times to the Present Century*, 1929, London: Hodder & Stoughton.

Keun, Odette, 'H. G. Wells – the player', *Time and Tide*, 13, 20 and 27 October 1934.

Lodge, David, *Language of Fiction*, 1966, London: Routledge & Kegan Paul.

Mitchell, Vic and Barbara, *Midhurst Town: Then and now*, 1983, Midhurst: Middleton Press.

Orel, Harold, *The Literary Achievement of Rebecca West*, 1986, London: Macmillan.

Parfitt, George, *Fiction of the First World War: A study*, 1988, London: Faber & Faber.

Parrinder, Patrick, (ed.) *H. G. Wells: The critical heritage*, 1972, London: Routledge & Kegan Paul.

Parrinder, Patrick and Robert Philmus, *H. G. Wells's Literary Criticism*, 1980, Hemel Hempstead: Harvester Wheatsheaf; New Jersey: Barnes & Noble.

Scheick, William J., *The Splintering Frame: The later fiction of H. G. Wells*, 1984, Victoria, BC: University of Victoria.

Weldon, Fay, *Rebecca West*, 1985, Harmondsworth: Penguin.

Wells, Frank, *H. G. Wells: A pictorial biography*, 1977, London: Jupiter.

Wolfe, Peter, *Rebecca West, Artist and Thinker*, 1971, London: Feffer & Simons; Carbondale: Southern Illinois University Press.

Index